A CHAUCER READER

A CHAUCER READER

SELECTIONS FROM

The Canterbury Tales

EDITED BY
CHARLES W. DUNN

University of Toronto

HARCOURT, BRACE & WORLD, INC.

New York · Chicago · San Francisco · Atlanta

PREFACE

The present selection from the poetry of Geoffrey Chaucer (*ca.* 1343–1400) has been prepared for readers who have no previous knowledge of the language of fourteenth-century England or of medieval literature.

The collection includes, in the language of the original, the *General Prologue* to the *Canterbury Tales*, six of the tales complete, and extracts from a seventh. To facilitate the reader's understanding of Chaucer's language, obscure words and phrases are glossed at the side of the page. A brief description of the outstanding features of the language is included in the Introduction, and a list of frequently recurring linguistic difficulties has been inserted on the inside covers of this volume for ready reference. A glossary has thus been rendered unnecessary.

To provide in readily accessible form some further indication of Chaucer's art and, in particular, to indicate the dramatic structure of the *Canterbury Tales*, three additional tales and all the links between tales have been included, in modern prose translation. Translations cannot, of course, adequately preserve the flavor of the original, but the editor hopes — to adapt a remark of Chaucer's — "he hath not done so grievously amiss to translate what a bygone author wrote," since the readers for whom this edition is intended may derive some profit from modern substitutes, the language of which, even if inferior, is at least entirely familiar.

Fourteen of the *Canterbury Tales* have been omitted entirely; but brief introductory comments have been considered indispensable for all the tales, whether included or not.

The University of Chicago Press graciously granted permission to the present editor to base his versions of the tales upon their monumental publication, *The Text of the Canterbury Tales Studied on the Basis of All Known Manuscripts*, 8 volumes (Chicago, 1940), edited by John M. Manly and Edith Rickert. No departures have been made here from the established text except for the inclusion of a few favored alternative readings, the addition of punctuation marks, the standardization of capital letters and ambiguous orthographical devices, and the renumbering of lines. (The standard line numbers are always indicated, however, in square brackets under the appropriate headings.)

Since we do not know definitely in what order Chaucer intended to arrange his tales, Robert A. Pratt's convincing recommendation in "The Order of the *Canterbury Tales*," *Publications of the Modern Language Association*, LXVI (1951), 1141–67, has here been followed because of its obvious artistic advantages over previous editorial arrangements.

The covers of this edition reproduce, in part, two pages from the *Canterbury Tales* as they appear in the Ellesmere Manuscript (now in the Huntington Library, California). The front cover shows the page containing a portrait of Chaucer and the text of his words to the Host (translated below, p. 58) and the beginning of his *Tale of Melibeus*. In view of the date of the manuscript (*ca.* 1400–10), the portrait may well have been drawn from life by an artist who had known the poet personally. The back cover reproduces part of a page containing the beginning of the *Franklin's Tale* (see pp. 128–29, ll. 15–38).

In the preparation of the Introduction and of the individual commentaries upon the tales and footnotes, the editor has derived assistance from several of the volumes mentioned below in the Selected Bibliography, and particularly from Professor F. N. Robinson's *Complete Works of Geoffrey Chaucer*. The latter contains not only a painstakingly prepared and definitive text of the poet's works and invaluable summaries of Chaucerian scholarship but also masterly appraisals of Chaucer's individual writings. The present editor takes an especial pleasure in acknowledging his indebtedness to this well-known edition since it is the work of an esteemed friend and former teacher.

In a eulogy of the *Canterbury Tales*, Elizabeth Barrett Browning once wrote concerning the Pilgrims: "Their laughter comes never to an end, and their talk goes on with the stars." The history of literary taste reminds us, however, that it is not a poet's worth alone which enables him to evade an undeserved oblivion, for, without the scholarly reinterpretations of the past so assiduously provided by scholars such as Professor Robinson, "y-loren were of remembrance the keye"—the key of memory would be lost.

C. W. D

University of Toronto
January, 1952

TABLE OF CONTENTS

PREFACE   v

INTRODUCTION:

    GENEALOGICAL TABLE   x

    CHAUCER'S CAREER   xi

    CHAUCER'S LITERARY DEVELOPMENT   xviii

    CHAUCER'S LANGUAGE   xxv

SELECTED BIBLIOGRAPHY   xxxvii

The General Prologue and Selected Tales

The italicized entries consist of linking passages translated into modern English and commentaries on omitted tales.

THE GENERAL PROLOGUE   3

    Knight's Tale, 32   Link, 32   Miller's Tale, 34   Link, 34 Reeve's Tale, 35   Link, 36   Cook's Tale, 37   Link, 37   Man of Law's Tale, 39   Link, 40   Shipman's Tale, 40   Link, 41

THE PRIORESS'S PROLOGUE AND TALE   41

    Link, 49

CHAUCER'S TALE OF SIR THOPAS   50

    Link, 57   Melibeus, 58   Link, 58

THE MONK'S TALE: FOUR MODERN INSTANCES   60

    Link, 65

THE NUN'S PRIEST'S TALE   66

THE WIFE OF BATH'S PROLOGUE AND TALE   85
Link, 120   *Friar's Tale,* 120   *Link,* 121   *Summoner's Tale,*
121   *Link,* 122   *Clerk's Tale,* 123   *Link,* 124   *Merchant's*
Tale, 125   *Link,* 125   *Squire's Tale,* 126   *Link,* 127

THE FRANKLIN'S TALE   127
Physician's Tale, 152   *Link,* 152

THE PARDONER'S PROLOGUE AND TALE   153
Second Nun's Tale, 172   *Link,* 172   *Canon's Yeoman's Tale,*
175   *Link,* 176   *Manciple's Tale,* 178   *Link,* 178   *Parson's*
Tale, 179

CHAUCER'S PRAYER   180

Three Tales in Prose Translation

THE REEVE'S TALE   185
THE CLERK'S TALE   192
THE CANON'S YEOMAN'S TALE   208

APPENDIX: The Pronunciation of Chaucer's Language   221

INTRODUCTION

SELECTIVE GENEALOGY

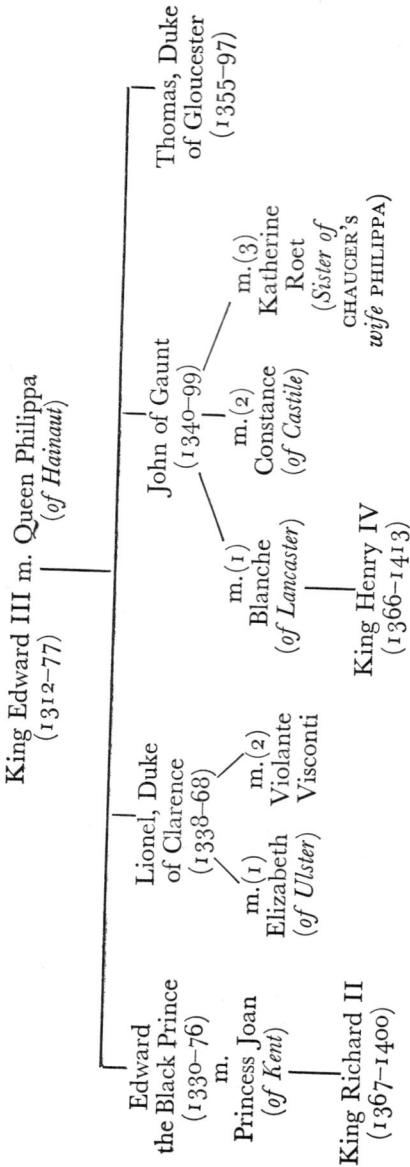

King Edward III m. Queen Philippa
(1312–77)   (of Hainaut)

Edward the Black Prince (1330–76)
m.
Princess Joan (of Kent)

King Richard II (1367–1400)

Lionel, Duke of Clarence (1338–68)
m.(1) Elizabeth (of Ulster)
m.(2) Violante Visconti

John of Gaunt (1340–99)
m.(1) Blanche (of Lancaster)
m.(2) Constance (of Castile)
m.(3) Katherine Roet (Sister of CHAUCER's wife PHILIPPA)

King Henry IV (1366–1413)

Thomas, Duke of Gloucester (1355–97)

REIGNS OF ENGLISH KINGS

Edward III	1327–77
Richard II	1377–99 (deposed)
Henry IV	1399–1413

REIGNS OF FRENCH KINGS

Philip VI	1328–50
John II	1350–64
Charles V	1364–80
Charles VI	1380–1422

INTRODUCTION

In the year 1386, during one of the periods of uneasy peace between England and France, the French poet Eustache Deschamps sent a poetic salutation to his English contemporary, Geoffrey Chaucer. In it he hailed his fellow poet as a Socrates in philosophy, a Seneca in morality, an Aulus Gellius in practical affairs, and an Ovid in poetry.

Such effusive praise, rarely accorded to a writer within his own lifetime, may, in perspective, seem somewhat excessive and certainly claims more credit for the unassuming Chaucer than he would have wished to acknowledge. Yet the comparisons suggest rather effectively the many-sided character of Chaucer, whose genial sense of humor was sharpened by his sense of morality and tempered by his enthusiasm for philosophy, and whose Ovidian gift for storytelling was accompanied by an astonishingly practical ability as a civil servant. To appreciate Chaucer's achievement as fully as Deschamps did, it is therefore useful for the modern reader to understand something of the interrelations between his development as a man of letters and his career as a man of affairs.

I. CHAUCER'S CAREER

As we piece together from the fragmentary records of the past the details of Chaucer's busy career as civil servant, we become increasingly aware of his paradoxical situation as a poet. In the fourteenth century, before the art of printing had been introduced into Europe, an author lacking resources of his own had to enlist the support of patrons sufficiently wealthy to defray the expense of having books prepared by hand. Chaucer wisely did not rely upon such uncertain aid, preferring to gain his livelihood by service variously as page-boy, valet, esquire, soldier, diplomat, customs officer, supervisor of public works, Justice of the Peace, Member of Parliament, and royal forester. But he served so industriously that it is easy to understand why some of his writing remained unfinished. Indeed, it is difficult to understand how he managed to write as much as he did.

Yet his civil posts gave him a familiarity with the world of people such as has fallen to the lot of few poets, and its effects can be traced throughout the entire development of his work. As Hazlitt aptly remarked, "Chaucer's intercourse with the busy world and collision with the actual passions and conflicting interests of others seemed to brace the sinews of his understanding and gave to his writings the air of a man who describes persons and things that he had known and been intimately concerned in."

Furthermore, in an age when books were few and expensive, and literary journals nonexistent, his access to the aristocratic society of both England and the Continent introduced him to the world of letters. He enjoyed an ideal opportunity of meeting contemporary authors, of acquiring copies of their works, and of listening to the literary judgments passed upon them by courtly connoisseurs, learned clerics, and wealthy book collectors.

Chaucer was born of a wealthy bourgeois family, and he was comfortably reared in London. His father, a successful wine importer who had at times held civil service positions under King Edward III, was evidently able to afford for his son an education sufficient for the work in which he later became engaged. Chaucer, so far as we know, did not attend either Oxford or Cambridge, which were in the fourteenth century the only universities in the British Isles. He may have studied civil law and business procedure at one of the law schools in London, though we cannot be sure. But he mastered the intricacies of medieval bookkeeping and, what was more important, acquired a knowledge of Latin, French, and Italian sufficient not merely for the negotiation of international diplomacy but also for the translation and adaptation of literary works written in all three languages.

We may assume that Chaucer acquired his intimate knowledge of the Latin classics from his early schooling. Deschamps complains that in his day men have lost interest in all but one of the Seven Arts, namely Arithmetic; but Chaucer shows a most uncommercial enthusiasm for the epics of Vergil, Lucan, and Statius, and he hails Ovid affectionately as "the clerk of Venus, who has sown wondrously wide the name of the great god of Love." [1]

Chaucer's native London was the wealthiest and most cosmopolitan of all the rapidly expanding cities in England. The city proper contained a population of about 40,000 and was enclosed within a defensive wall, bounded on the south by the River Thames, and surrounded by fertile farmlands. Though small by modern standards, London was nevertheless the hub of England's highways, and its river was a prosperous artery for shipping. The city and neighboring Westminster, the seat of government,

---

[1] Throughout the present Introduction and commentaries, quotations from Chaucer and other medieval writers have been rendered, whenever feasible, in modern English prose translation.

served as the gathering place of courtiers, the home of merchant princes, and the stronghold of English and foreign artisans.

The dynamic and complex life of London itself might very well have provided Chaucer with abundant inspiration for poetry, but his career early introduced him to the wider realm of western Europe. He was born in the midst of the Hundred Years' War (1338–1453) between England and France — an intermittent but destructive war which England was destined eventually to lose. In his youth he was appointed as page in the household of Elizabeth of Ulster, who was the wife of Lionel, Duke of Clarence, the second son of King Edward III. (See Genealogical Table.) His position must have brought him into close contact with the royal family and with their distinguished visitors both from England and from overseas.

Then, while still in his teens, he went to France with the English army, participated in the unsuccessful siege of Rheims (1359), was ignominiously captured, and in company with several of the Duchess of Clarence's officers and some of her horses had to be ransomed from the French by the King. Presumably, however, this mishap did not arouse in Chaucer any feeling of enmity against his captors, for, as the French chronicler Froissart remarked, the French and the English always agreed very amicably about the settlement of ransoms.

It would have been difficult, moreover, for any broad-minded Englishman to feel a personal sense of enmity against his French neighbors, whose language he knew well and whose culture he admired and imitated, for the war was in large part impelled, not by a clash of national interests, but by the dynastic rivalry of the two ruling houses. Indeed, to those not immediately affected, peace probably seemed more desirable than victory, or at least more desirable than the indecisive campaigns and expensive periods of rearmament which drained the resources of both countries.

By a curious irony, at the time when Chaucer was captured, Deschamps was living within the besieged city of Rheims, as was Guillaume de Machaut (ca. 1300–1377), the much admired poet whom Deschamps acknowledged as master. Yet in 1386 Deschamps, as we have seen, praised Chaucer, his former adversary — even, it may be added, after the English marauders had burned down his own favorite house in 1380; and in 1389 he implored the Kings of the two nations to make peace, reminding them that their wars were "impelled by avarice" and were destroying "nobles, people, and the Church; cities, castles, towns, lands, and palaces."

Reciprocally, Chaucer, who never speaks ill of the French in any of his writings, discovered his first poetic inspiration, not in English poetry, but in the poetry of Machaut, Deschamps, and Froissart, and in the *Romance of the Rose*, which was written in the thirteenth century by Guillaume de Lorris

and Jean de Meun. Nor were Chaucer and Deschamps the unique repre-
sentatives of cultural reciprocity between the two countries. Chaucer's
friend John Gower (*ca.* 1330–1408), for instance, wrote a 30,000-line poem
in French in addition to one in English and one in Latin. France's great
poet and greater chronicler, Jean Froissart (1338–*ca.* 1410), visited England in 1395 in order to present to King Richard II a French volume
dealing with matters of love, for which, he tells us, "The King was glad,"
looking in it and reading it in many places, "for he could speak and
read French very well."

    In keeping with this happy internationalism, Chaucer, at some time prior
to 1366, married a Flemish wife, Philippa Roet of Hainaut, who was lady-
in-waiting to King Edward's wife, Queen Philippa, also of Hainaut. New
opportunities opened before him. He became one of the King's valets
(*ca.* 1367) and subsequently rose to the rank of esquire in the Royal Household. From 1367 on, both he and his wife received stipends for life from the
royal exchequer, which were, theoretically at least, awarded annually,
though in fact they may have been paid only at such irregular intervals as
the precarious finances of England would permit.

    Nor were these Chaucer's only perquisites in the years that followed.
Like other civil servants, he occasionally received royal wardships over
heirs who had become orphans while not yet of age and were therefore
compelled, when they wished to marry, to purchase the royal consent from
the guardian appointed by the King. And, appropriately enough for the
son of a wine importer, Chaucer was in 1374 awarded by King Edward a
lifetime gift of a pitcher of Gascon wine, to be delivered daily by the King's
Butler. This picturesque but not uncommon gift he later commuted into
money, having found perhaps that hard cash was less readily available in
London than wine. And in 1397 he was awarded by King Richard II a like
gift — one butt of wine to be received from the Butler annually —, which
was renewed by King Henry IV after his accession in 1399.

    When Queen Philippa died in 1369, Chaucer's wife became lady-in-
waiting in another distinguished household, that of John of Gaunt, the
powerful young duke of Lancaster (1340–1399), whose first wife, Blanche
of Lancaster, had just died. (See Genealogical Table.) Son of one English
king, uncle of the next, and father of the third, the "time-honored Lancaster" acquired much of his unparalleled wealth by marriage. Through
his first wife, Blanche, he had secured the vast Lancastrian estates, which
extended from the south of England to the Scottish border and which he
protected by his own castles and administered through his own exchequer
and courts. By his second marriage in 1371 to Constance of Castile he also
won a claim to the kingship of Castile and Leon in Spain, but he never
succeeded in establishing himself on the throne.

Chaucer probably first became acquainted with John of Gaunt in 1357, when the latter was only seventeen and Chaucer himself somewhat younger, but the poet's dependence upon his wealthy contemporary seems to have commenced simultaneously with his wife's employment in the household. When in 1369 war with France broke out once more after a nine years' lull, Chaucer served in the army under Gaunt. And, from this date, the names of both Geoffrey and Philippa Chaucer appear with regularity in Gaunt's surviving account books as recipients of generous grants. Moreover, Philippa Chaucer's sister, Katherine, was made guardian of Gaunt's daughters; and after the death of her own first husband, she became Gaunt's mistress, bearing him the four distinguished Beaufort children, nicknamed the Fairborns, who were ultimately legitimized in 1396 when John of Gaunt took Katherine as his third wife.

John of Gaunt's rewards to Chaucer may have been bestowed in part because he was Katherine's brother-in-law, but it is likely that the pleasure-loving Gaunt, who was a connoisseur of the arts, also wished to encourage Chaucer as a writer. Although hardly any of Chaucer's works can be definitely dated, one of his earliest poems, the *Book of the Duchess,* was almost certainly addressed to the Duke after the death of his first wife in 1369. The style is strongly colored by the French poetry with which Chaucer had by now become familiar, perhaps through his travels in France; but the poet's sympathetic description of the recently bereaved knight is obviously a personal portrait of John of Gaunt.

Chaucer did not remain dependent upon Gaunt, however. He had begun to travel in France on the King's business as early as 1368, not as a soldier but as a diplomat, and he made frequent journeys thereafter. His duties introduced him also to Italy, which he visited, probably for the first time, in 1372 in order to offer English port and trade facilities to Genoese merchant shipping. Once again his official career provided him with direct access to new and important sources of literary inspiration. Although he might in any case have become acquainted with Italian literature solely through his avidity as a reader, yet the benefits of this and at least one other visit to Italy in 1378 seem to be clearly reflected in the considerable indebtedness of his subsequent works to the three great Italian poets, Dante (1265–1321), Petrarch (1304–1374), and Boccaccio (1313–1375). The lively eagle who serves as Chaucer's mentor in the *House of Fame* is suggested by a more modest eagle who appears briefly in the *Divine Comedy* as Dante's guide in Purgatory; and one of the tragedies ultimately combined in the *Monk's Tale* is derived from the *Inferno.* The *Clerk's Tale* is derived from Petrarch. The *Knight's Tale* is adapted from Boccaccio's *Teseida;* and Chaucer's brilliant tragic romance, *Troilus and Criseyde,* is a reworking of the material used by Boccaccio in his *Filostrato.*

Diplomatic missions required Chaucer's occasional presence on the Continent until at least the year 1387, according to the surviving records; but meanwhile he began to render more extensive civil services at home. In 1374 he was appointed by King Edward III as Controller of Customs and Subsidy of Wools, Skins, and Hides — a responsible position, for wool was England's most valuable dutiable export. And from this time to the end of his life, despite calamitous political upheavals, he derived his principal livelihood from service to the Crown in England.

Perhaps because of his shrewdness, perhaps because of his urbanity, Chaucer seems to have escaped political persecution. He did not suffer at the hands of those who disliked Edward III and his favorites, even though he and his wife were befriended by Edward's hated mistress Alice Perrers, whose reputation at the time of the King's death (1377) was scarcely enhanced by the rumor that she had stolen the rings from off the fingers of her dying lover.

When King Richard II ascended the throne at the age of ten, in the place of his grandfather Edward, Chaucer once again received royal favor. Princess Joan, Richard's mother and adviser, may have been Chaucer's patroness; certainly he became sufficiently familiar with the young King to speak plainly with him. Using the intimate pronoun *thou* rather than the formal *you*, he exhorts the King in a short, undated poem: "O Prince, desire to be honorable. Cherish thy people, and hate extortion. Allow nothing discreditable to thine estate to be done in thy realm. Show forth thy sword of castigation. Fear God, carry out the law, love truth and worth, and wed thy people again to steadfastness."

At the time of the Peasants' Revolt in 1381, violent popular uprisings broke out against King Richard, John of Gaunt, and other prominent men of wealth and power. One of Chaucer's superiors in the Customs, the rich merchant prince Nicholas Brembre, was knighted by the King for his bravery in repelling the mob which had invaded London; but Chaucer does not seem to have committed himself to action. Yet political favor is not necessarily enduring, as is demonstrated by the subsequent fate of Brembre and of other partisans such as Thomas Usk, a minor city official and literary disciple of Chaucer's, for both Brembre and Usk were executed in 1388 when the Duke of Gloucester and others gained temporary ascendancy over the King and his favorites.

During this uncomfortable period, possibly in order to remain inconspicuous, Chaucer moved temporarily from London to the neighboring countryside. He was made a Justice of the Peace in 1385, and in 1386 he represented the county of Kent, for one session only, as Member of Parliament. He evidently found time also to continue his writing. At some time probably prior to 1387 he had completed a prose translation of the sixth-century Latin *Consolation of Philosophy* by Boethius and written an unfinished poem entitled the *Legend of Good Women*, playfully celebrating those good women who, unlike his faithless Criseyde, had suffered martyrdom for the steadfastness of their love.

His wife apparently died in 1387, though he does not mention his loss. The only depression of spirit which we may sense in his writing is to be found in some brief lyrics lamenting, in guarded tones, the disorderliness of his age. "Alas, alas!" he cries in one such lyric. "Now may men weep and cry. For in our days there is nothing but greed, duplicity, treason, envy, poison, manslaughter, and murder of many kinds." But this somber note is certainly not characteristic of the products of his last years, which were his most notably creative, including as they did his most individual and original works. It is generally agreed, for instance, that he began to assemble his materials for the *Canterbury Tales* and wrote the brilliant *General Prologue* to this vast and ambitious project in 1387. And, in addition to the distinguished tales which he subsequently composed for it, he prepared his incomplete prose *Treatise on the Astrolabe*, a work quite unlike anything else he had written. Although it purports to be only a simplified account of astronomical computations intended for a youthful reader, it enjoys the sober distinction of being the earliest work in English to describe in detail the operations of a scientific instrument.

Good fortune continued to favor Chaucer. In 1389 he returned to London as Clerk of the Works, in charge of such eminently practical matters as building and repairs around Westminster Abbey, the Tower of London, Windsor Castle, and the King's manor at West Sheen (now Richmond on the Thames); surveying the dilapidated walls, ditches, sewers, and bridge on the South Bank of the Thames between Greenwich and Woolwich; and erecting scaffolds for the jousts held in 1390 at Smithfield. In 1391, by which time he had become by medieval standards an old man, he was removed, perhaps at his own request, from the strenuous Clerkship of the Works. Meantime he had become sub-Forester of the King's forest at North Petherton, 130 miles west of London. The appointment was presumably safe politically, and it is possible that he administered his duties from London with the convenient assistance of deputies.

Even when John of Gaunt's son, Bolingbroke, began to threaten King Richard's precarious hold on the throne, the King still continued his customary rewards to Chaucer and as late as 1398 gave him a letter of royal protection. Yet in 1399, when Bolingbroke deposed Richard and took the title of King Henry IV, Chaucer found no embarrassment in addressing a playful request for the replenishment of his purse to the new ruler, whom he hailed as the "true king," confirmed by both "lineage and free election." He was generously and immediately rewarded.

When Chaucer died in 1400, his fame as a poet was obviously assured. His death was deeply lamented in the verse of his two poetic admirers, Thomas Hoccleve and John Lydgate; and an Italian poet, Stephen Surigo of Milan, composed a highly eulogistic Latin epitaph for his tomb in Westminster Abbey. Appropriately, the section of the south transept of the Abbey where Chaucer was buried became the burial place of many other famous writers and was subsequently known as the Poets' Corner.

Chaucer's works had circulated widely in manuscript during his lifetime, and after his death new copies continued to appear in profusion. Eighty-four different manuscripts of the *Canterbury Tales* alone survive to the present time. His works were, moreover, among the first writings to be put into print by England's first printer, William Caxton, who hailed him as "the worshipful father and first founder and embellisher of ornate eloquence in our English" and as one who "ought eternally to be remembered."

II. CHAUCER'S LITERARY DEVELOPMENT

Other poets, Chaucer remarks with amusing diffidence, have already "reaped before me and carried away the grain. And I come after, gleaning here and there, and I'm very glad if I can find an ear of any goodly word which they have left behind." When Chaucer made this unduly modest remark in the *Legend of Good Women*, he was referring particularly to the authors of songs of love, but it provides a useful perspective in which to view all of his work, for the medieval writer, like any other apprentice, learned his craft by first imitating the acknowledged masters and then evolving his own technique from theirs.

Occupied though he may have been with affairs of the world, Chaucer was also an indefatigable reader. The omniscient eagle in the *House of Fame* maintains that Chaucer does not even know what his next-door neighbors are doing because, as he tells the poet, "when your work is all done and you've made all your reckonings, instead of rest and change, you go right home to your house and sit down as dumb as any stone at another book till your eyes are glazed." Naturally, such intensive reading influenced profoundly both the substance and the style of his writing. The brief notes introductory to the various works discussed in the present edition can indicate only partially the extent of Chaucer's indebtedness both to the Latin classics and to the more immediate works of his French and Italian predecessors and contemporaries. But Chaucer's achievement entirely transcends any indebtedness, for he attained the mastery of his craft early in his career, having learned the art of infusing fresh spontaneity into whatever he borrowed.

In an age of formalism, Chaucer subordinated formality to individuality, as his attitude toward medieval rhetoric plainly shows. He had read, perhaps more thoroughly than any contemporary English poet, the work of the theoreticians such as Geoffrey de Vinsauf and others who, from the end of the twelfth century on, began to codify the rules of poetry and to describe the figures of speech or "colors of rhetoric" appropriate to the art. Their teaching implied that the essence of poetry consisted in amplifying and adorning each subject by means of a profusion of suitable epithets and figures of speech — a deadly formula if applied without artistic restraint. The obvious dangers of becoming enslaved to it can be seen in some passages of the *Book of the Duchess*, as, for instance, when Chaucer's knight laments the loss of his lady:

> Whoever sees me tomorrow first can say that he has met with Sorrow, for I am Sorrow, and Sorrow is I. Alas! and I shall tell the reason. My song is turned to lamentation, and all my laughter to weeping, my glad thoughts to heaviness. In travail is my leisure and also my rest. My well is woe, my good is harm, and ever to wrath my sport is turned, and my delight to sorrowing. My health is turned to sickness, to doubt is all my security. To darkness all my light is turned. My wit is folly, my day is night, my love is hate, my sleep waking; my mirth and meals are fasting. My countenance is foolishness and all confounded wherever I be. My peace is turned to strife and war. Alas! how could I fare worse?

Even in this early poem, however, the poet's sympathy for his subject redeems the artificiality of the more rhetorical passages; and in his later work he became increasingly impatient with mechanical literary techniques. In the *Nun's Priest's Tale* (l. 527) he goes so far as to satirize Geoffrey de Vinsauf — gently, to be sure, but with telling effect — and elsewhere, in the *Franklin's Tale* (l. 310), for instance, he parodies rhetorical diction.

Similarly, Chaucer rejected the use of allegory, even though it was a favorite medieval poetic device. As an early literary exercise he himself had undertaken to translate, at least in part, the *Romance of the Rose*, a rambling French allegory of courtly love. The first section, written by Guillaume de Lorris in the 1230's, describes schematically the lover's hardships in the service of his lady, the Rose. The continuation, written by Jean de Meun in the 1270's, satirizes the code of courtly love and the society which cultivated such unrealistic conventions. But, although Chaucer subsequently borrowed ideas both from this and other medieval allegories, he

obviously preferred living realities to allegorical devices, for when he borrowed the familiar stock characters from what he had read, he remolded
them in accordance with his own observations of the actual men, women,
and children whom he had met in his career. The allegorical False Sem-
blance in the *Romance of the Rose* is transformed into the Pardoner in the
Canterbury Tales; the deceptive wife satirized as a type by French poets becomes the highly individual Wife of Bath; the anonymous martyr of shad-
owy legend becomes the engaging little schoolboy of the *Prioress's Tale.*
Even the birds in his *Parliament of Birds*, who in the earlier analogues tend
to resemble decorations upon a tapestry, break into speech.

In his more mature works, Chaucer does not, of course, entirely abandon
the literary resources suggested by the rules of rhetoric or the devices of
allegory, nor is there any reason why he should. And there are occasions,
such as that of Dorigen's extended lament (see the *Franklin's Tale*, l. 659,
n. 1), when modern taste would reject what Chaucer's audience may well
have admired. But, in general, like a true-born aristocrat, Chaucer knew
how to follow a code of manners without becoming the slave of fashion;
and, consequently, the most striking effect achieved by his descriptions of
setting and character is not their artifice but their immediacy and dramatic
appropriateness.

The quality of immediacy is everywhere apparent in Chaucer's poetry,
for, as an anonymous poet of the fifteenth century remarked, Chaucer's
language is "so fair and pertinent" that it seems "not only the word but
verily the thing." The portraits of the Canterbury pilgrims in the *General
Prologue* alone supply a complete set of brilliant examples of the poet's art
in bringing characters to life — the graceful young Squire with his "locks
curled as if they had been set in a press"; the belligerent Miller who could
"heave a door off its hinges or break it at a running with his head"; the
courtly Prioress who is "seemly" in all things, "seemly" in her manner of
entuning the divine service in her nose, "seemly" in her manner of reach-
ing for food at the table, "seemly" even in the way she pleats her head-
gear.

Examples of the immediacy of Chaucer's descriptions which may be so
copiously drawn from the tales serve also to illustrate the poet's pervasive
sense of dramatic appropriateness. In the *Nun's Priest's Tale*, for instance,
we hear the voice of the magnificent rooster, Chauntecleer, which "was
merrier than the merry organ which plays on mass-days in the church."
In the *Franklin's Tale* we see the "grisly, black rocks" of the Breton coast
which haunt the thoughts of Dorigen, the anxious wife. And then we learn
that these picturesque details are not mere rhetorical flourishes but integral
elements within the narrative. Chauntecleer's pride in his voice nearly

proves his undoing. Dorigen obtains a magical submergence of the menacing rocks, only to find herself threatened with a new disaster.

Chaucer accepted and retained one medieval convention, however, which to modern readers may seem strangely incongruous in the works of a poet whose delineation of human behavior is predominantly perceptive and realistic. This peculiar convention was the code of courtly love, which had appeared in French literature as early as the end of the twelfth century and had become familiar to English readers before Chaucer's time, particularly through translations of French romances and lyrics.

According to its doctrine, true love cannot exist between man and wife but only between a lover and his lady, and it is a matter of indifference whether the lady be unmarried or another man's wife. Love is an irresistible force which demands of the lover a complete servitude to the wishes of his adored one. The lover must not reveal her identity to anyone and must endure the pangs of love in patient silence, but the hope of ultimately attaining her favor will sustain him and exalt his courtesy, generosity, and valor.

Despite the idealism of these precepts, they were, of course, incompatible with Christian standards of morality. Actually, moreover, they may not have been followed in real life by either the French or the English, although illicit liaisons such as that between John of Gaunt and Chaucer's sister-in-law were common enough in the fourteenth century, at a time when marriages were not primarily made for love but were arranged by parents on a financial basis, sometimes between mere children who were unknown to one another.

But, in any case, whether the code of courtly love represents an actual mode of behavior or is merely a literary artifice, Chaucer often follows the French fashion in his portrayal of love affairs, and occasionally, in his early lyrics, even speaks as if he were himself a courtly lover. "Though you are one of the worthiest alive, and I the most unlikely to prosper, yet, despite all this, know well," he assures his lady, "that you shall not drive me from your service, no longer to serve you faithfully with all my five wits, whatever woe I may feel."

Personally, however, Chaucer seems to have felt more amused than convinced by the exaggerations of courtly love. In the *Parliament of Birds*, for instance, his attitude is distinctly irreverent, even if not openly satirical. Three courtly eagles plead before Nature's parliament for the favor of a lady eagle, whose coyness deters her from making any choice between them, even though the occasion is St. Valentine's Day. The first eagle claims that no one loves her so well as he; the second eagle claims that no one has loved her longer than he; and the third claims that no one has loved her more faithfully than he.

In the ensuing argument the opinion of the assembly is sharply divided between the aristocratic and the plebeian birds. The cackling goose, grossly ignorant of courtly refinement, argues in favor of common sense. "Listen to what reasoning I'll bring forth! My wit is sharp, and I don't like delay. I'd advise anyone, I say, even if he were my brother — unless she's willing to love him, let him love someone else."

Such impatience in the service of an unresponsive lady would, of course, be unpardonable; and the aristocratic sparrowhawk sarcastically retorts: "Listen to the perfect reasoning of a goose! . . . Heavens, fool! It would have been better yet for you to have held your peace than to show your stupidity." And, as Chaucer puts it, "laughter arose from all the aristocratic birds." But the realistically minded author, we suspect, found amusement in both extremes.

From the point of view of literary history, then, Chaucer's paramount achievement in his development from apprentice to master lies in his rejection of all that is lifeless and merely formal, in favor of the immediacy and actuality of life as he knew it. The judgments of literary criticism, however, cannot be so succinctly stated. As Caroline Spurgeon has demonstrated in her *Five Hundred Years of Chaucer Criticism*, the critics in each age have tended to look for and discover in Chaucer those qualities which they particularly desired to praise. The imitative authors of the fifteenth century, uncertain of linguistic standards, signalized his eloquence. The religious reformers of the sixteenth and early seventeenth centuries admired his morality, while the scholars of the Renaissance especially admired his learning. The frivolous courtiers of the Restoration (1660) enjoyed his wit, especially in its more licentious manifestations. He was condemned by the elegant rationalists of the eighteenth century on the grounds that his language was archaic and his meter barbarous, only to be justified in the nineteenth century through the researches of philologists and restored to fame once more by a multitude of sympathetic critics. And the readers of today admire Chaucer's surprising modernity, while the scholars emphasize his originality.

In general, however, it may safely be said that Chaucer's poetry is distinguished by at least two characteristics which, even if not consistently acknowledged by the criticism of five-and-a-half centuries, have never been seriously denied. One is the effectiveness of his storytelling; another is the geniality which his personality sheds upon what he writes.

Concerning Chaucer's narrative technique, John Dryden, his most sympathetic critic in the seventeenth century, dryly remarked: "As he knew what to say, so he knows also when to leave off — a continence which is practised by few writers." An analysis of any of the tales included here will amply demonstrate the truth of this generalization, for Chaucer's economy is indeed remarkable, though his narrative is never a bald recital. He may linger with affectionate relish over dramatic details concerning the unwilling bridegroom and the sardonic hag in the *Wife of Bath's Tale*, for instance, or the faithful wife and desperate lover in the *Franklin's Tale*, or the callous rioters and Death in the *Pardoner's Tale*, or the rash but ingenious rooster, the dogmatic hen, and the subtle fox in the *Nun's Priest's Tale*; but, when once he has established the background of the tale and developed the conflict to his own satisfaction, he then unfolds the denouement swiftly and deftly and, when necessary, remorselessly. It is only when we have finished our reading that we fully realize how ingeniously the various components of the tale have been fitted together.

Behind the tale, moreover, there always lurks the teller himself, the interpreter of human behavior, the commentator upon life, whose personality defies any simple summary. Chaucer is generally thought of as a comic poet, but we must remember that his tone is often primarily serious, and that almost half of the narrators in the *Canterbury Tales* are, like the Clerk, sober-minded pilgrims, intent upon "moral virtue."

Chaucer himself frequently dwells on the cruel fact, lamented by his favorite philosopher, Boethius, and starkly revealed by the experiences of his own contemporaries, that Fortune may whirl a man on high at one moment and then as quickly hurl him low again. In one of his lyrics he steels himself against the blows of the heartless goddess by arguing: "No man is wretched unless he think so himself; and he that has himself, has sufficiency." In another lyric he admits that "the wrestling for this world demands a fall. Here is no home; here there is nothing but wilderness." And he therefore counsels a friend: "Thank God for all. Hold the high way, and let your spirit lead you; and truth shall set you free, without a doubt."

At such moments Chaucer expresses in a manner that is obviously neither perfunctory nor insincere the more serious side of his character; but the majority of his works, whether written "in earnest or in game," are illuminated by what Coleridge calls "the inborn kindly joyousness of his nature." The irrepressible sense of humor which particularly endears Chaucer to modern readers is very wide indeed in its range. Sometimes Chaucer laughs happily and uncritically at what he feels to be essentially ludicrous, as in the Reeve's boisterous tale concerning the schemes of the crafty miller of Trumpington and the counter-schemes of the spirited Cambridge students. Sometimes he finds amusement in the ironies of life, as when in the *Nun's Priest's Tale* Chauntecleer's dream accurately forecasts the future even though his wife has proved scientifically that it cannot, or when the avaricious Pardoner in his tale eloquently condemns avarice.

And occasionally, but only occasionally, as in his portrait of the Summoner, Chaucer's ironic perceptions reflect a moral indignation more generally characteristic of the uncompromising satirist.

Even in the *General Prologue* to the *Canterbury Tales*, where he deals in unusually critical terms with some of the current problems of his age — a topic which few poets can view with detachment —, his predominant tone is one of amused tolerance, which is all the more striking when his work is compared with the fulminations of his contemporaries, William Langland and John Gower.

Langland's *Vision of Piers Plowman*, which was written in 1362, was so popular that two revisions were called for during Chaucer's lifetime, and in it there is no trace of sympathy with such corrupt members of society as, for instance, fraudulent pardoners or the negligent bishops who tolerate them, or even with the victims whose gullibility encourages further fraudulence. Langland complains: "Thus you give your gold in aid of gluttony and hand it to wastrels who hanker after lechery. Were the bishop holy and worth both his ears, they should not be so bold to deceive the people so."

Similarly, Chaucer's friend and fellow poet, Gower, in a long diatribe against the corruption of his age, entitled the *Mirror of Man (ca.* 1378), condemns all ranks and conditions of men — the Pope, cardinals, bishops, archdeacons, other ecclesiastics, parish priests, chantry priests, candidates for the priesthood, monks, friars, emperors, kings, lords, knights, men-at-arms, men of law, barristers, judges, sheriffs, reeves, jurymen, merchants, traders, artificers such as doctors and druggists, victualers, and laborers alike.

Langland and Gower and all the religious reformers of the age would certainly have condemned vehemently the attempts of such an unrepentant sinner as Chaucer's Monk to excuse his disregard of monastic vows by means of specious arguments; yet Chaucer is content to rely upon quiet irony. Innocently he remarks: "I said his opinion was good. Why should he study and make himself crazy, poring all the time over a book in the cloister, or toil and labor with his hands as St. Augustine demands?" This single comment in the *General Prologue* well exemplifies the subtlety of tone which characterizes much of Chaucer's writing. By the effect of his own comic detachment, the author leaves us free to conclude that the Monk is sinful and we should condemn him, or that the Monk is very human and we should sympathize with him, or that we ourselves are ludicrously tolerant toward what we officially condemn. Understandably, the utterances of the vehement Langland and the overanxious Gower seldom attain such suggestiveness.

Chaucer's sense of humor is so pervasive that, as author, he sometimes finds the elements of comedy in circumstances which the characters in his tale can only consider to be serious or pathetic. Thus, in the *Knight's Tale*, even when the courtly lover Arcite has just died for the sake of his ladylove Emily, Chaucer slyly invites us to smile at the incongruities of human behavior. When the women of the city hear the news, they cry: "Why would you be dead, when you had gold enough and Emily?" The chivalric idealist has died for love, and for love alone; and yet the insensitive mourners speak as if his ladylove and his worldly wealth were of equal moment!

Such superimposition of the comic upon the tragic is not equivalent to the sort of comic relief which, for instance, Shakespeare's drunken porter provides in *Macbeth*. Rather it is a product of Chaucer's literary attitude — and, presumably, of his personal attitude, too — toward the mingled tragedy and comedy of life. Fundamentally, Chaucer is neither a satirist intent upon ridiculing folly and vice nor a cynic addicted to heaping ironic contempt upon human behavior. His humor is of the gentler kind. As a diplomat, he accepts and tolerates the irrational ways of the world; and as a Christian, he sympathizes with the human frailty of his fellow mortals during their sojourn in what the spirit of Troilus, removed to a cosmic perspective, calls "this little spot of earth." In short, he seems to believe that laughter, not loathing, is the best and most practical response to the errors of mankind and the conflicts of this world.

The real personality of the author himself must, of course, always remain somewhat inscrutable. As the perceptive Host of the Canterbury pilgrimage remarked, Chaucer is "elvish" — that is, elflike, remote from man in an otherworldly way; he does not, as the Muse of Sir Philip Sidney advised, look in his heart and write. He is a poet of the heart in another sense. The word "heart" is itself a favorite of his, occurring in his writing ten times more often than the word "mind," but it is the heart of his fellows, not his own, whose sorrows and joys he so penetratingly reveals.

III. CHAUCER'S LANGUAGE

The language which Chaucer wrote and spoke is different from modern English, and we must therefore make an initial effort to familiarize ourselves with it. The scholars of our day call the language of Chaucer's age, in retrospect, Middle English, thereby differentiating it both from its ancestor, Old English or Anglo-Saxon, spoken before 1066, and from its descendant, our modern English, spoken after 1500. But Chaucer, we must remember, would have considered *his* language normal, modern English. And he would have had every right to do so, for his particular dialect, among the diverse regional and class dialects of England, was that spoken by the educated classes of London during the fourteenth century, and it later became the model for standard modern English when other dialects began to lose prestige.

Unfortunately for the subsequent appreciation of his work, however, language is ever changing. Consciously or unconsciously, speakers effect minor innovations within the limited sets of distinctive sounds, intonations, grammatical forms, sentence patterns, and words currently in use; and in time the subtle balance within these sets of interdependent speech elements is changed so that the language of yesterday seems unnatural or obscure. The changes which the English language underwent, particularly in its pattern of contrasting sounds, were remarkably extensive in the century after Chaucer's death in 1400. Our conservative and arbitrary English spelling system affords a most inadequate clue to the actual facts, but, presumably, if Chaucer had reappeared in the age of Shakespeare, two centuries later, Elizabethans would have found his speech almost incomprehensible, not merely because he used some words that had become archaic but particularly because an extensive shift of vowel sounds had rendered the still surviving words and grammatical forms which he used unrecognizable in sound. By contrast, three and a half centuries after the death of Shakespeare, we ourselves should find the English spoken in the Elizabethan age still intelligible.

By a process of ingenious deductions from the mute and ambiguous written records of Chaucer's language, scholars have established the principal features of sound, intonation, form, arrangement, and vocabulary characteristic of the language actually spoken in his time. The following simplified account of these findings offers a practical working guide for those who wish to understand what Chaucer wrote and to read his poetry aloud in somewhat the manner in which the poet himself would have read it. No hypothetical reconstruction can be absolutely correct in all its details; but, if we are to appreciate the flavor of an author's language, whether we are reading Chaucer's poetry or Burns's lyrics or the tales of Uncle Remus, some sort of imaginative projection into a dialect other than our own is necessary.

SOUNDS

To transform the written transcript of Chaucer's language consistently into spoken words, the first requirement is a readjustment of our sense of relationship between spelling symbols and spoken sounds. A complete table of correspondences will be found in an Appendix to this edition, but *three practical rules are sufficient for a rough approximation.*

(1) Pronounce all written consonants as we do those in modern English. However, *gh* as in *night*, though now silent, was pronounced like the *ch* in the Scottish pronunciation of *loch* or in the German pronunciation of *Bach*. This unfamiliar sound is like the initial sound in modern English *how* but more strongly breathed. Further exceptions are explained in the Appendix.

(2) Pronounce all the syllables in a word, even those which are represented only by a final *–e* and are no longer pronounced in modern English. Thus, pronounce Chaucer's *damè* with two syllables as *dah-meh*, and his *damès* as *dah-mess*. This final unstressed vowel probably had the same sound as the final unstressed vowel, when unemphatic, in modern English *Stella* or *raven*.

It is most important for our understanding of Chaucer's meters to note that, as in classical French poetry, all final syllables were pronounced, including those ending in *–e*, *–ed*, *–en*, *–es*, *–eth*. In this Introduction and the Appendix these have been marked with a dot over the *e*.

(3) Pronounce all written vowels according to their so-called "Continental" values, that is, according to the sounds which they represent in modern French or Italian, or in our modern pronunciation of Latin.

Thus, pronounce the vowel spelled *a* in Chaucer's *damè* as the *ah* sound of modern French *dame* (or modern English *father*), not as the *ay* sound of modern English *dame*. Other instances are Chaucer's *barè, carè, famè, gamè, hatè, lamè, makè, namè, pagè, ragè, savè, takè, wakè.*

Pronounce the vowel spelled *e* or *ee* in Chaucer's *regioun* as the *ay* sound of modern French *région* (or modern English *able*), not as the *ee* sound of modern English *region*. Other instances are Chaucer's *be, me, thee.* There are a large number of exceptions in this case, as explained in the Appendix, but the important fact to remember is that Chaucer's *e* is never pronounced as the *ee* sound of modern English *region, be,* and so on.

Pronounce the vowel spelled *i* or *y* in Chaucer's *finè* as the *ee* sound in modern French *fine* (or modern English *machine*), not as the *eye* sound in modern English *fine*. Other instances are *bitè, glidè, kyndè* (modern English *kind*), *minè, primè, ridè, strivè, thinè, wyn* (modern English *wine*).

Pronounce the vowel spelled *ou* or *ow* in Chaucer's *doute* as the *ou* sound in modern French *doute* (or modern English *soup*), not as the *ow* sound in modern English *doubt*. Instances are *bour* (modern English *bower*), *doute* (modern English *doubt*), *foul, hous, mous, tour* (modern English *tower*), *out.*

The vowels represented by *o, u,* and diphthongs diverge less notably from modern usage and need not be described here.

FORMS

The grammatical forms used by Chaucer are less troublesome for the modern reader than the now-vanished pronunciation, for contrasting forms can be positively identified from the written record, and most of them survive, at least as archaisms, in modern English.

NOUNS

The numerous declensional systems derived from the earliest stages of the English language had by the time of Chaucer become reduced, with but few exceptions, to two contrasting forms:

dissh (*dish*)	*disshės* (*dishes*)
disshės (*dish's*)	*disshės* (*dishes'*)

It must be noticed that the ending spelled *–ės* was pronounced with an *s*, not, as in modern English *dishes* (*dishez*), with a *z*. Nor was the termination conditioned, as it is in modern English, by the phonetic nature of the noun's final sound. Compare Chaucer's *disshės*, *cattės*, and *doggės* with the modern three-type system: *dishes* (*ez*), *cats* (*s*), and *dogs* (*z*).

Exceptions to the above declensional system are either still familiar, such as *goos — gees* (*goose — geese*) and *oxė — oxėn* (*ox — oxen*), or are so rare that when they occur they can best be explained in the notes.

PRONOUNS

There are several important differences between Chaucer's pronouns and those used in modern English, as the following chart will show.

I	*thou*	*we*	*ye*
myn	*thyn*	*our*	*your*
me	*thee*	*us*	*you*

he	*(h)it*	*she*	*they*
his	*his*	*her(ė), hir(ė)*	*her(ė), hir(ė)*
him	*him* (dat.)	*her(ė), hir(ė)*	*hem*
	(h)it (acc.)		

The only serious difficulty offered by the above set of pronouns lies in the fact that *her(ė)* or *hir(ė)* may mean, depending on context, either *her* or *their;* and *his* may, as in Shakespeare, mean either *his* or *its*.

ADJECTIVES

Chaucer still observed a distinction, now lost, between two different inflections of the adjective, the so-called strong and weak inflections, which were inherited from earlier English. The strong inflection of adjectives consists of a contrast between an absence of ending in the singular (*yong*) and the presence of a final *e* in the plural (*yongė*). It occurs after the indefinite article (*a* or *an*), or before an otherwise unmodified plural noun, or after a preposition, or as a predicate:

a *yong* knight	*yongė* knightes
of *yong* folk	of *yongė* knightes
he is *yong*	they been (arė) *yongė*

The weak inflection, which has a final *e* in both the singular and the plural (*yongė*), occurs in all other situations:

the (this, myn) *yongė* knight	the (thesė, mynė) *yongė* knightės
O *yongė* knight	O *yongė* knightės

With adjectives, such as *swete*, which have inherited a final *e* etymologically as part of their uninflected form, however, no such distinction can be made because the final *e* appears in all situations:

a *swetė* knight	*swetė* knightės
the *swetė* knight	the *swetė* knightės

VERBS

In Chaucer's English the past tense of verbs was formed in two basically different patterns, which still survive. Weak verbs (*love*) added a *d* or *t* to the stem; strong verbs (*drinkė*) changed their stem vowel. The conjugational endings of the two classes differed, as they no longer do, only in the indicative singular of the past tense. The final *n* of the conjugational endings and the prefix *y*– of the past participle (here inserted in parenthesis) were beginning to disappear from the language. Chaucer used them or not at will.

PRESENT INDICATIVE

I *lovė*	*drinkė*		we *lovė*(n)	*drinkė*(n)
thou *lovėst*	*drinkėst*		ye *lovė*(n)	*drinkė*(n)
he *lovėth*	*drinkėth*		they *lovė*(n)	*drinkė*(n)

SUBJUNCTIVE

I, thou, he *lovė* *drinkė*	we, ye, they *lovė*(n) *drinkė*(n)

PAST INDICATIVE

I *lovedè*	drank	we *lovedè*(n)	*dronkè*(n)
thou *lovedèst*	*dronkè*	ye *lovedè*(n)	*dronkè*(n)
he *lovedè*	drank	they *lovedè*(n)	*dronkè*(n)

SUBJUNCTIVE

I, thou, he *lovedè   dronkè*   we, ye, they *lovedè*(n)   *dronkè*(n)

IMPERATIVE

lovè   drink(è) (thou)   *lovèth   drinkèth* (ye)

PAST PARTICIPLE   INFINITIVE

I have (*y*–)*lovèd*   (*y*–)*dronkè*(n)   to *lovè*(n)   *drinkè*(n)

Some verbs with stem ending in *d* or *t* regularly contracted the conjugational ending –*eth*, as in the following particularly common examples: he **bit** (biddeth), *fint* (findeth), *holt* (holdeth), *list* (listeth), *rit* (rideth), *stant* (standeth).

The only other irregularities of frequent occurrence likely to seem unfamiliar to the modern reader are the verb *to be*, which has the forms *we*, *ye*, *they be* or *been* in addition to the familiar *arè*(n); and the following group of verbs which are peculiar both in form and meaning:

I *can*, thou *canst*, he *can*; we, ye, they *connè*(n)   (I can, know how)
   I *coudè*, we *coudè*(n) (conjugated like *lovedè*)
I *may*, thou *mayst*, he *may*; we *mowè*(n)   (I can, am able)
   I *mightè*
I *moot*, thou *moost*, he *moot*; we *mootè*(n)   (I may, must)
   I *mostè*
I *woot*, thou *woost*, he *woot*; we *witè*(n)   (I know)
   I *wistè*

SYNTAX

Modern readers will find little in Chaucer's syntax that seems unfamiliar. Chaucer, like other poets before and since, in composing verse takes the liberty of inverting the word order normal to a prose sentence, but one of the chief characteristics of his style is its clarity. And when, on rare occasions, the logic of his sentence is irregular (see *General Prologue*, ll. 173–75 and note), it merely matches the unconscious illogicalities of everyday speech.

VOCABULARY

Most of Chaucer's words, especially those of most frequent occurrence, have survived into modern English and have not notably changed in meaning. Some of his words have, however, become completely archaic, and their meanings must now be learned just as if they were words in a foreign language. And some apparently familiar words have subtly shifted in meaning since Chaucer's day and must therefore be reinterpreted.

The following literal translation of the opening lines of the *General Prologue* will exemplify the kind of problem in interpretation which faces the modern reader; and it can, at the same time, serve as an illustration of Chaucer's sentence construction.

> Whan that Aprill with his shoures soote
> The droghte of March hath perced to the roote
> And bathed every veyne in swich licour
> Of which vertu engendred is the flour,
> Whan Zephirus eek with his sweete breeth
> Inspired hath in every holt and heeth
> The tendre croppes, and the yonge sonne
> Hath in the Ram his half cours y-ronne,
> And smale foweles maken melodye
> That slepen al the nyght with open eye,
> So priketh him Nature in hir corages,
> Than longen folk to goon on pilgrymages,
> And palmeres for to seken straunge strondes,
> To ferne halwes kouthe in sondry londes.

(l. 1) When (*whan that* is more common than *whan* in Chaucer) April with its (the word *its* had not yet appeared in English) sweet showers has pierced the drought of March to the root and has bathed every vein in such liquid through the power of which the flower is engendered; (l. 5) when Zephyrus (the West Wind) also with its sweet breath has inspired (either in the etymological sense "breathed into," or "made to live," or both) the tender shoots in every wood and heath, and the young sun has run its half-course in the Ram (in the first stage of its annual journey through the signs of the zodiac), and small birds (not domestic *fowls* in the modern sense) make melody which sleep all the night with open eye — so much does Nature stir them in their hearts —; (l. 12) then people long to go on pilgrimages, and palmers (pilgrims who have carried back a palm leaf from Jerusalem) to seek unfamiliar shores, to distant shrines known in various lands.

The first sentence runs to a length and complexity quite unusual in Chaucer, but its structure, though loose, is effectively planned.

(1) *When* April has pierced . . . and bathed . . . ;
(5) *when* Zephyrus has inspired . . . ,
      (7) and the sun has run . . . ,
      (9) and birds make melody . . . (so much does Nature stir . . .);
(12) *then* people long to go . . . (and palmers [long] to seek . . .) to distant shrines . . . .

The problem of the meaning of words is obviously more serious than that of syntax. Only two words in the whole selection, *ferne* ("distant") and *halwes* ("shrines"), can be said to be extinct, and the latter is still familiar indirectly through the verb *to hallow* and the word *Halloween*, which means "Eve of All Hallows" ("hallowed persons" or saints). But several words such as *soote* ("sweet") do not immediately suggest their modern survivals because of extensive sound changes; and other words such as *licour* ("liquor"), because of subsequent extensions of meaning, are no longer familiar in the sense intended by Chaucer.

It is always difficult, moreover, to think within the frame of reference of a bygone age, yet we must attempt to if we wish to appreciate Chaucer's use of a word such as *corage* (l. 11). It is the ancestor of our word *courage* and can be roughly translated by the word "heart." But it suggested, for Chaucer's contemporaries, the animating spirit within the body which responds to the heart as the center of feelings rather than to the brain as the center of thought. It represents in medieval thought a counterpart to our current concept of the "autonomic nerve system," but only a partial counterpart. Chaucer's concept was in turn connected both with the theory of the four humors and with the belief in the influence of the planets (see *General Prologue*, l. 411, note), whereas our concept is allied with the theory of conditioned and unconditioned reflexes, and the like.

Chaucer himself was well aware of the relativity of language and of culture. "You know . . . that in form of speech there is change within a thousand years," he remarks in *Troilus and Criseyde*, "and that words that then had value now seem remarkably quaint and strange to us." "And yet," the people of the past "spoke them so and," he adds shrewdly, "succeeded as well . . . as men do now."

Ironically but inevitably, Chaucer's writing has suffered misunderstanding and neglect from posterity because of the apparent quaintness and strangeness of its language. In the seventeenth century, for instance, the brilliant poet and critic John Dryden, even though he admired and imitated

Chaucer, failed to recognize Chaucer's metrical skill merely because he did not realize that his final *e*'s were to be pronounced. And, despite all the technical assistance afforded by modern scholarship, the reader of today must still make some adjustment of mind if he is to enjoy the feeling that, when he reads Chaucer's poetry, he is reading the language once spoken by living men and women with minds and hearts like our own.

VERSIFICATION

Chaucer's copious repertoire of meters, hitherto unparalleled in English poetry, must have been inspired by his French and Italian contemporaries, whose techniques he probably learned not merely by close observation of their writings but also by personal conversations. The first known French treatise on the composition of vernacular rather than Latin poetry was written in 1392 by Eustache Deschamps, long after Chaucer had already displayed his own versatility; but the problems of versification must already have been discussed orally in France, just as they had been in Italy from the time of Dante, and we may be sure that Chaucer, while traveling on the Continent, sought every opportunity for guidance on the subject.

In meter, rime, and verse-form he shows a consistent skill which appears particularly striking when compared with that of his English contemporaries. In England two entirely different types of versification were currently popular, though the pious Parson repudiates both in the preamble to his tale. (See p. 179, n. 1.) The one, representing a native tradition dating back before the Norman Conquest (1066), was based not upon rime or a fixed pattern of stressed syllables but upon alliteration. Surviving examples of its application contemporary with Chaucer are not numerous, although they include such poems as the brilliant anonymous romance *Sir Gawain and the Green Knight* and the widely read *Piers Plowman*. But the other type, which Chaucer adopted, was the familiar combination of rime and fixed stress-patterns which had gradually been adopted from the French after the Conquest and had become the dominant type of English versification.

The particular verse-form most commonly used in England during Chaucer's youth for purposes of narrative poetry was the four-beat couplet, and it was in this measure that Chaucer cast some of his earlier poetry, such as the *House of Fame*. But there is a danger that short lines with rime recurring every eight syllables will lapse into a tedious jog-trot, as indeed they did in the hands of lesser poets of the fourteenth century, and Chaucer with fine artistic sense departed from this limited verse-form early in his career. He became one of the first poets to introduce into English poetry the five-beat line, and he experimented in it with a variety of riming combinations.

In the *Canterbury Tales*, among other meters, Chaucer used, apparently for the first time in English poetry, a five-beat, seven-line stanza, riming *ababbcc* (later known as the rime royal), for the *Man of Law's Tale*, the *Clerk's Tale*, the *Prioress's Tale*, and the *Second Nun's Tale*. A song in the *Clerk's Tale* is composed in five-beat, six-line stanzas riming *ababcb;* and the *Monk's Tale* is composed in five-beat, eight-line stanzas riming *ababbcbc*. Both of these meters were also new to English poetry. In *Sir Thopas* he used a medley of stanzaic forms. But the verse-form which he used most widely in the *Canterbury Tales* is the most famous, the five-beat couplet, later to be known as the heroic couplet.

Whatever verse form he uses, Chaucer gives the impression of being at ease. In one of his lyrics he complains of the scarcity of riming words in English as compared to French, but he rimes accurately, hardly ever allowing himself to use a farfetched word or an imperfect rime. On occasions, it is true, he does use identical rime, as in the *General Prologue*, ll. 17–18:

> The holy, blisful martir for to *seke*
> That hem hath holpen whan that they were *seeke*.

But here, as elsewhere, the two riming words (one the ancestor of modern English *seek*, and the other of modern English *sick*) though identical in sound differ in origin and meaning. And he is certainly imitating the practice of French poets, who considered identical rime an adornment, not a fault.

Metrically, Chaucer is equally sure in his control of the underlying pattern which he has adopted, and here also he follows the practices of French poetry. He uses both masculine and feminine endings:

> Bifel that in that sésoun on a day
>
> In Southwerk at the Tabard, as I lay
>
> Redy to wenden on my pilgrymage
>
> To Caunterb(u)ry with ful devout corage.
> (*General Prologue*, ll. 19–22)

Here both lines of the first couplet end on a stressed tenth syllable (a masculine ending); both lines of the second couplet, on a stressed tenth syllable followed by an unstressed eleventh syllable (a feminine ending). He also varies at will the position of the stress within a metrical foot, as in *Redy to* wénden. Variations involving the insertion of extra syllables or the omission of syllables are perhaps often intended but may sometimes have resulted either from Chaucer's failure to revise his writing or from a scribe's careless recopying of a normal line.

As in French classical poetry, a final unstressed e, which in Chaucer's English was usually but not always pronounced, counted as one of the syllables of the meter, unless the e could be elided with a following word beginning either with a vowel or with an h followed by a vowel.

> And which(e) they weren, and of what degree,
>
> And eek in what array that they wer(e) inne.
>
> (General Prologue, ll. 40–41)

Here the e of whiche was apparently not pronounced though written in most manuscripts. The final e of were (in the second line), which might have been pronounced, is here elided before a following vowel. In the first line, however, Chaucer uses the form weren instead of were and thereby avoids an unwanted elision with the vowel of and, availing himself, as he often does, of the optional variation in the conjugational ending –e(n), which appears not merely, as here, in the past tense but also in the present, the infinitive, and the participle.

Chaucer usually allows each line to terminate some unit of a sentence, although less frequently than the next great master of the heroic couplet, John Dryden; but, like Dryden, he attains freedom within the line by skillful variation in his use of the sentence pause or caesura. The rapid phrasing of the comic lines describing a widow's pursuit of a fox who has stolen her rooster may be compared, for instance, with the tragic lines describing a widow's vain search for her missing son:

> The sely widw(e) and eek hir(e) doghtres two
>
> Herden this(e) hennes cry(e) and maken wo,
>
> And out att(e) dores stirten they anon.
>
> (Nun's Priest's Tale, ll. 555–57)

> This poure wydw(e) awaiteth al that nyght
>
> After hir litel child,‖ but he cam noght.
>
> (Prioress's Tale, ll. 134–35)

Chaucer's versification is in itself masterly, but it derives its effectiveness from his larger mastery of poetic creativity. A superficial reading of Chaucer's poetry may suggest simplicity, but the sensitive reader soon comes to realize that Chaucer has cunningly concealed the pains bestowed upon his art. We might, in fact, apply to it the words which in the *Parliament of Birds* he applies to the art of love: "The life so short, the craft so long to learn! The attempt so hard, so keen the victory!"

SELECTED BIBLIOGRAPHY

EDITIONS AND COMMENTARIES

Muriel A. Bowden, *Commentary on the General Prologue to the Canterbury Tales*, Macmillan, 1948.

W. F. Bryan and Germaine Dempster, eds., *Sources and Analogues of Chaucer's Canterbury Tales*, University of Chicago Press, 1941. A somewhat technical work containing the texts of works that Chaucer followed in writing the tales and of works similar in content to various of the tales. The introductory comments, written by various editors, are, however, often highly readable.

J. M. Manly, ed., *Canterbury Tales by Geoffrey Chaucer*, Holt, 1928. The introductory summary of Chaucer's grammar is particularly useful.

F. N. Robinson, ed., *The Works of Geoffrey Chaucer*, Houghton Mifflin, 1957. A new edition of the work mentioned in the Preface. For reasons specified there, indispensable.

W. W. Skeat, ed., *Complete Works of Geoffrey Chaucer*, 7 vols., Oxford University Press, 1894–1900. Still useful for its copious notes and glossary.

J. S. P. Tatlock and A. G. Kennedy, *Concordance to the Complete Works of Geoffrey Chaucer*, Washington, Carnegie Institute, 1927. Can provide illuminating guidance to Chaucer's use of words, concepts, and images.

The Ellesmere Chaucer Reproduced in Facsimile, 2 vols., Manchester University Press, 1911. A superb facsimile, unfortunately not widely accessible, of a richly illuminated manuscript of the *Canterbury Tales*, which contains portraits of all twenty-three narrators. An instructive example of a book written by hand prior to the introduction of printing.

LITERARY HISTORY AND CRITICISM

H. S. Bennett, *Chaucer and the Fifteenth Century*, Oxford University Press, 1947. Contains a comprehensive guide to Chaucerian bibliography.

Nevill Coghill, *The Poet Chaucer*, Oxford University Press, 1949.

R. D. French, *Chaucer Handbook*, 2d ed., Crofts, 1947.

G. L. Kittredge, *Chaucer and His Poetry*, Harvard University Press, 1915. Contains outstanding and influential critical pronouncements.

W. W. Lawrence, *Chaucer and the Canterbury Tales*, Columbia University Press, 1950.

T. R. Lounsbury, *Studies in Chaucer*, 3 vols., Harper, 1892. The survey in Chapter 5 of Chaucer's literary affiliations remains unrivaled.

J. L. Lowes, *The Art of Geoffrey Chaucer*, Oxford University Press, 1930.

Kemp Malone, *Chapters on Chaucer*, Johns Hopkins University Press, 1951.

R. K. Root, *The Poetry of Chaucer*, rev. ed., Houghton Mifflin, 1922.

Caroline F. E. Spurgeon, *Five Hundred Years of Chaucer Criticism and Allusion, 1357–1900*, 3 vols., Oxford University Press, 1925. An invaluable collection of copious excerpts from the ever changing literary criticism of five centuries, prefaced by an informative analysis of the shifts in taste.

J. S. P. Tatlock, *The Mind and Art of Chaucer*, Syracuse University Press, 1950.

J. E. Wells, *Manual of the Writings in Middle English*, Yale University Press, 1916; with *Supplements*, 1919 ff. An indispensable bibliographical guide containing analyses of works contemporary with Chaucer such as *Piers Plowman* and Gower's poetry.

HISTORICAL STUDIES

Marchette Chute, *Geoffrey Chaucer of England*, Dutton, 1946. An unauthoritative but readable popular account of Chaucer's life.

G. G. Coulton, *Chaucer and His England*, 7th ed., Dutton, 1950. An informative description of Chaucer's background.

Edith Rickert, comp., *Chaucer's World*, Columbia University Press, 1948. An original and illuminating anthology of contemporary records, many hitherto unavailable.

G. M. Trevelyan, *Illustrated English Social History, I: Chaucer's England and the Early Tudors*, Longmans, 1949. A skillfully condensed survey of the cultural life of Chaucer's age. The numerous well-chosen illustrations include the famous *Troilus* miniature showing Chaucer reading his works to his courtly audience.

THE GENERAL PROLOGUE

AND SELECTED TALES

THE GENERAL PROLOGUE

[A 1–858] [1]

Every age is a Canterbury Pilgrimage; we all pass on, each sustaining one or other of these characters; nor can a child be born who is not one of these characters of Chaucer. — WILLIAM BLAKE (1809)

It is a striking tribute to Chaucer's skill that a work so realistic and immediate as the *Prologue* to the *Canterbury Tales* should also appeal to the mystical mind of the poet Blake as a universal allegory. To Chaucer's contemporaries, no setting could have been more familiar than the London-to-Canterbury pilgrimage route; and Chaucer was obviously concerned to achieve verisimilitude in his description.

The scene opens in the month of April, and from subsequent astronomical allusions in the tales it seems likely that Chaucer was thinking specifically of the year 1387. He tells us that he was staying at the Tabard Inn at Southwark with the intention of setting out the next day on a pilgrimage to the shrine of St. Thomas Becket at Canterbury, and that the season was so inviting that thirty [2] more pilgrims arrived that night bound for the same popular destination. The innkeeper's name, we learn later, was Harry Bailly.

The details are eminently plausible. Southwark, located on the south bank of the River Thames opposite London, was connected with the city by London Bridge, which served as a principal artery for cross-country traffic. In the Southwark of Chaucer's day there was an actual innkeeper by the name of Henry Bailly, and there was at least one inn by the name of the Tabard, although we do not know whether there was one near another inn called the Bell, as line 719 specifies.

In the Middle Ages throughout Europe members of all ranks of society traveled to religious shrines, some because they sought remission of their sins, some because they sought healing through the miraculous powers of the shrines, and some, despite the church's disapproval of worldly frivolities, merely because springtime awakened the wanderlust in their hearts. The English were accustomed to visit native shrines such as the chapel of Our Lady at Walsingham; or if, like the Wife of Bath, they

---

[1] For the sake of cross reference to other editions of Chaucer, the standard group-letter and line numbers of the *Canterbury Tales* are indicated in brackets after each heading. Each tale included here is, however, numbered independently. It is not known how Chaucer intended to arrange the separate groups of tales; the order suggested by Robert A. Pratt (see Preface above, p. vi) has been followed here for convenience.

[2] Chaucer says that there were "a good nine-and-twenty," but in the individual portraits which follow he includes thirty characters, not counting himself and the innkeeper.

could afford to do so, they ventured to more distant places — to Boulogne-sur-mer in France, Cologne in Germany, Santiago de Compostela in Spain, and even Rome and Jerusalem. But, within England itself, the popularity of Canterbury Cathedral, the nation's mother church, was unrivaled.

Canterbury lay only sixty miles distant from London, an easy three or four days' ride on horseback over a much traveled and well-known route, which we can reconstruct from Chaucer's occasional references to the places passed by the pilgrims:

> From Southwark
> 2 miles to Watering-place of St. Thomas
> 5 miles to Deptford
> 6 miles to Greenwich
> 30 miles to Rochester
> 40 miles to Sittingbourne
> 55 miles to Boughton under Blean
> 58 miles to Harbledown
> 60 miles to Canterbury

The popularity of the Cathedral as a pilgrimage center arose from the fame attached to the memory of Archbishop Thomas Becket, whose feud with King Henry II had led to his martyrdom in 1170. When the Cathedral was rebuilt after a fire in 1174, the shrine which was erected in honor of the "holy, blissful martyr" was the most magnificently adorned of any within the entire structure, and its splendor was increased from year to year by donations. When the shrine was destroyed in 1538 by King Henry VIII, the gold and jewels stripped from it were said to have filled two large chests, each of which required six men to lift it.

Chaucer recognized that some of his companions might be motivated by sentiments other than those of pure religion, but he did not blame them as did the follower of the reformer John Wyclif who complained that "what with the noise of their singing, and with the sound of their piping, and with the jangling of their Canterbury bells, and with the barking out of dogs after them, they make more noise than if the King came there away, with all his clarions and many other minstrels."

In the *Canterbury Tales* the solemn Cathedral remains in the background as a silent reminder of the common goal of all pilgrims, pious and impious alike; but it is unlikely, if Chaucer had lived to complete his work, that he would have felt it either necessary or desirable to describe their arrival at the shrine. His work, despite its otherworldly moments, is a human comedy, springing to birth in a common meeting place at the crossroads of England under the inspiration of a very worldly innkeeper.

Appointing himself as organizer of the gathering, the Host offers to join Chaucer and the thirty other pilgrims on their journey and stipulates that each of the thirty-one shall recite two tales on the way to Canterbury and two on the return trip to London, a plan calling for one hundred and twenty-four tales.

Chaucer, however, apparently lacked either the time or — less likely — the inspiration necessary to complete his ambitious plan, for only twenty-four tales survive. In the extant manuscripts two of these, for reasons unknown, remain incomplete; and another two are left unfinished intentionally because the narrators are silenced by the other pilgrims. Chaucer himself is the only person who has an opportunity to tell two tales instead of one, and his first tale is one of those discontinued by request. No tale is provided for seven of the pilgrims, though an extra member who later joins the pilgrimage is allotted one; nor is there any evidence to suggest that, during the thirteen or so years between the composition of the *Prologue* and Chaucer's death in 1400, he completed more tales than have survived.

It was also part of Chaucer's plan to link all the tales together in a narrative sequence, but only occasional sections are so linked, and it is not even possible to determine precisely in what order Chaucer intended to arrange them. But, despite the fragmentary nature of the *Canterbury Tales*, Chaucer managed to reveal the wide scope of his poetic craftsmanship, and subsequent readers have willingly concurred with the verdict of the seventeenth-century poet John Dryden, who remarked, "Here is God's plenty."

The device of setting a series of stories within a narrative framework is by no means unique with Chaucer, but no writer who had used the device before him had succeeded in making the characters of his framework play so integral and lively a role. In the *Prologue* Chaucer suggests, though sometimes rather guardedly, his own opinion of his fellow pilgrims; in the links between the tales, he indicates their opinions of each other; and the style and content of the individual tales are usually appropriate to the narrator's rank, calling, and personality. Thus the reader's feeling of previous personal acquaintance with the narrator enhances the effect of the tale, and the nature of the tale intensifies the individuality of the pilgrim who tells it.

In the *Prologue* the pilgrims are all consistently identified, not by their personal names, but by the titles of their callings, except for two: the author himself who, throughout, remains an anonymous and unidentified "I," and the Wife of Bath, who is actually a clothmaker. However, since she has been married five times, the term "wife" might quite fittingly be said to describe her primary calling. Despite a few omissions, the array of pilgrims gathered together by Chaucer provides an extraordinarily representative survey of medieval society, embracing the three large categories — feudal, ecclesiastical, and urban.

The members of the feudal order ultimately belong to and depend upon the land. The Knight holds land of agricultural value from an overlord and in return provides him with military support. His son, the Squire, is learning to follow in the steps of his father. The Yeoman serves the Knight in peace and war. The rich and epicurean Franklin lives on the land and aids in the administration of justice. The Miller holds a monopoly upon the preparation of the grain produced in his locality. The Reeve is the business manager of a country estate. The Plowman works on the land but cannot own it outright.

The members of the ecclesiastical order play various roles in the complex structure of the medieval Catholic church. The Parson is in charge of one of the parishes into which the entire country is divided and is responsible to the bishop within whose jurisdiction his parish lies. The Summoner, a layman, acts as officer of the ecclesiastical court of the archdeacon, whose authority at this period sometimes conflicted with that of the bishop. The Monk, who supervises a group of members of a religious order living in a monastery, is subordinate to the abbot who rules the central abbey of the order. The Prioress is in charge of a nunnery. The Second Nun acts as her secretary. One of the Prioress's three Priests (Chaucer possibly intended to include only one priest in her retinue, not three as the surviving manuscripts say) presumably says mass in her nunnery and hears the nuns' confessions. The Friar belongs to a religious order of mendicants who were originally dedicated to a life of willing poverty and depended upon alms for their livelihood; he, however, intrudes upon the operations of the local parish and the interests of the local monastery by begging for money within their precincts in exchange for the hearing of confessions and the granting of penances. The Pardoner belongs to an organization founded to raise extra funds for the emergent needs of the Catholic church by distributing indulgences or pardons from the Pope; but he, like the Friar, competes illicitly with the normal parish organization of the church. The Clerk, although eligible for the priesthood or for membership in a religious order or for lucrative secular employment, prefers to continue his quest for higher academic degrees at the university. And the two characters who later join the pilgrimage, the Canon and his Yeoman, are also part of the ecclesiastical group. The Canon, like the Monk, is dedicated to a religious life but is not obliged to live in a monastic residence and is therefore able to spend his time in conducting experiments in alchemy; and the Yeoman, his manservant, acts as his assistant.

The third and largest group of pilgrims consists entirely of laymen, both professional and mercantile, who, unlike the members of the feudal group, reside in the ever expanding and increasingly wealthy English towns of Chaucer's day. The professional men are two, the Physician and the Man of Law, or more properly the Sergeant of the Law, who has been appointed directly by the King as justice to serve in the regular local or assize courts of the English counties. The Manciple manages the purchasing of provisions required for a law society's residence in London. The others depend for their living ultimately upon manufacture and commerce. The Merchant makes his living by selling English produce on the Continent and (illegally) by speculating in foreign exchange. The Shipman is engaged in carrying cargoes and, incidentally, in piracy and wine smuggling. The Haberdasher, the Carpenter, the Weaver, the Dyer, the Tapestry-maker, and the Cook who accompanies them, the Clothmaker (the Wife of Bath), and the Innkeeper are likewise all characteristic townspeople.

The pilgrims are not, however, depicted as a set of abstract universals, as we might have expected from a poet steeped in the prevalent medieval tradition of allegory. Although writing within a schematic framework, Chaucer succeeds in suggesting that he is a member of a real pilgrimage and that the pilgrims whom he describes are real human beings. At the same time, he carefully avoids rigidity of method in his portraiture, sometimes arranging his comments in a deliberately haphazard order, and sometimes even suggesting that it is difficult to glean as much information as he would like. Thus, concerning the pilgrims' names, for instance, he has managed to discover that the Friar's name is Huberd and that the

Reeve's horse's name is Scot, but he is silent as to the name of the Reeve himself, and he goes out of his way to remark that he has not learned the name of the secretive Merchant. In the minor matter of beards, on the other hand, he is able to tell us that the Merchant has a forked beard, the Franklin's beard is white as a daisy, the Shipman's beard has been shaken by many a tempest, the Miller's beard is as red as a sow or fox and as broad as a spade, the Reeve's beard is close-shaven, the Summoner's beard is wispy, and the Pardoner has no beard at all and never will have. Thus by means of random and apparently artless comments Chaucer paints such distinctive portraits that modern scholars have attempted to discover historical figures who might have served as actual models.

But, one must add, the essence of Chaucer's technique, both in the *General Prologue* and in his other writing, is that there is nothing automatic about it, even about its randomness. Chaucer does not attempt to individualize *all* the characters in the *Prologue*. The five prosperous artisans who, as fellow members of the same religious fraternity, all wear an identical livery are complete anonymities, submerged in the uniformity of their dress and of their political ambition — or, rather, as Chaucer slyly suggests, the political ambition of their absent wives. But, after all, what more do we need to know about them? The Prioress's discreet companions, the nun and the three Priests, are not described at all, although it has often been suggested that Chaucer intended ultimately to provide portraits of them; but their very silence, even if it supplies no positive information about their own characters, emphasizes the dominating character of their superior.

The framework of the *Canterbury Tales* is remarkable, however, not merely because it is universal in scope and realistic in treatment but also because the underlying tone is comic. The wide range of Chaucer's comedy cannot readily be described in terms of a few simple techniques; but, within the *Prologue* and links at least, the author's predominant tone may be said to be one of self-effacing comic detachment. Chaucer, the only pilgrim whose calling is not revealed, suggests the same portrait of himself in the *Canterbury Tales* which appears in his other writings — that of an amiable but slow-thinking, middle-aged man, bookish but unskilled in poetry, inept in matters of love, and naïve in judging his fellow men. Such is the guise he assumes from the outset in the *Prologue* by innocently implying from time to time that he is incapable of distinguishing truth from falsehood in the conversation of his companions and that he is therefore compelled to record their own self-evaluations. Hence the large number of superlatives in the portraits. No one has traveled farther than the Knight; no member of all the four orders of mendicants knows more of fair language than the Friar; no one understands navigation better than the Shipman; no one in all the world can speak of medicine and surgery so well as the Physician; no auditor can discredit the Reeve's accounting; there is no fairer citizen in Cheapside than the Host.

Chaucer's tone is also capable of changing unexpectedly from comic detachment to indignation and converting comedy into irony or even into satire. When he calls the Knight a "true, perfect, gentle knight," most readers accept his judgment; but when he calls the Physician a "true and perfect practitioner," his undertone is obviously ironic. Here again he is deliberately unsystematic; his tone may vary from mild irony to astringent satire. Readers disagree, for instance, as to whether Chaucer intends his portrait of the Prioress as a compliment to her graciousness or as an ironic rebuke to her breach of religious discipline. But his satire of such an unpopular member of society as the Pardoner is unambiguous, for he levels no mere charge of fraudulence and hypocrisy but a sweeping imputation of spiritual degradation and physical degeneracy.

In general, however, Chaucer's tone is colored by his geniality and his zest for human nature. In the *Prologue* he portrays his characters neither as saints nor as sinners but as creatures of flesh and blood with whom he is willing to sympathize. And, throughout the dramatic links which knit the *Canterbury Tales* together, whenever he converts the static portraiture of the *Prologue* into a dynamic representation of life, he evinces the same sympathy for his fellow man. "Pity runneth soon in gentle heart," is a saying which Chaucer uses on four different occasions, and it is evidently his motto as a poet.

Whan that° Aprill with his shoures soote°	When sweet
The droghte of March hath perced to the roote	
And bathed every veyne in swich licour°	such liquid
Of which vertu° engendred is the flour,	By power of which
Whan Zephirus eek° with his sweete breeth	also
Inspired hath in every holt° and heeth°	wood heath
The tendre croppes,° and the yonge sonne	shoots
Hath in the Ram his half cours y-ronne,[1]	
And smale foweles maken° melodye	birds make
That slepen al the nyght with open eye, 10	
So priketh hem° Nature in hir corages,°	stirs them their hearts
Than longen° folk to goon° on pilgrymages,	Then long go
And palmeres° for to seken° straunge strondes,°	pilgrims seek strands
To ferne halwes kouthe° in sondry londes.	distant shrines known
And specially, from every shires ende	
Of Engelond, to Caunterbury they wende,	
The holy, blisful martir [2] for to seke	

[1] "Has run his half-course in the Ram." At the time Chaucer was writing, the "young sun" of spring moved through the *first* half-course (approximately) of the Ram (Aries, the first of the twelve signs into which the zodiac is divided) during the period between March 12 to March 31, and the *second* half-course between April 1 and April 11, and then entered the Bull (Taurus). The reference here is to the sun's completion of its second half-course on April 11.

[2] Thomas Becket, Archbishop of Canterbury, was martyred in 1170 and canonized as a saint in 1172. The Roman missionary Augustine, the first archbishop, had established Canterbury in Kent in 597 as the metropolis of the church in England.

That hem hath holpen° whan that they were   helped
    seeke.°   sick
Bifel° that in that sesoun, on a day   It befell
In Southwerk at the Tabard, as I lay   20
Redy to wenden on my pilgrymage
To Caunterbury with ful devout corage,°   heart
At nyght was come into that hostelrye
Wel nyne-and-twenty in a compaignye
Of sondry folk by aventure y-falle°   chance fallen
In felaweshipe, and pilgrymes were they alle
That toward Caunterbury wolden° ryde.   intended to
The chambres and the stables weren wyde,°   spacious
And wel we weren esed atte beste°;   entertained at the best
And shortly, whan the sonne was to reste,
So hadde I spoken with hem everichon°   every one
That I was of hir° felaweshipe anon;   their
And made forward° erly for to ryse   (we) made agreement
To take oure wey ther-as° I yow devyse.°   where tell
    But, nathelees,° whil I have tyme and space, nevertheless
Er that° I ferther in this tale pace,°   Before pass
Me thynketh it° acordant to resoun   It seems to me
To telle yow al the condicioun
Of ech of hem° so as it semed me,   them
And whiche they weren, and of what degree, 40
And eek° in what array that they were inne;   also
And at a knyght than wol I first bigynne.
    A KNYGHT ther was, and that a worthy man,
That, fro the tyme that he first bigan
To riden° out, he loved chivalrye,   ride (in expeditions)
Trouthe and honour, fredom and curteisye.
Ful worthy was he in his lordes werre,°   war
And ther-to hadde he riden, no man ferre,°   farther
As wel in Cristendom as in hethenesse,°   heathendom
And evere honoured for his worthynesse.[1] 50
    At Alisaundre° he was whan it was wonne.   Alexandria (Egypt)
Ful ofte tyme he hadde the bord bigonne°   table headed

[1] The historical allusions indicate that the Knight was a veteran of more than forty years'
service. In accordance with his feudal duty to his over-lord, the King, he had fought in
"his lord's war," a term presumably referring to the campaigns of the Hundred Years'
War between England and France. Chaucer could have mentioned specifically the famous
victories of Crécy (1346) and Poitiers (1356) and the less happy expeditions of 1359-60

Aboven alle nacions in Pruce.° *Prussia*
In Lettow° hadde he reysed,° and in Ruce,° *Lithuania served Russia*
No Cristen man so ofte of his degree.
In Gernade° at the seege eek° hadde he be° *Granada (Spain) also been*
Of Algezir,° and riden in Belmarye.° *Algeciras Benmarin (Morocco)*
At Lyeys° was he and at Satalye° *Ayas (Armenia) Adalia (Turkey)*
Whan they were wonne; and in the Grete° See *Mediterranean*
At many a noble armee° hadde he be.   60 *armada*
At mortal batailles hadde he been fiftene,
And foghten for oure feith at Tramyssene° *Tlemçen (Algeria)*
In lystes° thries, and ay° slayn his foo. *tournaments always*
This ilke° worthy Knyght hadde been also *same*
Som tyme with the lord of Palatye° *Balat (Turkey)*
Agayn° another hethen in Turkye. *Against*
    And evere moore° he hadde a sovereyn prys,° *always reputation*
And, though that he were worthy, he was wys
And of his port° as meke as is a mayde. *deportment*
He nevere yet no vileynye° ne sayde   70 *anything boorish*
In al his lyf unto no maner wight.° *any kind of person*
He was a verray,° parfit, gentil knyght. *true*
    But for to tellen yow of his array,
Hise hors° were goode, but he was nat gay. *horses*
Of fustian° he wered a gypoun° *rough cotton blouse*
Al bismotered° with his habergeoun,° *stained coat of mail*
For he was late y-come from his viage° *journey*
And wente for to doon his pilgrymage.
    With hym ther was his sone, a yong SQUYER,
A lovere and a lusty bacheler,[1]   80
With lokkes crulle as° they were leyd in presse.° *curled as if curlers*
Of twenty yeer of age he was, I gesse.
    Of his stature he was of evene° lengthe, *medium*
And wonderly delyvere,° and of greet strengthe; *agile*
And he hadde been som tyme in chivachye° *on a raid*

and 1369, in which he himself took part; but it is possible that as an admirer of French culture he saw nothing worthy in these wars. The Knight had also enlisted voluntarily against the Mohammedans both in the Moorish realms of the western Mediterranean and in the Turkish realms of the eastern, and against the pagan hordes of north-eastern Europe.

[1] In obedience to the customs of the aristocracy, the Squire as a "bachelor" or candidate for knighthood had dedicated himself not merely to military training but also to courtly love, and he therefore undertook as a "lover" to win the approval of a lady by valor in war and devotion in love.

In Flaundres, in Artoys, and Picardye,[1]
And born° hym wel, as of so litel space,°   conducted   time
In hope to stonden° in his lady° grace.   stand   lady's
    Embrouded° was he as it were a meede°   Embroidered   meadow
Al ful of fresshe floures white and reede.   90
Syngynge° he was or floytynge° al the day.   fluting
He was as fressh as is the monthe of May.
Short was his gowne with sleves longe and wyde.
Wel koude he sitte on hors and faire° ryde.   gracefully
He koude songes make and wel endite,°   compose words
Juste,° and eek° daunce, and wel purtreye,° and   Joust   also   draw
    write.
So hoote he lovede that by nyghtertale°   nighttime
He slepte namoore than dooth a nyghtyngale.
    Curteys he was, lowely, and servysable,
And carf° biforn his fader at the table.   100   carved
    A YEMAN° hadde he° and servantz namo°   yeoman   he (the knight)   no more
At that tyme, for hym liste° ryde so,   he liked to
And he was clad in coote and hood of grene.
A sheef of pecok arwes° bright and kene   arrows
Under his belt he bar° ful thriftily.°   carried   neatly
Wel koude he dresse° his takel° yemanly;   prepare   equipment
His arwes drouped noght with fetheres lowe.
And in his hand he bar a myghty bowe.
A not° heed hadde he, with a broun visage.   close-cropped
Of wodecraft wel koude° he al the usage.   110   knew
Upon his arm he bar a gay bracer,°   archer's guard
And by his syde a swerd° and a bokeler,°   sword   buckler
And on that° oother syde a gay daggere,   the
Harneysed° wel, and sharp as poynt of spere,   Mounted
A Cristofre° on his brest of silver shene.°   St. Christopher medal   bright
An horn he bar, the bawdryk° was of grene.   carrying-belt
A forster° was he soothly,° as I gesse.   forester   truly
    Ther was also a nonne, a PRIORESSE,
That of hir smylyng was ful symple° and coy.°   unpretentious   quiet

¶ Under the pretext of aiding the Pope at Rome against the rival pope supported by the French at Avignon, an English raiding party plundered Flanders, Artois, and Picardy in 1383. If this is the expedition alluded to, it would have provided suitable experience to the Squire without any hazard more serious than he might meet while jousting in practice tournaments.

Hir gretteste ooth was but by Seint Loy [1];   120
And she was cleped° Madame Eglentyne.   called
   Ful wel she soong° the servyce dyvyne,   sang
Entuned° in hir nose ful semely,°   Intoned properly
And Frenssh she spak ful faire, and fetisly°   elegantly
After the scole of Stratford atte Bowe,[2]
For Frenssh of Parys was to hire unknowe.°   unknown
   At mete wel ytaught was she with alle;
She leet° no morsel from hir lippes falle,   let
Ne wette hir fyngres in hir sauce depe;   deeply
Wel koude she carie a morsel, and wel kepe°   130   take care
That no drope ne fille° upon hir brest.   fell
In curteisie was set ful muchel° hir lest.°   much concern
Hir over lippe wyped she so clene
That in hir coppe ther was no ferthyng° sene   particle
Of grece whan she dronken hadde hir draughte.
Ful semely after hir mete she raughte,°   reached
And sikerly° she was of greet desport,°   surely/certainly fun
And ful plesaunt and amyable of port,°   deportment
And peyned hire° to countrefete cheere°   strove imitate appearance
Of court, and to been estatlich° of manere,   140   stately
And to been holden digne° of reverence.   considered worthy
   But for to speken of hir conscience,
She was so charitable and so pitous,°   sympathetic
She wolde wepe if that she sawe a mous
Caught in a trappe, if it were deed or bledde.
Of smale houndes [3] hadde she that she fedde
With rosted flessh, or mylk and wastel° breed;   white wheat
But soore wepte she if oon of hem were deed,
Or if men° smoot it with a yerde smerte.°   someone stick severely
And al was conscience and tendre herte.   150
   Ful semely° hir wympel pynched° was,   gracefully head-dress fluted

[1] The talented goldsmith St. Loy (or Eligius) served as treasurer in the luxurious French court of King Dagobert in the seventh century and was appointed bishop by the King.

[2] The allusion would suggest either that the Prioress had been educated at the Benedictine nunnery of St. Leonard's or that she was in charge of it. It was situated beside Stratford at the Bow on the outskirts of London and served as a finishing school for the daughters of London's middle class. Appropriately, we learn from what follows that she was preoccupied with matters of etiquette.

[3] It was contrary to religious discipline for a nun to have a pet dog, but evidently the Prioress kept lap dogs and pampered them indulgently with meat and milk and the second-best grade of bread, even at a time when food was scarce.

Hir nose tretys,° hir eyen° greye as glas,   shapely eyes
Hir mouth ful smal, and ther-to softe and reed,
But sikerly° she hadde a fair forheed;   certainly
It was almoost a spanne brood, I trowe,°   believe
For hardily° she was nat undergrowe.   undeniably
Ful fetys° was hir cloke, as I was war°;   graceful aware
Of smal coral aboute hir arm she bar°   carried
A peyre of bedes, gauded al with grene,[1]
And ther-on heng a brooch of gold ful shene,° 160   bright
On which ther was first writen a crowned A,
And after *Amor vincit omnia.*°   *Love conquers all.*
   Another NONNE with hire hadde she,
That was hir chapeleyne, and preestes thre.
   A MONK ther was, a fair for the maistrye,°   an extremely fine (one)
An outridere° that lovede venerye,°   supervisor hunting
A manly man, to been an abbot able.
Ful many a deyntee° hors hadde he in stable,   valuable
And whanne he rood, men myghte° his brydel heere   could
Gynglen° in a whistlynge wynd as cleere   170 Jingle
And eek° as loude as dooth the chapel belle   also
Ther-as° this lord was kepere of the celle.°   Where group
   The reule of Seint Maure or of Seint Beneit,[2]
By cause that it was old and somdel streit,°   somewhat strict
This ilke° Monk leet olde thynges pace   same
And heeld after the newe world, the space.°   for the meanwhile
He yaf° nat of that text a pulled° hen   gave plucked
That seith that hunters been° nat holy men,   are
Ne that a monk, whan he is recchelees,°   without a care
Is likned til° a fissh that is waterlees,   180 like to
This is to seyn,° a monk out of his cloystre.   say
But thilke° text heeld he nat worth an oystre; that same
And I seyde his opinioun was good.
What° sholde he studie and make hymselven wood° Why himself insane
Upon a book in cloystre alwey to poure,°   pore

---

[1] "A set of beads (a rosary), with every *gaud* (large bead among smaller beads) colored green."

[2] The Monk, though a *keeper* or guardian of a local *cell* or group of monks, and an *out-rider* or supervisor of the monastery's property, no longer followed the rule of behavior incumbent upon Benedictine monks. This rule was first formulated in Italy in the sixth century by St. Benedict (*Beneit*), the originator of the order, and subsequently brought to France in the same century by his disciple St. Maur. (Two sentences are here run together: — "This . . . monk let . . . the rule . . . pass by," and "This . . . monk let old things pass by.")

Or swynken° with his handes and laboure — work

As Austyn bit?° How shal the world be served?[1] — commands (*biddeth*)

Lat Austyn have his swynk° to hym reserved. — work

Therfore he was a prikasour° aright. — fast rider

Grehoundes he hadde as swift as fowel° in flight. 190 — bird

Of prikyng° and of huntyng for the hare — tracking (the hare)

Was al his lust,° for no cost wolde he spare. — pleasure

  I seigh° his sleves y-purfiled° at the hond — saw trimmed

With grys,° and that the fyneste of a lond; — gray fur

And for to festne his hood under his chyn

He hadde of gold wroght a ful curious pyn;

A love knotte in the gretter° ende ther was. — larger

His heed was balled,° that shoon as any glas, — bald

And eek° his face as° he hadde been enoynt.° — also as if anointed

He was a lord ful fat and in good poynt,° 200 — condition

Hise eyen stepe° and rollynge in his heed, — eyes bulging

That stemed° as a forneys° of a leed,° — glowed furnace boiler

His bootes souple, his hors in greet estat.

  Now certeynly he was a fair prelat.

He was nat pale as a forpyned goost.° — tormented spirit

A fat swan loved he best of any roost.

His palfrey was as broun as is a berye.

  A FRERE° ther was, a wantowne° and a merye, — friar gay

A lymytour,° a ful solempne° man. — limiter splendid

In alle the ordres foure [2] is noon that kan° 210 — knows

So muche of daliaunce° and fair langage. — flirtation

---

[1] St. Augustine (*Austyn*) of Hippo in the fifth century criticized monks for their sloth. The query "How is the world to be served" means "Who will perform worldly services such as require a cleric's education if monks withdraw themselves from the world to the life of spiritual contemplation required of them?" Throughout this portrait Chaucer acquiesces ironically with the Monk's argument.

[2] The four orders of friars, which were all established in the thirteenth century, were intended to combat the abuses of the earlier monastic orders. Friars renounced property and undertook, when necessary, to earn money by manual labor; and they followed an active life of service to mankind rather than, as the monks did, a contemplative life. But the need of their organization became such that they were forced to become mendicants and beg for alms; and they were subsequently licensed to raise funds by hearing confessions and granting absolutions. In the fourteenth century priests came to object to the infringements on their parishes made by limiters, or friars assigned to particular limits; and reformers began to accuse them of corruption. The outspoken advocate of reform, John Wyclif, called the friars "the children of Caim," punning on the medieval form of the name of Cain, Abel's murderer, and the initial letters of the four orders: Carmelites, Augustines, Iacobins (Dominicans), and Minorites (Franciscans).

He hadde maad° ful many a mariage   *arranged*
Of yonge wommen at his owene cost.
    Unto his ordre he was a noble post.°   *pillar*
Ful wel biloved and famulier was he
With frankeleyns over-al° in his contree   *rich landholders everywhere*
And with worthy wommen of the toun,
For he hadde power of confessioun,
As seyde hymself, moore than a curat,°   *parish priest*
For of his ordre he was licenciat.   220
Ful swetely herde he confessioun,
And plesaunt was his absolucioun.
He was an esy man to yeve° penaunce   *give*
Ther-as he wiste° to have a good pitaunce.°   *Where he knew gift*
For unto a poure ordre for to yive°   *give*
Is signe that a man is wel y-shryve°;   *confessed*
For if he yaf,° he dorste make avaunt,°   *gave (the Friar) dared to avow*
He wiste° that a man was repentaunt;   *knew*
For many a man so hard is of his herte,
He may not wepe, althogh hym° soore smerte.°   230 *he smart*
Therfore, in stede of wepynge and preyeres,
Men moote yeve° silver to the poure freres.   *One ought to give*
    His typet° was ay farsed° ful of knyves   *cape always stuffed*
And pynnes for to yeven faire wyves.
    And certeynly he hadde a murye note.
Wel koude he synge and pleyen on a rote°;   *stringed instrument*
Of yeddynges° he bar outrely° the prys.   *ballads carried off completely*
His nekke whit was as the flour de lys°;   *fleur-de-lis*
Ther-to° he strong was as a champioun.   *In addition*
    He knew the tavernes wel in every toun   240
And every hostiler° and tappestere°   *innkeeper bar-maid*
Bet° than a lazar° or a beggestere,°   *Better leper female beggar*
For unto swich° a worthy man as he   *such*
Acorded nat,° as by his facultee,°   *It was not suitable capacity*
To have with sike° lazars aqueyntaunce.   *sick*
It is nat honeste,° it may nat avaunce,°   *proper benefit*
For to deelen with no swich poraille°   *such poor folk*
But al with riche and selleres of vitaille.°   *victuals*
And, over-al ther-as° profit sholde arise,   *everywhere where*
Curteys he was and lowely of servyse.   250
Ther was no man nowher so vertuous.°   *gifted*
He was the beste beggere in his hous,°   *friary*

For thogh a wydwe° hadde noght a sho,°   widow   shoe
So plesant was his *In principio*,[1]
Yet wolde he have a ferthyng er° he wente.   farthing before
His purchas° was wel° bettre than his rente.°   pickings   much   regular
                                                          income
And rage° he koude as it were right° a whelpe.   frolic   just like

   In lovedayes° ther koude he muchel° helpe,   arbitration-days   much
For ther he was nat lyk a cloysterer
With a thredbare cope,° as is a poure scoler,   260   cloak
But he was lyk a maister° or a pope;   Master of Arts
Of double worstede was his semycope,°   short cloak
That rounded as a belle out of the presse.

   Somwhat he lipsed° for his wantownesse°   lisped   playfulness
To make his Englissh sweete upon his tonge;
And in his harpyng, whan that he hadde songe,
Hise eyen° twynkled in his heed aright   eyes
As doon the sterres in the frosty nyght.
This worthy lymytour was cleped° Huberd.   called

   A MARCHANT° was ther with a forked berd,   merchant
In motlee,° and hye on hors he sat,   felt   271   figured cloth
Upon his heed a Flaundryssh° bevere hat, hat   Flemish
His bootes clasped faire and fetisly.°   elegantly

   Hise resons° he spak ful solempnely,°   views   impressively
Sownynge° alwey the encrees of his wynnyng.°   Relating   profit
He wolde the see were kept° for any thyng   guarded
Bitwixe Middelburgh° and Orewelle.°   Middelburg (Holland)
                                                         Orwell Harbor (England)
Wel koude he in eschaunge sheeldes selle.[2]

   This worthy man ful wel his wit bisette.°   applied
Ther wiste° no wight° that he was in dette,   280   knew   person
So estatly was he of his governaunce
With his bargaynes and with his chevysaunce.°   manipulation

   For sothe,° he was a worthy man with alle,   Truly
But, sooth to seyn,° I noot° how men hym calle.   say   don't know

   A CLERK° ther was of Oxenford° also   student   Oxford
That unto logyk [3] hadde longe y-go.°   long since gone

---

[1] "In the beginning" — the first words of *St. John's Gospel*, used in the Middle Ages as a
religious and even magic formula.

[2] "He well knew how to sell *shields* or *écus* (French coins) in (illegal) exchange (at a profit
allowed only to the royal money-changers)." Presumably the Merchant was a wholesale
exporter and, as such, knew how to evade foreign exchange restrictions.

[3] Medieval university courses in arts were based on a study of the Seven Arts. The B.A.
required the study of the trivium, a group of three topics, grammar, logic, and rhetoric.
The M.A. required further, prolonged study of the quadrivium, a group of four topics,

As leene was his hors as is a rake,
And he was nat right° fat, I undertake,° — particularly vow
But looked holwe° and ther-to sobrely. — hollow
Ful thredbare was his overeste courtepy,°   290 — outer short coat
For he hadde geten hym yet no benefice,° — ecclesiastical appointment
Ne was so worldly for to have office,° — secular position
For hym was levere° have at his beddes heed — he would rather
Twenty bookes clad in blak or reed
Of Aristotle and his philosophie
Than robes riche or fithele° or gay sautrie.° — fiddle psaltery (harp)
 But, al be that he was a philosophre,[1]
Yet hadde he but litel gold in cofre,° — coffer
But al that he myghte of his frendes hente,° — get
On bookes and on lernynge he it spente,   300
And bisily gan for the soules preye° — prayed (*gan . . . preye*)
Of hem that yaf° hym wher-with to scoleye.° — gave study
 Of studie took he moost cure° and moost heede. — care
Noght oo° word spak he moore than was neede, — one
And that was seid in forme and reverence° — formally and respectfully
And short and quyk and ful of heigh sentence.° — significance
Sownynge in° moral vertu was his speche, — Tending toward
And gladly wolde he lerne and gladly teche.
 A SERGEANT OF THE LAWE, war° and wys, — wary
That often hadde been at the Parvys,[2]   310
Ther was also, ful riche of excellence.
Discreet he was and of greet reverence —
He semed swich,° hise wordes weren° so wyse. — such were
 Justice he was ful often in assise° — local assize court
By patente° and by pleyn° commissioun. — public full
For° his science° and for his heigh renoun, — In reward for knowledge
Of fees and robes hadde he many oon.° — a one

---

arithmetic, geometry, music, and astronomy, to which both natural philosophy (science) and moral philosophy had been added by Chaucer's time. The Clerk was presumably engaged in completing his M.A., and if he then intended to qualify for a degree in theology, he would be obliged to spend another ten years at the university.

[1] Natural philosophy, which the Clerk probably neglected in favor of moral philosophy, embraced all the sciences, one of which was alchemy, and alchemists claimed to be able to transmute base metals into gold.

[2] The Sergeant of the Law was one of a small and select group of eminent lawyers specially appointed by the King. He had often appeared at the "Parvys" (perhaps St. Paul's porch, London) where clients consulted their lawyers, and he had also traveled on circuit as a justice.

So greet a purchasour° was nowher noon;   *buyer of land*
Al was fee symple° to hym in effect.   *unrestricted possession*
His purchasyng myghte° nat been infect.°   320   *could invalidated*
  Nowher so bisy a man as he ther nas,°   *was*
And yet he semed bisier than he was.
  In termes° hadde he caas° and doomes° alle   *Precisely cases judgments*
That from the tyme of Kyng William° were falle.   *William I (1066–87)*
Ther-to° he koude endite° and make a thyng°;   *In addition compose draw up a document*
Ther koude no wight pynchen° at his writyng.   *person find fault*
And every statut koude° he pleyn by roote.°   *knew fully by memory*
  He rood but hoomly° in a medlee° coote,   *plainly striped*
Girt with a ceynt° of silk with barres smale.   *belt*
Of his array telle I no lenger tale.   330
  A FRANKELEYN was in his compaignye.
Whit was his berd as is the dayesye°;   *daisy*
Of his complexioun he was sangwyn.°   *blood-red*
Wel loved he by the morwe° a sop° in wyn.   *morning piece of bread*
To lyven in delyt was evere his wone,°   *custom*
For he was Epicurus owene sone,
That heeld opynyoun that pleyn° delit   *complete*
Was verray° felicitee parfit.°   *true perfect*
  An housholdere, and that a greet,° was he;   *great (one)*
Seint Julyan he was in his contree.[1]   340
His breed, his ale, was alweys after oon.°   *consistently good*
A bettre envyned° man was nevere noon.   *wined*
Withoute bake-mete° was nevere his hous   *pie*
Of fissh and flessh,° and that so plentevous°   *meat plentiful*
It snewed° in his hous of mete° and drynke,   *snowed food*
Of alle deyntees that men koude thynke,
After° the sondry sesons of the yeer,   *According to*
So chaunged° he his mete and his soper.°   *varied supper*
Ful many a fat partrich hadde he in muwe,°   *coop*
And many a breem and many a luce° in stuwe.°   350   *pike pond*
Wo was his cook but if° his sauce were   *unless*
Poynaunt° and sharp, and redy al his geere.°   *Pungent utensils*
His table dormaunt in his halle alway
Stood redy covered al the longe day.[2]

Final (margin note)

---

[1] A rich land-owner and householder, the Franklin was the local counterpart of St. Julian, the traditional patron saint of hospitality.

[2] He kept a permanent (*dormaunt*) table (rather than a removable board and trestles) in his main room (*halle*).

At sessions ther he was lord and sire [1];
Ful ofte tyme he was knyght of the shire.° — *Member of Parliament*
An anlaas° and a gipser° al of silk — *dagger   purse*
Heeng° at his girdel whit as morne° mylk. — *Hung   morning*
A shirreve° hadde he been and a countour°; — *sheriff   auditor*
Was nowher swich a worthy vavasour.°   360 — *squire*
   An HABERDASSHERE and a CARPENTER,
A WEBBE,° a DYERE, and a TAPYCER° — — *weaver   tapestry-maker*
And they were clothed alle in oo° lyveree — *one*
Of a solempne° and a greet fraternytee.° — *important   religious guild*
Ful fressh and newe hir geere apiked was°; — *their accessories were trimmed*
Hir knyves were chaped° noght with bras — *mounted*
But al with silver; wroght ful clene and wel
Hir girdles and hir pouches everydel.° — *altogether*
Wel semed ech of hem a fair burgeys° — *citizen*
To sitten in a yeldehalle° on a deys.° (*dais*)   370 — *guildhall   platform*
Everych° for the wisdom that he kan° — *Each one   knows*
Was shaply° for to been an alderman, — *suited*
For catel° hadde they ynogh and rente,° — *property   income*
And eek° hir wyves wolde it wel assente, — *also*
And elles° certeyn they were to blame. — *otherwise*
It is ful fair to been y-cleped° "madame" — *called*
And goon to vigilies° al bifore — *festivals on eves of saints' days*
And have a mantel roialliche y-bore.° — *carried*
   A COOK they hadde with hem for the nones° — *occasion*
To boille the chiknes° with the marybones,°   380 — *chickens   marrowbones*
And poudre-marchaunt° tart, and galyngale.° — *flavoring   spice*
Wel koude he knowe° a draughte of Londoun ale. — *judge*
He koude rooste and sethe° and broille and frye, — *boil*
Maken mortreux,° and wel bake a pye. — *Make stews*
But greet harm was it, as it thoughte° me, — *seemed to*
That on his shyne a mormal° hadde he. — *shin an ulcer*
For blankmanger° that made he with the beste. — *sweet creamed fowl*
   A SHIPMAN° was ther wonyng fer by° weste; — *merchant-ship owner   living far to the*
For aught I woot,° he was of Dertemouthe.° — *know   Dartmouth (Devon)*
He rood upon a rouncy as he kouthe°   390 — *nag as best he could*
In a gowne of faldyng° to the knee. — *serge*
A daggere hangynge on a laas° hadde he — *lanyard*

[1] He presided at sessions of the local Justices of the Peace, who would deal with minor
matters. More serious cases would be brought before local assize courts (l. 314) conducted
by circuit justices such as his companion the Sergeant of the Law.

Aboute his nekke, under his arm adoun.
The hoote somer had maad his hewe al broun.
  And certeynly he was a good felawe.°   rascal (*good felawe*)
Ful many a draughte of wyn hadde he drawe
Fro Burdeuxward° whil that the chapman sleep.°   From Bordeaux (France)
                                                           dealer slept
Of nyce° conscience took he no keep°;   tender   heed
If that he faught and had the hyer hond,
By water he sente hem hoom° to every lond.   400   them home (overboard)
  But of his craft to rekene wel his tydes,
His stremes,° and his daungers hym bisydes,°   currents   around
His herberwe,° and his moone, his lodemenage,°   harbor   pilotage
Ther nas noon swich° from Hulle to Cartage.°   was none such   Cartagena
                                                           (Spain)
Hardy he was and wys to undertake.°   conduct an enterprise
With many a tempest hadde his berd been shake.
He knew alle the havenes as they were
Fro Gootland° to the cape of Fynystere°   Gottland (off Sweden)
                                                           Finisterre (Spain)
And every cryke° in Britaigne° and in Spayne.   creek   Brittany
His barge y-cleped° was the Mawdelayne.   410   called
  With us ther was a DOCTOUR ¹ OF PHISIK°;   medicine
In al this world ne was ther noon hym lyk,
To speke of phisik and of surgerye,
For he was grounded in astronomye.°   astrology
He kepte° his pacient a ful greet deel   watched
In houres° by his magik natureel.   (astrologically important)
                                                           hours
Wel koude he fortunen the ascendent°   determine the correct point
Of hise ymages° for his pacient.   of the zodiac
                                                         curative images
He knew the cause of every maladye,
Were it of hoot or coold or moyste or drye,   420
And where engendred, and of what humour.
He was a verray,° parfit practisour.°   true   practitioner
  The cause y-knowe° and of his harm the roote,   known
Anon° he yaf° the sike man his boote.°   Immediately   gave   remedy
Ful redy hadde he hise apothecaries

---

¹ To qualify as a doctor in Chaucer's time, a student, after acquiring a B.A., usually
spent five years of reading and two years of practice at medical school. He studied the time-
honored Greek theories concerning the choleric, melancholy, sanguine, and phlegmatic
complexions or temperaments and the bodily fluids or humors, which were supposed to
engender them and to arise in turn from the proportions of hot, cold, wet, or dry within
the body. He also studied astrology, because it was still believed that the planets influenced
the equilibrium of the humors in the body, and that their effects could therefore be predicted by the calculation of horoscopes and modified by the use of natural or legitimate,
not black, magic.

To sende hym drogges and his letuaries,°   remedies
For ech of hem made oother for to wynne°;   gain
Hir° frendshipe nas nat° newe to begynne.   Their   was not
   Wel knew he the olde Esculapius,
And Deiscorides, and eek Rufus,   430
Old Ypocras, Haly, and Galyen,
Serapion, Razis, and Avycen,
Averrois, Damascien, and Constantyn,
Bernard, and Gatesden, and Gilbertyn.[1]
   Of his diete mesurable° was he,   moderate
For it was of no superfluitee
But of greet norissynge° and digestible.   nourishment
His studie was but litel on the Bible.
   In sangwyn° and in pers° he clad was al,   red   Persian blue
Lyned with taffata and with sendal,°   440 silk
And yet he was but esy° of dispence.°   cautious   spending
He kepte that° he wan in pestilence.   what
For° gold in phisik is a cordial,°   Because   heart-remedy
Therfore he loved gold in special.[2]
   A good WYF was ther of biside BATHE,
But she was somdel° deef, and that was scathe.°   somewhat   a pity
   Of clooth-makyng she hadde swich an haunt,° such a skill
She passed hem° of Ypres and of Gaunt.°   surpassed them (the Flemish
In al the parisshe, wyf ne was ther noon   weavers)   Ghent
That to the offrynge bifore hire sholde goon°; 450 go
And if ther dide, certeyn, so wrooth was she
That she was out of alle charitee.
   Hir coverchiefs° ful fyne were of ground°;   head-coverings   texture
I dorste° swere they weyeden ten pound   would dare
That on a Sonday weren upon hir heed.
Hir hosen weren of fyn scarlet reed,
Ful streite y-teyd,° and shoes ful moyste and newe. tightly tied
Boold was hir face and fair and reed of hewe,
She was a worthy womman al hir lyve.

[1] The Doctor has consulted the most reputable medical authorities, five Greek writers
(ll. 429–431) from the legendary Aesculapius through Hippocrates, Dioscorides, Rufus, to
Galen in the second century A.D.; seven Arabic writers (ll. 431–433) from the ninth to the
twelfth century; and three British writers (l. 434) from the mid-thirteenth century up to
John Gaddesden of Oxford, who died in 1361.

[2] The Doctor had profited by the severe plagues (l. 442) which ravaged England during
the second half of the fourteenth century. He liked gold, Chaucer ironically remarks, because of its heart-restoring properties when mixed in medicine.

Housbondes at chirche dore she hadde fyve,[1]   460
Withouten° oother compaignye in youthe —   Not to mention
But ther-of nedeth nat to speke as nouthe.°   now (*as nouthe*)
    And thries° hadde she been at Jerusalem.   thrice
She hadde passed many a straunge° strem.   foreign
At Rome she hadde been, and at Boloyne,°   Boulogne (France)
In Galice° at Seint Jame,° and at Coloyne.°   Galicia   James (of
                                                                 Compostela) Cologne
She koude° muche of wandrynge by the weye.   knew
Gat-tothed° was she, soothly° for to seye.   Gap-toothed   truly
    Upon an amblere esily she sat,
Y-wympled wel,° and on hir heed an hat   470   Well hooded
As brood as is a bokeler° or a targe,°   buckler   shield
A foot-mantel° aboute hir hipes large,   outer skirt
And on hir feet a peyre of spores° sharpe.   spurs (because she rode
                                                                 astride)
    In felawshipe wel koude she laughe and carpe°;   talk
Of remedies° of love she knew par chaunce,   restoratives
For she koude° of that art the olde daunce.   knew
    A good man was ther of religioun
And was a poure PERSOUN° of a toun,   parson
But riche he was of holy thoght and werk.
He was also a lerned man, a clerk,°   480   scholar
That Cristes gospel trewely° wolde preche.   faithfully
His parisshens° devoutly wolde he teche.   parishioners
Benygne he was and wonder° diligent,   remarkably
And in adversitee ful pacient,
And swich he was preved° ofte sithes.°   proved   times
    Ful looth were hym° to cursen° for his tithes,°   was he   excommunicate
                                                                 church dues
But rather wolde he yeven° out of doute   give
Unto his poure parisshens aboute
Of his offrynge° and eek° of his substaunce.°   voluntary gifts   also
                                                                 income
He koude in litel thyng have suffisaunce.   490
Wyd was his parisshe and houses fer asonder,
But he ne lafte° nat for reyn ne° thonder,   neglected   nor
In siknesse nor in meschief,° to visite   misfortune
The ferreste° in his parisshe, muche° and lite,°   furthest (members) great
                                                                 small
Upon his feet, and in his hond a staf.
    This noble ensample° to his sheep he yaf,°   example   gave
That first he wroghte, and afterward he taughte.
Out of the gospel he tho° wordes caughte.°   those   took
And this figure° he added eek ther-to,   parallel

---

[1] Medieval marriages took place at the church door, preceding nuptial mass at the altar.

That if gold ruste, what sholde iren do? 500
For if a preest be foule on whom we truste,
No wonder is a lewed° man to ruste. — unlearned
And shame it is, if a preest take keep,° — heed
A shiten° shepherde and a clene sheep. — defiled
Wel oghte a preest ensample for to yive° — give
By his clennesse how that his sheep sholde lyve.
    He sette nat his benefice to hyre
And leet° his sheep encombred in the myre — left
And ran to Londoun unto Seint Poules° — St. Paul's (Cathedral)
To seken° hym a chauntrye° for soules, 510 — secure endowment to sing masses
Or with a bretherhede° to been withholde,° — religious fraternity retained (as chaplain)
But dwelte at hoom and kepte° wel his folde — watched
So that the wolf ne made it nat myscarye.
He was a shepherde and noght a mercenarye.
    And thogh he hooly were and vertuous,
He was noght to synful men despitous,° — scornful
Ne° of his speche daungerous ne digne,° — Nor domineering or pompous
But in his techyng discreet and benigne.
To drawen folk to hevene by fairnesse,
By good ensample, this was his bisynesse.° 520 — concern
But it° were any persone obstinat, — if there
What so° he were of heigh or lowe estat, — Whether
Hym wolde he snybben° sharply for the nonys.° — reprove occasion
    A bettre preest I trowe° that nowher noon ys. — believe
He wayted after° no pompe and reverence, — expected
Ne maked hym a spiced° conscience, — Nor assumed an over-scrupulous
But Cristes loore° and his apostles twelve — teaching
He taughte, but first he folwed it hymselve.
    With hym ther was a PLOWMAN, was his
        brother,
That hadde y-lad° of donge° ful many a fother.° 530 — hauled manure load
A trewe swynkere° and a good was he, — laborer
Lyvynge in pees and parfit charitee.
God loved he best with al his hoole herte
At alle tymes, thogh hym gamed or smerte,° — he rejoiced or grieved
And thanne his neighebore right° as hymselve. — just as much
He wolde thresshe and ther-to dyke° and delve° — ditch dig
For Cristes sake for every poure wight
Withouten hire,° if it lay in his myght. — payment
His tithes payde he ful faire and wel

Bothe of his propre swynk° and his catel.°   540   own work   property
In a tabard° he rood, upon a mere.°   smock   (unfashionable) mare
   Ther was also a REVE° and a MILLERE,   reeve
A SOMNOUR° and a PARDONER also,   summoner
A MAUNCIPLE° and myself; ther were namo.°   manciple   no more
   The MILLER was a stout carl for the nones.°   an especially stout fellow
Ful big he was of brawn and eek of bones.
That proved wel, for over-al ther° he cam,   everywhere
At wrastlynge he wolde have alwey the ram.°   ram (as prize)
He was short-sholdred, brood, a thikke knarre.°   knot of a fellow
Ther was no dore that he nolde° heve of harre° 550 would not   off its hinges
Or breke it at a rennyng with his heed.
His berd as any sowe or fox was reed°   red
And ther-to brood° as though it were a spade.   as broad
Upon the cop right° of his nose he hade   very top
A werte,° and ther-on stood a tuft of herys,°   wart   hairs
Reed as the bristles of a sowes erys.°   ears
His nosethirles° blake were and wyde.   nostrils
A swerd and a bokeler bar° he by his syde.   wore
   His mouth as greet was as a greet fourneys.°   furnace
He was a jangler° and a goliardeys.°   560   talker   jester
And that was moost of synne and harlotries.°   ribaldries
   Wel koude he stelen corn and tollen thries,°   levy a toll thrice
And yet he hadde a thombe of gold,[1] pardee.°   certainly
   A whit cote and a blew hood wered° hee.   wore
A baggepipe wel koude he blowe and sowne,°   play
And ther-with-al he broghte us out of towne.
   A gentil MAUNCIPLE° was ther of a temple°   purchasing agent   law society's residence
Of which achatours° myghte take exemple   From whom buyers
For to be wys in byynge of vitaille,°   victuals
For wheither that he payde or took by taille,° 570 tally (of the debit)
Algate° he wayted° so in his achaat°   In any case   watched buying
That he was ay biforn° and in good staat.   always ahead
   Now, is nat that of God a ful fair grace
That swich a lewed° mannes wit shal pace°   such an unlearned   surpass
The wisdom of an heep of lerned men!
Of maistres hadde he mo° than thries ten   more
That weren of° lawe expert and curious,°   in   ingenious
Of whiche° ther were a dozeyne in that hous   Among whom

[1] That is, "For a miller, he was honest," in ironic reference to the ambiguous proverb, "An honest miller has a golden thumb."

Worthy to been stywardes° of rente° and lond   be stewards   income
Of any lord that is in Engelond,   580
To make hym lyve by his propre good°   own resources
In honour detteles, but if° he were wood,°   unless   insane
Or lyve as scarsly° as hym list° desire;   sparingly   he wishes to
And able for to helpen° al a shire   aid (legally)
In any caas that myghte falle or happe.
And yet this Maunciple sette hir aller cappe.°   on them all the dunce cap
    The REVE° was a sclendre, colerik man.   estate-manager
His berd was shave as neigh° as ever he kan;   close
His heer was by his erys° ful round y-shorn;   ears
His top was dokked° lyk a preest byforn.   590   cropped (because he was a serf)
Ful longe were his legges and ful lene;
Ylik a staf,° ther was no calf y-sene.   Like a stick
    Wel koude he kepe a gerner° and a bynne;   watch a granary
Ther was noon auditour koude on hym wynne.
Wel wiste° he by the droghte and by the reyn   knew
The yeldynge of his seed and of his greyn.
His lordes sheep, his neet,° his dayerye,   cattle
His swyn, his hors, his stoor,° and his pultrye   stock
Was hoolly in this Reves governynge,
And by his covenant yaf° the rekenynge   600   (he) gave
Syn° that his lord was twenty yeer of age.   Since the time
Ther koude no man brynge hym in arrerage.°   arrears
Ther nas baillif,° ne hierde,° ne oother hyne°   was not overseer   herd servant
That he ne knew his sleighte° and his covyne.°   whose tricks he didn't know fraud
They were adrad° of hym as of the deeth.   afraid
    His wonyng° was ful faire upon an heeth;   dwelling
With grene trees shadwed was his place.
He koude bettre than his lord purchace;
Ful riche he was astored pryvely.°   stocked in secret
His lord wel koude he plesen subtilly   610
To yeve° and lene° hym of his owene good°   give   lend   property
And have a thank and yet° a coote and hood.   also
    In youthe he hadde lerned a good myster°:   trade
He was a wel good wrighte, a carpenter.
    This Reve sat upon a ful good stot,°   stallion
That was al pomely° grey and highte° Scot.   dapple   was called
A long surcote of pers° upon he hade,   overcoat of Persian blue
And by his syde he baar° a rusty blade.   wore
Of Northfolk° was this Reve of which I telle,   Norfolk

Biside a toun men clepen Baldeswelle.°   620   Bawdswell
Tukked he was as is a frere° aboute;   friar
And evere he rood the hyndreste° of oure route.°   hindermost company
    A SOMNOUR° was ther with us in that place,   constable of a church court
That hadde a fyr-reed cherubynnes face,[1]
For saucefleem° he was, with eyen° narwe.   pimpled eyes
As hoot he was and lecherous as a sparwe,°   sparrow
With scaled° browes blake and piled° berd.   scabby scanty
Of his visage children were aferd.°   afraid
Ther nas quyksilver, lytarge,° ne brymstoon,   lead ointment
Boras,° ceruce,° ne oille° of tartre noon,   630   Borax white lead cream
Ne oynement that wolde clense and byte,
That hym myghte helpen° of his whelkes° white,   could rid (leprous) sores
Nor of the knobbes sittynge on his chekes.
    Wel loved he garlek, oynons, and eek lekes,
And for to drynke strong wyn reed as blood;
Thanne wolde he speke and crye as° he were wood°;   as if mad
And whan that he wel dronken hadde the wyn,
Thanne wolde he speke no word but Latyn.
    A fewe termes hadde he, two or thre,
That he had lerned out of som decre.   640
No wonder is! He herde it al the day;
And eek ye knowen wel how that a jay
Kan clepen "Watte"° as wel as kan the Pope.   call out "Walter" (like "Polly")
But who so koude in oother thyng hym grope,°   examine
Thanne hadde he spent al his philosophie.
Ay° "*Questio, quid juris?*"[2] wolde he crie.   Always
    He was a gentil harlot° and a kynde;   an obliging rascal
A bettre felawe sholde men noght fynde.
He wolde suffre,° for a quart of wyn,   allow
A good felawe° to have his concubyn°   650   A rascal mistress
A twelf monthe and excuse hym atte fulle.°   fully
Ful pryvely° a fynch eek koude he pulle°;   secretively fornicate (*pulls a fynch*)
And if he foond owher° a good felawe,   found anywhere
He wolde techen hym to have noon awe
In swich caas of the ercedekenes curs°   archdeacon's curse (of excommunication)
But if° a mannes soule were in his purs,   Unless

---

[1] The Summoner had a "fire-red cherub's face," like the faces of cherubim colored red in ecclesiastical ornamentation. He evidently had, in medieval terms, a "sanguine complexion" and suffered from a leprous disease known as *alopicia*.

[2] "Query, what of the law (here)?" That is, "What law applies to this case?"

For in his purs he sholde y-punysshed be.
"Purs is the ercedekenes helle," seyde he.
But wel I woot° he lyed right in dede;   *know*
Of cursyng oghte ech gilty man drede, —   660
For curs wol slee,° right as assoillyng° savith, —   *slay absolution*
And also war hym of° a *significavit.*°   *beware writ for arrest*

In daunger° hadde he at° his owene gyse°   *subjection in way*
The yonge gerles° of the diocise,   *people (male and female)*
And knew hir counseil,° and was al hir reed.°   *their secrets adviser of all of them*

A gerland° hadde he set upon his heed,   *garland*
As greet as it were for an ale stake°;   *alehouse sign*
A bokeler hadde he maad hym of a cake.

With hym ther rood a gentil PARDONER
Of Rouncival, his freend and his comper,°   670   *comrade*
That streight was comen fro the court of Rome.[1]
Ful loude he soong,° "Com hider,° love, to me."   *sang hither*
This Somnour bar° to hym a stif burdoun,°   *carried strong accompaniment*
Was nevere trompe° of half so greet a soun.°   *trumpet sound*

This Pardoner hadde heer° as yelow as wex,°   *hair wax*
But smothe it heeng° as dooth a strike of flex.°   *hung hank of flax*
By ounces° henge his lokkes that he hadde,   *In wisps*
And ther-with he his shuldres overspradde,
But thynne it lay by colpons oon and oon.°   *in single strands*
But hood, for jolitee,° wered° he noon,   680   *jauntiness wore*
For it was trussed up in his walet.
Hym thoughte he rood al of the newe jet.°   *style*
Dischevelee,° save his cappe he rood al bare.   *With loose hair*
Swiche glarynge eyen hadde he as an hare.

A vernycle° hadde he sowed upon his cappe,   *souvenir of St. Veronica*
His walet biforn hym in his lappe,
Bret° ful of pardoun comen from Rome al hoot.°   *Cram hot*

A voys he hadde as smal as hath a goot.°   *goat*
No berd° hadde he, ne nevere sholde have;   *beard*
As smothe it was as° it were late y-shave.°   690   *as if newly shaved*
I trowe° he were a geldyng° or a mare.   *believe must have been a gelding*

But of his craft fro Berwyk into Ware
Ne was ther swich another pardoner,

[1] The Pardoner evidently belonged to a fraternity located at the religious hospital of the Blessed Mary of Rouncivalle, just outside London. The pardons (remissions of punishment) which he was prepared to dispense were, allegedly at least, issued by the Pope at Rome. Many of the pardoners in Chaucer's England, however, were fraudulent and unlicensed.

For in his male° he hadde a pilwe-beer°   bag pillowcase
Which that he seyde was Oure Lady veyl.°   Lady's veil
He seyde he hadde a gobet° of the seyl°   piece sail
That Seint Peter hadde whan that he wente°   walked
Upon the see til Jesu Crist hym hente.° ¹   caught
He hadde a croys of latoun° ful of stones,   copper alloy
And in a glas he hadde pigges bones.   700
But with thise relikes, whan that he fond
A poure persoun° dwellyng upon lond,°   parson (to aid him) the country
Upon a° day he gat hym moore moneye   one
Than that the persoun gat in monthes tweye.
And thus with feyned flaterye and japes°   tricks
He made the persoun and the peple his apes.°   fools
    But trewely to tellen, atte laste,
He was in chirche a noble ecclesiaste.
Wel koude he rede a lessoun or a storie,°   Bible story (*or* saint's life)
But alderbest° he song° an offertorie,   710   best of all sang
For wel he wiste° whan that song was songe,   knew
He moste° preche and wel affile° his tonge   must make smooth
To wynne silver, as he ful wel koude.
Ther-fore he song the murierly° and loude.   more merrily
    Now have I told yow soothly in a clause°   truly in brief
Th' estaat, th' array, the nombre, and eek the cause
Why that assembled was this compaignye
In Southwerk at this gentil hostelrye,
That highte° the Tabard, faste° by the Belle.°   was called close Bell Inn
But now is tyme to yow for to telle   720
How that we baren us° that ilke° nyght   conducted ourselves same
Whan we were in that hostelrie alyght°;   alighted
And after wol I telle of oure viage°   journey
And al the remenant of oure pilgrymage.
    But first I pray yow of youre curteisye
That ye n' arette it nat° my vileynye°   won't blame it on boorishness
Thogh that° I pleynly speke in this matere   Even if
To telle yow hir° wordes and hir cheere°   their behavior
Ne thogh° I speke° hir wordes proprely.°   And if repeat literally
For this ye knowen also° wel as I,   730   as
Who so shal telle° a tale after a man,   retell
He moot reherce° as neigh° as evere he kan   must repeat closely
Everich a° word if it be in his charge,   Every single

¹ *Matt.*, xiv, 29.

Al° speke he nevere so rudeliche° and large,°   Even though rudely broadly
Or ellis° he moot telle his tale untrewe,   else
Or feyne thyng,° or fynde wordes newe.   invent something
He may nat spare° al thogh he were his brother;   hold back
He moot° as wel seye o° word as another.   must one
Crist spak hymself ful brode° in holy writ,   freely
And wel ye woot,° no vileynye is it.   740   know
Eek° Plato seith, who so kan hym rede,   Also
The wordes mote° be cosyn° to the dede.   must cousin
   Also, I pray yow to foryeve° it me,   forgive
Al° have I nat set folk in hir degree°   Even if their order of rank
Here in this tale as that° they sholde stonde.°   just as stand
My wit is short, ye may° wel understonde.   can
   Greet cheere made oure HOOST us everichon,°   for each of us
And to the soper sette he us anon.°   immediately
He served us with vitaille° at the beste.   victuals
Strong was the wyn, and wel to drynke us leste.°   750   it pleased
   A semely° man oure Hoost was with alle   suitable
For to been a marchal in an halle.°   banquet hall
A large man he was, with eyen stepe.°   bulging
A fairer burgeys° was ther noon in Chepe,°   citizen Cheapside (London)
Boold of his speche, and wys, and wel y-taught,
And of manhode hym° lakked right naught.   he
   Eke ther-to he was right° a murye man,   truly
And after soper pleyen° he bigan   to joke
And spak of myrthe,° amonges othere thynges,   amusement
Whan that we hadde maad° oure rekenynges,°   760   paid bills
And seyde thus, "Now, lordynges,° trewely,   sirs
Ye been° to me right welcome, hertely,   are
For by my trouthe, if that I shal not lye,
I saugh nat this yeer so murye a compaignye
At ones° in this herberwe° as is now.   once lodging
Fayn° wolde I doon° yow myrthe, wiste I° how.   Gladly provide if I knew
And of a myrthe I am right now bythoght
To doon yow ese,° and it shal coste noght.   comfort
   "Ye goon° to Caunterbury, God yow spede!   are going
The blisful martir quyte° yow youre mede°!   770   grant reward
And wel I woot° as ye goon by the weye,   know
Ye shapen yow to talen° and to pleye,   intend to tell tales
For trewely confort ne° myrthe is noon°   nor none
To ryde by the weye domb as a stoon.

And ther-fore wol I maken yow disport,° amusement
As I seyde erst,° and doon yow som confort. before
And if yow liketh alle by oon° assent one
For to stonden at° my juggement abide by
And for to werken° as I shall yow seye, do
Tomorwe, whan ye riden by the weye,   780
Now, by my fader° soule, that is deed, father's
But° ye be murye, I wol yeve yow myn heed.° Unless   head
Hoold up youre hondes withouten moore speche."
    Oure conseil was nat longe for to seche.° seek
Us thoughte it was nat worth to make it wys,° difficult
And graunted° hym withouten moore avys° (we) yielded to
      consideration
And bad hym seye his voirdit° as hym leste.° verdict   it pleased
    "Lordynges," quod° he, "now herkneth° for the said   listen
    beste,
But taketh it not, I pray yow, in desdeyn.° contemptuously
This is the poynt, to speken short and pleyn,   790
That ech of yow, to shorte with oure weye,° cut short our way with
In this viage° shal telle tales tweye,° — journey   two
To Caunterburyward° I mene it so, — toward Canterbury
And homward he shal tellen othere two
Of aventures that whilom° have bifalle. once upon a time
And which° of yow that bereth° hym best of alle, whichever   conducts
That is to seyn, that telleth in this caas
Tales of best sentence° and moost solaas,° significance   delight
Shal have a soper at oure aller cost° the expense of all of us
Here in this place, sittyng by this post,   800
Whan that we come agayn fro Caunterbury.
And, for to make yow the moore mury,
I wol myself goodly with yow ryde
Right at myn owene cost and be your gyde;
And who so° wole my juggement withseye° whosoever   resist
Shal paye al that we spende by the weye.
And if ye vouchesauf that it be so,
Tel me anoon° withouten wordes mo,° immediately   more
And I wol erly shape° me ther-fore." prepare
    This thyng was graunted, and oure othes swore° sworn
With ful glad herte, and preyden° hym also   811 (we) begged
That he wolde vouchesauf for to do so,
And that he wolde been oure governour,
And of oure tales juge and reportour,° critic

And sette a soper at a certeyn prys,
And we wol reuled been at his devys°   discretion
In heigh and lough.° And thus by oon assent   In all matters
We been acorded to his juggement;
And ther-upon the wyn was fet anoon.°   fetched immediately
We dronken,° and to reste wente echon°   820   drank   each one
Withouten any lenger taryynge.
   A morwe,° whan that day bigan to sprynge,   The next morning
Up roos oure Hoost and was oure aller cok°   the cock (who crowed) for
                        us all
And gadred° us togidre° in a flok,   gathered   together
And forth we riden,° a° litel moore than pas,°   rode   at a   foot-pace
Unto the wateryng° of Seint Thomas,   watering-place
And there oure Hoost bigan his hors areste°   to halt
And seyde, "Lordynges, herkneth,° if yow leste.°   listen   it pleases
Ye woot° youre forward° and it yow recorde.°   know   agreement
                        remember it
If evensong and morwesong acorde,°   830   morning-song agree
Lat se° now who shal telle the firste tale.   Let's see
As evere moot° I drynke wyn or ale,   may
Who so be rebel to my juggement
Shal paye for al that by the wey is spent.
Now draweth cut er that we ferrer twynne.°   lots before we further depart
He which that hath the shorteste shal bigynne.
Sire Knyght," quod he, "my mayster and my lord,
Now draweth° cut, for that is myn acord.°   draw a   agreement
Cometh neer," quod he, "my lady Prioresse,
And ye, sire Clerk, lat be° youre shamefastnesse,°   lay aside   modesty
Ne studieth noght. Ley hond to, every man."   841
   Anoon° to drawen every wight bigan,   Immediately
And shortly for to tellen as it was,
Were it by aventure° or sort° or cas,°   chance   lot   destiny
The sothe° is this: the cut fil° to the Knyght,   truth   fell
Of which ful blithe and glad was every wight,°   person
And telle he moste° his tale, as was resoun°   must   right
By forward° and by composicioun,°   agreement   compact
As ye han° herd. What nedeth wordes mo?   have
   And whan this goode man saugh that it was so,
As he that wys was and obedient   851
To kepe his forward by his free assent,
He seyde, "Syn° I shal bigynne the game,   Since
What,° welcome be the cut, a° Goddes name!   Why   in
Now lat us ryde, and herkneth what I seye."

7777777

And with that word we ryden forth oure weye,
And he bigan with right a murye° cheere   a very merry
His tale anoon° and seyde as ye may heere.   thereupon

THE KNIGHT'S TALE

[A 859–3108. Here omitted.]

The *Knight's Tale* is perhaps somewhat less realistic than we might have expected from such a widely experienced veteran as the Knight, but it is entirely in keeping with what we know of the literary taste prevalent among the members of his class of society in Chaucer's day. Chaucer borrowed his plot from a graceful romance composed by the Italian poet Giovanni Boccaccio (1315–1375), from whom he also borrowed material on other occasions. The setting is ancient Athens, but Chaucer's rendering of the characters is entirely medieval, and the chivalric theme is appropriate to the narrator.

While imprisoned in Athens, two friends, Theban knights, both fall in love simultaneously with the Queen's sister. They suffer the pangs of love in the stereotyped manner of the many courtly lovers whose woes are described in the romances composed especially for the delight of the aristocracy. They settle the question of their rival claims by a tournament, the details of which the Knight, of course, finds extremely absorbing. And to this adaptation Chaucer adds philosophic touches suitable to the reflective side of the Knight's nature, utilizing the work of the sixth-century philosopher Boethius, whose *Consolation of Philosophy* he had previously translated from Latin into English.

LINK

[A 3109–3186. Here translated.]

When the Knight had thus told his tale, in all the company everyone, whether young or old, said that it was a noble story and worthy to be held in memory, and particularly the gentry one and all. Our Host laughed and swore: "As I live, this goes well. The pack is unbuckled. Let's see now who shall tell another tale, for the game has certainly started well. Now you, sir Monk, if you can, tell something to match the Knight's tale."

The Miller, who was so pale from drinking that he could hardly sit on his horse, would doff neither hood nor hat, nor stand aside for any man out of courtesy, but in a voice like Pilate's [1] cried out and swore: "By arms, and

[1] Medieval religious plays assigned both to Pontius Pilate and to Herod violent characterizations in their respective roles as examiner and judge of Christ.

by blood and bones, I know a noble tale for the occasion, which I'll now match the Knight's tale with."

Our Host saw that he was drunk with ale and said: "Wait, Robin, my dear brother. Some better man shall tell us another first. Wait, and let's act sensibly."

"By God's soul," said he, "I won't. For I'll either speak or else go my way."

Our Host answered, "Tell away, the Devil take it! You're a fool. You've lost your senses."

"Now listen," said the Miller, "one and all. But first I protest that I am drunk. I know by the way I sound. And so if I should speak amiss, blame it on the Southwark ale, I beg you. For I'm going to tell a life and legend [1] about a carpenter and his wife and how a clerk made a fool of the wright."

The Reeve answered and said, "Hold your tongue. Give up your stupid, drunken ribaldry. It's a sin, and a great folly besides, to belittle a man or to defame him, and to bring wives into such bad repute too. You can say plenty about other things."

The drunken Miller immediately spoke back and said, "Dear brother Oswald, he is no cuckold [2] who has not any wife. But I don't mean to say therefore that you're one. There are many very good wives and always a thousand good ones for every bad one. You well know that yourself if only you wouldn't get cross. Why are you angry with my tale now? I have a wife, God knows, as well as you; but, for all the oxen in my plow, I wouldn't needlessly jump at the conclusion that I'm a cuckold. I'd rather believe that I'm not. A husband mustn't be inquisitive about God's secrets or about his wife. As long as he finds God's plenty there, there's no need to inquire about the rest."

What more should I say than that the Miller wouldn't withhold his words for any man but told his churlish tale in his own manner. I'm sorry that I must repeat it here. And therefore I beseech all gentlefolk, for goodness' sake, don't think that I speak with any evil intention but only because I must either repeat all their tales, be they better or worse, or else falsify some of my matter. And therefore whoever doesn't care to hear it, let him turn over the page and chose another tale, for he shall find enough, great and small, of story-telling about gentility and also about morality and holiness. Don't blame me if you choose amiss. The Miller is a churl, as you well know. So was the Reeve, and many another more. And both of them

---

[1] In medieval usage the terms *life* and *legend*, irreverently misapplied here, signify devotional biographies of martyrs or saints.

[2] A husband whose wife is unfaithful.

told ribaldries. Be advised, and put no blame on me. Besides, men must not make earnest out of game.

THE MILLER'S TALE

[A 3187–3854. Here omitted.]

From the *General Prologue* it is clear that there is a temperamental difference between the Miller and the Reeve. When the pilgrims set out from Southwark, the stout and rubicund Miller characteristically rides at their head, playing the bagpipes; while the lean and choleric Reeve, we are told, rides always the hindermost. Now we gather that the Miller knows the Reeve personally. In his tale, which is probably an adaptation of a French comic narrative poem or *fabliau*, he tells how the youthful Nicholas, an Oxford student, seduces a jealous carpenter's young wife. The Carpenter on the pilgrimage raises no objection to the tale; but the Reeve, also a carpenter by training, betrays himself by taking personal offence.

LINK

[A 3855–3920. Here translated.]

When people had laughed at the nice case of Absolom and gentle Nicholas, various people spoke variously, but for the greater part they laughed and jested, nor did I see anyone grieve over the tale except for Oswald the Reeve. Because he was of the carpenter's craft, a little anger was left in his heart. He began to grumble and find some fault with it.

"As I thrive," said he, "I could very well requite you with the blearing of a proud miller's eye if I cared to speak of ribaldry. But I am old. Because of age I don't care to play. Grass time is done; my fodder is now stable-fare. This white top proclaims my old years. My heart has moldered like my hair, unless I fare like the medlar-fruit, which gets worse the older it is until it lies rotten in muck or straw. So do we old men fare, I'm afraid. Until we are rotten, we cannot be ripe. We always hop as long as the world will pipe. For our wishes ever stick upon a snag: we have a hoar head and a green tail, like a leek; for though our powers are gone, our wishes still hanker after folly just the same. For when we cannot act, then we talk. In our old ashes fire still lies raked.

"We have four embers, which I'll enumerate: boasting, lying, anger, and cupidity. These four sparks belong to old age. Our old limbs may well be unwieldy, but, in truth, desire will never fail. And even now I still have a colt's tooth, many as is the year that has passed away since my tap of life began to run. For certainly the moment that I was born, death drew the tap of life and let it go, and the tap has run ever since till the barrel is almost empty. The stream of life now drops to the bottom. The hapless tongue may just as well ring and chime of misery that has passed in days bygone. With old people, apart from dotage, there is nothing more!"

When our Host had heard this sermonizing, he spoke as haughtily as a king. He said, "What does all this wisdom amount to? Why must we always speak of Holy Writ? The Devil himself made a reeve to preach or turned a carpenter into a shipman or physician. Go ahead and tell your tale, and don't waste time. There's Deptford, and it's half past seven in the morning. There's Greenwich, and many a shrew lives in it! [1] It's high time to begin your tale."

"Now, sirs," said Oswald the Reeve, "I beg you all not to be grieved if I answer and turn him somewhat to scorn, for it's allowable to match force with force. This drunken Miller has told us here how a carpenter was deceived, perhaps in mockery since I am one. And by your leave, I shall pay him back now. I'm going to speak in his same churlish language. Pray God, he may break his neck. He can well see a mote in my eye, but in his own he can't see a beam."

THE REEVE'S TALE

[A 3921–4324. Translated on pp. 185–91.]

Here, as in the *Miller's Tale*, Chaucer has refashioned a French comic narrative poem or *fabliau* to suit the context. This time, the stock role of the deceptive clerk in the *fabliau* is played not by an Oxford student, like the Miller's "gentle Nicholas," but by two lusty Cambridge men. With a restraint proper to his philosophic temperament, the Clerk of Oxford, though perhaps not entirely satisfied by such a one-sided representation of university life, makes no comment; and the other proper-minded members of the group, though they have been willing enough to praise the Knight's courtly romance, also maintain a dignified silence.

The *Reeve's Tale* must have seemed somewhat crude even to a society less restrained in speech than our own, but Chaucer minimizes the potentially bawdy tone of the forthright story by placing its narrator in dramatic perspective. He has warned us that the Reeve is a churl; he has portrayed the Reeve's mounting surge of anger against the Miller; and we know that the Reeve now hopes to gain the offensive by telling the nastiest tale he can think of about a miller. Consequently, while we may laugh at the neat wit of the tale itself, we can laugh equally heartily at the narrator's indignation.

[1] Deptford is situated on the south bank of the Thames, to the north of the road which the pilgrims were following from Southwark to Canterbury, some five miles from their starting point. Greenwich, where Chaucer may have been living at the time of writing, lies next to Deptford on the east.

Moreover, Chaucer deliberately provides an anticlimactic outcome to the Reeve's onslaught. The Reeve has allowed his bad temper to discredit his case beyond repair and yet has failed to arouse any indignant protest from his intended victim, the Miller; and the only result of all his fury is that he unintentionally encourages the Cook, a totally uninvolved listener, to divert the course of the argument.

The tale is remarkable also for the appropriateness of its style to the unscholarly and practical-minded narrator. Unlike the elaborate tale told by the cultured Priest, for instance, here the plot is unfolded directly, and virtually without the assistance of literary references and allusions. For perhaps the first time in English literature, however, rustic speech is used to secure a comic effect (which unfortunately cannot be adequately represented in modern translation). The two students speak a broad Northumbrian dialect which, for Chaucer's London audience, would unquestionably intensify the humor of their lines.

LINK

[A 4325–4364. Here translated.]

While the Reeve was speaking, for very delight the Cook of London felt just as if he were being scratched on the back. "Ha ha," said he. "By the suffering of Christ, this miller had a sharp conclusion to his argument about lodging! Solomon [1] well said in his language, 'Bring not every man into thine house,' for lodging by night is perilous. A man should well consider whom he brings into his privacy. May God give me care and sorrow, I pray, if ever since I was first named Hodge of Ware, I heard of a miller put better to work. He had a malicious jest played on him in the dark. But God forbid that we should stop here; and so, if you are willing to listen to a tale from me, who am a poor man, I'll tell you as best I can a little joke that happened in our city."

Our Host answered and said, "I permit you. Now tell on, Roger. See that it's good, for you've let the blood [2] from many a pasty, and you've sold many a Dover pie that's been twice heated and twice cold. You've been cursed by many a pilgrim who still feels the worse from eating your parsley with your stubble-fattened goose, for many a fly is loose in your shop. Now tell on, gentle Roger. But still, I beg you, don't be angry over fun. A man may speak full truly in fun and play."

"You speak full truly," said Roger, "by my faith! But 'True jest is no

---

[1] Actually not Solomon but the author of the apocryphal book of the Old Testament called *Ecclesiasticus* (xi, 29).

[2] Like a physician letting a patient's blood, he has drawn the gravy out of unsold pastries, which he will refill the next day for sale.

jest,' as the Fleming says. And so, Harry Bailly, by your faith, don't be angry if I tell a tale about an innkeeper before we depart from here. Nevertheless, I won't tell it yet; but before we leave, you'll be paid back!'' And at that he laughed and became cheerful again and told his tale as you shall now hear.

THE COOK'S TALE

[A 4365–4422. Here omitted.]

The *Cook's Tale* consists of a lively fragment concerning low life in London; if completed, it would obviously have matched the two preceding tales both in substance and in tone.

The narrative unit following hereafter (B1–4636) is not directly linked to any other group of tales.

LINK

[B 1–98. Here translated.]

Our Host clearly saw that the bright sun had run through one quarter of the arc of its artificial day, and half an hour and more beyond it; and though he wasn't deeply steeped in learning, he knew that it was the eighteenth day of April, which is the messenger of May; and he saw clearly that the shadow of every tree was the same quantity in length as the upright body which caused it; and so by the shadow he decided that Phoebus, which was shining so clear and bright, had risen forty-five degrees; and he concluded that for that date and latitude it was ten o'clock; and abruptly he wheeled his horse about.[1]

"My lords," said he, "I warn you, all this company, that the fourth part of this day is gone. Now for the love of God and of St. John, in so far as you can, don't lose any time. My lords, time is wasting night and day, and it steals away from us while we're sleeping in privacy and, because of our negligence, even while we're awake, just as does the stream that never turns back, descending from the mountain to the plain. Well may Seneca [2] and

[1] Chaucer, himself an enthusiastic student of astronomy and the translator of a treatise on the use of the astrolabe, comically suggests that the Host was able to compute time without the use of tables by merely estimating the height of the sun in the course of the artificial day (that is, the period of daylight, not the twenty-four hour day).

[2] Medieval writers frequently attributed proverbial lore inaccurately, as Chaucer does here, to Seneca, a Roman philosopher of the first century.

many another philosopher bewail time more than gold in coffer, for he says, 'Loss of chattels can be recovered, but loss of time destroys us.' Beyond a doubt, it won't come back any more than Malkin's maidenhood when she has lost it through her wantonness. So let's not molder in idleness.

"Sir Man of Law," said he, "may you have bliss. Tell us a tale now according to agreement. You've submitted through your free assent to abide by my judgment in this case. Acquit yourself of your behest now; then you'll at least have done your duty."

"Host," said he, "*par Dieu*, I assent. It's not my intention to break my agreement. A behest is a debt, and I'll gladly fulfill my entire behest. I can't say better than that. For such law as a man gives another person he should properly use himself. That's our text. But none the less, right now I certainly can't tell any apt tale which Chaucer hasn't already told long since in the best English he can, as many know, although he's but ignorantly skilled in meters and in effective riming.[1] And if, dear brother, he hasn't told them in one book, he has told them in another. For he has told more about lovers up and down than Ovid mentions in his *Epistles*,[2] which are very old. Why should I tell them since they've been told?

"In youth he told about Ceyx and Alcione,[3] and since then he has spoken about every single person, both noble women and lovers also. Whoever cares to search out his large volume called the *Legend of Cupid's Saints*[4] may there see the large, wide wounds of Lucretia, and of Thisbe of Babylon; the sword of Dido for the false Aeneas; the tree of Phyllis for her Demophon; the complaint of Dejanira and of Hermione, of Ariadne and of Hypsipyle; the barren isle standing in the sea; Leander drowned for his Hero; the tears of Helen, and also the woe of Briseis and of you, Laodamia; the cruelty of you, Queen Medea, hanging your little children by the neck for your Jason, who was so false in love. O Hypermnestra, Penelope, Alcestis, your womanhood he praises with the best!

"But certainly he doesn't write a word about the wicked example of Canace, who sinfully loved her own brother — I say fie upon such accursed stories — or about Apollonius of Tyre, which is such a horrible tale to read, about how the cursed King Antiochus bereft his daughter of her

---

[1] The pilgrims never realize that their reticent companion is the poet Chaucer.

[2] The *Heroides*, one of Chaucer's favorite sources.

[3] Chaucer retold this story from Ovid's *Metamorphoses* in one of his earliest poems, *The Book of the Duchess*.

[4] Chaucer's *Legend of Good Women*, as it is usually called, consists of an incomplete series of narratives about women who were faithful in love, avowedly written in order to atone for the harm spoken of women in his translation of the French *Romance of the Rose* and in his *Troilus and Criseyde*. The Man of Law, however, characteristically relishes the tragic elements of the *Legend* and not its semi-comic tone.

maidenhood when he threw her upon the pavement.[1] And so with proper judgment he would never write in any of his discourses about such unnatural abominations, nor will I repeat any if I can help it.

"But what shall I do about my tale this day? I'd certainly hate to be compared to those Muses called the Pierides [2] — the book of *Metamorphoses* knows what I mean. But nevertheless, I don't care a straw even if I do come after him with humble fare. I speak in prose and leave him to make rimes." [3]

And with that word he began his tale with sober countenance, as you shall hereafter hear.

THE MAN OF LAW'S TALE

[B 99–1162. Here omitted.]

The tale ascribed to the Man of Law, whether originally intended for him or not, is suited to the moralistic tone of his preceding remarks. The prologue to the tale consists largely of a paraphrase of a section of Pope Innocent the Third's *Contempt of the World*, one of the most ascetic works of the middle ages; and further passages from it are quoted throughout the tale. The tale itself is derived from an Anglo-Norman chronicle and deals with the Christian patience and piety of Constance, the daughter of the Emperor of Rome, who is miraculously and repeatedly rescued from malicious pagans and finally restored to her family. Chaucer's contemporary, John Gower, tells the identical tale in his English poem, the *Lover's Confession*, following the same source; but where Gower uses the material as an illustration of the triumph of love over detraction, Chaucer molds the material according to the devotional pattern of the martyr's or saint's life.

[1] The stories here repudiated — the former derived from Ovid, the latter from some version of a prose romance widely known throughout medieval Europe — are both told in the *Lover's Confession*, a long English poem by Chaucer's friend, the "moral Gower." Perhaps Chaucer is here teasing Gower, or perhaps he is merely delineating the austere taste of the Man of Law.

[2] Not the real Muses of Pieria but the would-be Muses, daughters of King Pierus, who were turned into magpies, according to Ovid's *Metamorphoses*, after losing a contest with the real Muses.

[3] This line might possibly mean that the Man of Law usually spoke as a lawyer only in prose; but more likely Chaucer wrote these words at a time when he intended to supply a prose tale for the Man of Law and then forgot to correct them after he had altered his plan.

LINK

[B 1163–1190. Here translated.]

Our Host rose up at once on his stirrups and said, "Good men, hear me everyone. This was a most suitable tale. Sir Parish Priest," said he, "for God's bones, tell us a tale, as was your agreement previously. I clearly see that you men steeped in learning know many good things, by God's dignity!"

The Parson answered him, "*Benedicite!* What ails the man to swear so sinfully?"

Our Host answered, "O Jankin, are you there? I smell a Lollard in the wind.[1] Now, good men," said our Host, "hear me. By the worthy suffering of God, just wait, for we're going to have a sermon. This Lollard here is going to preach something at us."

"No, by my father's soul," said the Shipman, "he shall not. He shall not preach here. He shall not interpret or teach any gospel here. We all believe in the great God," said he. "He would sow some difficulty or sprinkle cockles among our pure wheat. And therefore, Host, I forewarn you, my jolly body shall tell a tale, and I'll ring you so merry a bell that I'll awaken this entire company. But it won't be about philosophy or phislyas [2] or obscure terms of law. There is but little Latin in my gullet."

THE SHIPMAN'S TALE

[B 1191–1624. Here omitted.]

The *Shipman's Tale* is presumably derived from a French comic poem or *fabliau*. Because of some unrevised lines in the *Shipman's Tale* in which Chaucer allows the narrator to speak from the point of view of a married woman, it seems likely that he originally intended the tale for a female pilgrim, presumably the Wife of Bath; but its theme is perfectly suited to the type of story traditionally expected from sailors, for it describes the ingenious manner in which a young monk succeeds in seducing the wife of a niggardly merchant.

[1] Surprised by the Parson's blunt reproach, the Host gently ridicules his critic's piety. He applies to him a contemptuous nickname for a priest, Jankin, and labels him a Lollard, that is, a follower of Wyclif, the advocate of ecclesiastical and political reform.

[2] The Shipman so thoroughly garbles the pronunciation of whatever unfamiliar term he may have had in mind that it is impossible to determine what he intended to say.

LINK

[B 1625–1642. Here translated.]

"Well said, by *corpus Dominus*," [1] said our Host. "Now long may you sail along the coast, sir gentle master, gentle Mariner. God give the monk a thousand cartloads of bad years! Aha, fellows! Beware of such a trick! The monk made an ape of the man and of his wife, too, by Saint Augustine. Invite no more monks into your home. But now, pass on, and let us find out who next of all this group shall tell another tale."

And with that word he said as courteously as if a maiden spoke, "My lady Prioress, by your leave, if I knew that it wouldn't vex you, I'd judge that you should tell a tale next, providing that you were willing. Now, will you condescend, my dear lady?"

"Gladly," said she, and spoke as you shall hear.

THE PRIORESS'S TALE

[B 1643–1880]

The *Prioress's Tale*, one of the briefest of the *Canterbury Tales*, is notable not merely for the skillful economy of its narrative but also for its suitability to the narrator's character. The Prioress has ignored the boisterous tales preceding hers, and her courtly manner shields her from all irreverent jibes such as those which the brash Host later aims at the Monk. When she recites her story of a miracle performed by the Virgin Mary, she remains gracefully oblivious of the rude members of her audience, speaking indeed very much as she might have if she were addressing a community of pious nuns. Throughout the preliminary invocation and the legend proper, she mingles phrases drawn from the divine services, which, as Chaucer has remarked, she can entune so well.

Her theme — the Virgin's compassion for a nameless little boy who suffers martyrdom because of his devotion to her — is doubly appropriate, first because the Prioress herself is vowed to a life of chastity and devotion, and also because she is the sort of woman who would weep even over a dead mouse or a whipped dog. Her character is all compounded of "conscience and tender heart," and her motto proclaims that "love conquers all."

Ironically, we also discover, as Wordsworth remarked, "the fierce bigotry of the Prioress." Her tale is derived from a vague but ancient and widespread libel,

---

[1] Despite his rich vocabulary of expletives the Host is no Latin scholar. *Corpus Domini* (the Lord's body) is the correct form.

already current in England before Chaucer was born, that Jews were accustomed
to murder Christian children for ritualistic purposes. She does not, it is true, claim
any first-hand acquaintance with the Jews and is, in fact, unlikely to have had it,
for they were expelled from England in 1290 and were not readmitted until the
seventeenth century; and she sets the scene of action in an unidentified part of
distant Asia. But she accepts without question the validity of the legend underlying her tale and, in her epilogue, quite gratuitously cites an equally legendary
English story of the boy named Hugh of Lincoln, who was reported in the
thirteenth century to have been murdered by the Jews.

The striking feature of the tale, however, is its pathos. The pilgrims are understandably silenced by its effect and do not seize upon her argument as they do
upon the Wife of Bath's. Even the Host, who abruptly changes the subject at the
end of her tale, for once appears to feel ill at ease.

PROLOGUE

"O Lord, oure Lord, thy name how merveillous°   marvelously
Is in this large worlde y-sprad,°" quod° she;   spread   said
"For nat oonly thy laude° precious   praise
Parfourned° is by men of dignytee,   Celebrated
But by the mouth of children thy bountee
Parfourned is, for on the brest soukynge°   suckling
Som tyme shewen° they thyn heriynge.° 1   show forth   praise

Wher-fore in laude, as I best kan or may,
Of thee and of the white lilye flour 2
Which that° thee bar,° and is a mayde° alway, 10   Who bore virgin
To telle a storie I wol do my labour,
Nat that I may encressen hir honour,
For she hirself is honour and the roote°   source
Of bountee, next hir Sone, and soules boote.°   salvation

O moder Mayde, O mayde Moder free°!   gracious
O bussh unbrent, brennyng in Moyses sighte,³
That ravysedest° doun fro the Deitee,   ravished
Thurgh thyn humblesse, the Goost° that in th'   (Holy) Spirit
    alighte,°   in you alighted

---

¹ The substance of the first stanza is derived from Psalm viii, 1–2, which would have been
particularly familiar to the Prioress since it forms part of the Office of the Blessed Virgin.

² The white lily flower, which symbolizes the Virgin, is derived from the *Song of Solomon*,
ii, 2.

³ "O bush unburnt, burning in Moses's sight." The bush which God made appear to be
burning before Moses (*Exod.*, iii, 2) was interpreted as the symbolic foreshadowing of the
Virgin, upon whom the Holy Ghost descended.

Of whos vertu, whan he thyn herte lighte,°   lightened
Conceyved was the Fadres sapience,[1]   20
Help me to telle it in thy reverence!

Lady, thy bountee, thy magnificence,
Thy vertu, and thy grete humylitee
Ther may° no tonge expresse in no science.°   can   in any learned manner
For somtyme, Lady, er° men praye to thee,   before
Thow goost biforn,° of thy benygnytee,   precede
And getest us the light of thy prayere
To gyden us unto thy Sone so deere.

My konnyng° is so wayk,° O blisful Queene,   skill   weak
For to declare thy grete worthynesse   30
That I ne may the weighte nat sustene.
But as a child of twelf month old or lesse,
That kan unnethe° any word expresse,   hardly
Right so fare I, and therfore, I yow preye,
Gydeth° my song that I shal of yow seye."   Guide

THE PRIORESS'S TALE —

Ther was in Asye,° in a greet citee,   Asia
Amonges Cristen folk a Jewerye,°   ghetto
Sustened by a lord of that contree
For foul usure [2] and lucre of vileynye,°   villainous lucre
Hateful to Crist and to his compaignye.   40
And thurgh this strete° men myghte ryde and   street
    wende,°   go
For it was free and open at eyther ende.

A litel scole of Cristen folk ther stood
Doun at the ferther ende, in which ther were
Children an heep,° y-comen of Cristen blood,   a lot
That lerned in that scole yeer by yere
Swich manere doctrine° as men used there,   Such kind of teaching
This is to seyn,° to syngen and to rede   say
As smale children doon in hir° childhede.   their

---

[1] The "Father's sapience" is Christ, whom Paul calls "the wisdom of God" (I *Cor.*, i, 24).
[2] Medieval church law prohibited Christians from charging interest (*usure*) on loans but exempted Jewish moneylenders, as non-Christians. from this restriction because their loans facilitated trade.

Among thise children was a wydwes° sone,   50   widow's
A litel clergeoun,° seven yeer of age,   pupil
That day by day to scole was his wone°;   custom
And eek also, wher-as he say° th'ymage   where he saw
Of Cristes moder, hadde he in usage,
As hym was taught, to knele adoun and seye
His *Ave Marie* as he goth by the weye.

Thus hath this wydwe hir litel sone y-taught
Oure blisful Lady, Cristes moder deere,
To worshipe ay,° and he forgat it naught,   ever
For sely° child wol alwey° soone lere.°   60   a good   always   learn
But ay whan I remembre on this matere,
Seint Nicholas stant° evere in my presence,   stands
For he so yong to Crist dide reverence.[1]

This litel child, his litel book lernynge,
As he sat in the scole at his prymer,[2]
He *Alma redemptoris* [3] herde synge
As children lerned hir Antiphoner,[4]
And, as he dorste,° he drow hym ner° and ner   dared   drew nearer
And herkned ay the wordes and the note
Til he the firste vers koude° al by rote.   70   knew

Noght wiste° he what this Latyn was to seye,°   knew   meant
For he so yong and tendre was of age,
But on a day his felawe gan he preye°   companion he begged
T'expounden hym this song in his langage
Or telle hym why this song was in usage.
This preyde he hym to construen and declare
Ful ofte tyme upon his knowes° bare.   knees

His felawe, which that elder was than he,
Answerde hym thus: "This song, I have herd seye,
Was maked of° oure blisful Lady free,   80   for
Hire to salue° and eek hire for to preye   salute
To been oure help and socour° whan we deye. succor

[1] It was claimed that, as an infant, St. Nicholas (Santa Claus) voluntarily abstained from suckling on fast days.
[2] Latin prayer-book studied at school.
[3] Anthem in the Breviary beginning "Blessed Mother of the Redeemer."
[4] Book of psalms, hymns, or prayers sung responsively.

I kan namoore expounde in this matere.
I lerne song, I kan° but smal gramere."   *know*

"And is this song maked° in reverence   *made*
Of Cristes moder?" seyde this innocent.
"Now, certes,° I wol do my diligence   *certainly*
To konne° it al er° Cristemasse be went.   *know before*
Thogh that I for my prymer shal be shent°   *scolded*
And shal be beten thries° in an houre,   90   *thrice*
I wol it konne, oure Lady for to honoure."

His felawe taughte hym homward° pryvely   *on the way home*
Fro day to day til he koude° it by rote,   *knew*
And thanne he song° it wel and boldely   *sang*
Fro word to word acordyng with the note.
Twyes a day it passed thurgh his throte,
To scoleward° and homward whan he wente.   *Toward school*
On Cristes moder set was his entente.

As I have seyd, thurghout the Juerye
This litel child as he cam to and fro   100
Ful murily wolde he synge and crye
O Alma redemptoris everemo.
The swetnesse his herte perced so
Of Cristes moder that, to hire to preye,
He kan nat stynte of° syngyng by the weye.   *stop from*

Oure firste foo, the serpent Sathanas,
That hath in Jewes herte his waspes nest,
Up swal° and seyde, "O Hebrayk peple, allas!   *swelled*
Is this to yow a thyng that is honest°   *honorable*
That swich° a boy shal walken as hym lest,°   110   *such it pleases*
In youre despit,° and synge of swich sentence,°   *scorn of you such a theme*
Which is agayns oure lawes reverence?"

Fro thennes forth the Jewes han° conspired   *have*
This innocent out of the world to chace.
An homycide° therto han they hired,   *murderer*
That in an aleye° hadde a pryvee place.   *alley*
And as the child gan° forby for to pace°   *began pass*
This cursed Jew hym hente,° and heeld hym faste,   *seized*
And kitte° his throte, and in a pit hym caste.   *cut*

I seye that in a wardrobe° they hym threwe,   120   privy
Wher-as° thise Jewes purgen hir° entraille.   Where   their
O cursed folk of Herodes al newe,[1]
What may youre yvel entente yow availle?
Mordre° wol out, certeyn, it wol nat faille,   Murder
And namely ther-as° th'onour of God shal sprede.   particularly where
The blood out crieth on youre cursed dede.

O martir, souded° to virginitee,   attached
Now maystow° syngen, folwyng evere in oon°   you can   consistently
The white Lamb celestial — quod she —
Of which the grete evangelist seint John   130
In Pathmos° wroot, which° seith that they that gon Patmos   who
Biforn this Lamb and synge a song al newe,
That nevere, flesshly,° wommen they ne knewe.[2]   carnally

This poure wydwe awaiteth al that nyght
After hir litel child, but he cam noght;
For which, as soone as it was dayes lyght,
With face pale of drede and bisy thoght,
She hath at scole and elleswhere° hym soght   elsewhere
Til fynally she gan so fer espie°   so far discovered
That he last seyn was in the Jewerie.   140

With modres pitee in hir brest enclosed
She goth as° she were half out of hir mynde   as if
To every place wher she hath supposed
By liklyhede° hir litel child to fynde,   likelihood
And evere on Cristes moder meke and kynde
She cryde, and at the laste thus she wroghte,°   did
Among the cursed Jewes she hym soghte.

She frayneth,° and she preyeth pitously   inquires
To every Jew that dwelte in thilke° place   that same

---

[1] The "folk of Herod cursed anew" are the Jews, who are held responsible for crimes committed by various members of the Herod family. After Christ's birth King Herod the Great had the infants of Bethlehem killed (*Matt.*, ii, 16). Herod Antipas the Tetrarch, Herod's son, had John the Baptist beheaded (*Matt.*, xiv, 10) and assented to the crucifixion of Christ (*Luke*, xxiii, 11). King Herod Agrippa, Herod's grandson, killed the apostle James (*Acts*, xii, 2).

[2] "They sung . . . a new song before the throne. . . . These are they which were not defiled with women." (*Rev.*, xiv, 3-4.)

To telle hire if hir child wente oght forby.°   150   went past at all
They seyde "Nay," but Jesu of his grace
Yaf in hir thought,° inwith° a litel space,   Gave her insight   within
That° in that place after hir sone she cryde   So that
Wher he was casten in a pit bisyde.°   nearby

O grete God, that parfournest° thy laude   celebrate
By mouth of innocentz, lo, here thy myght!
This gemme of chastitee, this emeraude°   emerald
And eek° of martirdom the ruby bright,   also
Ther° he with throte y-korven° lay upright,°   Where   cut   face-upward
He *Alma redemptoris* gan° to synge   160   began
So loude that al the place gan to rynge.

The Cristen folk that thurgh the strete wente
In coomen° for to wondre upon this thyng,   Gathered
And hastily they for the provost° sente.   magistrate
He cam anon withouten tariyng,
And herieth° Crist, that is of hevene kyng,   praises
And eek his Moder, honour of mankynde,
And after that the Jewes leet he bynde.°   he caused to be bound

This child with pitous lamentacioun
Up taken was, syngynge his song alway,   170
And with honour of greet processioun
They carien hym unto the nexte° abbay.   nearest
His moder swownyng by his beere° lay.   bier
Unnethe° myghte the peple that was there   Hardly
This newe Rachel [1] bryngen fro his beere.

With torment and with shameful deth echon°   each one
This provost dooth° thise Jewes for to sterve°   causes   die
That of this mordre wiste,° and that anon.   murder knew
He nolde no swich° cursednesse observe.°   wouldn't any such   tolerate
Yvel shal have that° yvel wol deserve.   180   who
Therfore with wilde hors he dide hem drawe,°   horses he had them drawn
And after that he heng° hem by the lawe.   hung

[1] Jeremiah's reference (xxxi, 15) in the Old Testament to the weeping of Jacob's wife, Rachel, for her children is interpreted in the New Testament (*Matt.*, ii, 18) as a prophetical parallel to the lamentation of the mothers whose children were slain by King Herod's command.

Upon this beere ay lith° this innocent · ever lies
Biforn the chief auter° whil the masse laste. · altar
And after that, the abbot with his covent° · convent
Han sped hem° for to burien hym ful faste; · Have hastened
And whan they holy water on hym caste,
Yet° spak this child, whan spreynd° was holy water, · Still sprinkled
And song° *O Alma redemptoris mater.* · sang

This abbot, which that was an holy man,   190
As monkes ben, or elles oghten° be, · else ought to
This yonge child to conjure° he bigan · beseech
And seyde, "O deere child, I halsen° thee · implore
In vertu of the holy Trinitee,
Tel me what is thy cause for to synge
Sith that° thy throte is kit to my semynge°?" · Since cut apparently

"My throte is kit unto my nekke boon,"
Seyde this child, "and, as by wey of kynde,° · nature
I sholde have dyed, ye,° longe tyme agoon. · yea
But Jesu Crist, as ye in bokes fynde,   200
Wol° that his glorie laste and be in mynde,° · Wishes be remembered
And for the worship of his Moder deere
Yet may° I synge *O Alma* loude and clere. · Still can

"This welle of mercy, Cristes moder swete,
I loved alwey, as after my konnynge,° · according to my ability
And whan that I my lyf sholde forlete,° · was to give up
To me she cam and bad me for to synge
This anteme, verraily,° in my deiynge, · truly
As ye han herd; and whan that I had songe,
Me thoughte she leyde a greyn° upon my tonge. 210 · pearl

"Wher-fore I synge, and synge moot,° certeyn, · must sing
In honour of that blisful Mayden free,
Til fro my tonge of° taken is the greyn. · off
And, after that, thus seyde she to me:
'My litel child, now wol I fecche thee
Whan that° the greyn is fro thy tonge y-take. · When
Be nat agast. I wol thee nat forsake.'"

This holy monk, this abbot, hym mene I,
His tonge out caughte and took awey the greyn,

And he yaf° up the goost ful softely.   220   gave
And whan this abbot hadde this wonder seyn,
His salte teerys° trikled doun as reyn,   tears
And gruf° he fil al plat° upon the grounde,   face-down   all flat
And stille he lay as he hadde been y-bounde.

The covent° eek lay on the pavement,   convent
Wepynge and herying° Cristes moder deere.   praising
And after that they ryse, and forth been went,°   have gone
And toke awey this martir from his beere,
And in a tombe of marbil stones cleere
Enclosen they this litel body swete.   230
Ther° he is now, God leve° us for to meete.   Where   grant

Epilogue

O yonge Hugh of Lyncoln,[1] slayn also
With° cursed Jewes, as it is notable,   By
For it is but a litel while ago,
Preye eek for us, we synful folk unstable,
That, of his mercy, God so merciable
On us his grete mercy multiplie
For reverence of his moder Marie. Amen.

LINK

[B 1881–1901. Here translated.]

When this miracle was all told, everyone was so sober that it was a
wonder to see, till our Host began to joke, and then he first looked at me
and said, "What sort of man are you? You look," said he, "as if you
wanted to find a hare, for I see you always staring at the ground. Draw
near, and look up merrily. Now watch out, sirs, and let this man have
place. He's as well shaped in the waist as I. This would be a puppet
for any woman slim and fair of face to embrace in her arm! He seems as
distant as an elf, to judge by his behavior, for he doesn't dally with a soul.

[1] In 1255 a boy named Hugh, aged eight, was found dead in a well in Lincoln. Excited
by the widely accepted belief that the Jews crucified a Christian child annually as part of
their ritual, the townspeople seized Copin, a Jew in whose house Hugh had last been seen,
and forced him to confess that a local group of Jews had murdered the child. Although
the confession had been extorted under a guarantee of life and limb, Copin was immediately
hanged. Hugh of Lincoln's shrine soon became a pilgrimage resort.

Tell something now, since other folk have spoken. Tell us a mirthful tale, and right away."

"Host," said I, "don't be displeased, for indeed I don't know any other tale except for a rime I once learned long ago."

"Yes, that's good," said he. "Now we shall hear something rare, judging by the look of him."

CHAUCER'S TALE OF SIR THOPAS

[B 1902–2108]

Chaucer's interrupted *Tale of Sir Thopas* is a parody of the medieval romances of knight errantry. Indirectly, it is also a defense of Chaucer's own literary sources of inspiration; for, in disregarding native writers in favor of French and Italian models, Chaucer turned his back on a genre which in his day had reached the acme of its development. Romances were as widely admired as are murder mysteries today, and several, such as the anonymous *Sir Gawain and the Green Knight*, were unquestionably works of great literary distinction. But the future of the genre was doomed, and Chaucer perceptively exposed those very limitations which caused its decline within a century after his death.

Chaucer had obviously read many romances attentively and some, perhaps, enthusiastically, and he was therefore familiar with their conventional patterns — the knight who is wandering on a quest, the remote lady who inspires him to sacrificial acts of courtly love, and the pagan giant who unsuccessfully tries to bar his way. But Chaucer unmercifully reduces the accepted commonplaces to incongruities and absurdities.

The unpromising knight Sir Thopas, whose name suggests the gem of chastity, the topaz, belongs to Flanders — a country well suited to produce the three scoundrels in the *Pardoner's Tale*, but little reputed by the English for military brilliance. His appearance is elaborately described, but his face, as white as the best white bread, and his hair and waist-length beard, as yellow as saffron, smack more of the kitchen than the battlefield. The "merry men" who attend him might be fit company for Robin Hood or some other ragged outlaw extolled by the common people in their ballads, but they entirely lack that dignity proper to the unsmiling squires of aristocratic romance.

The plot also is full of false promise. Superficially, it is reminiscent of an enduringly popular romance, *Sir Thomas of Erceldoune*, which was highly admired by Sir Walter Scott, a competent judge of romances. But the difference of treatment is more significant than the similarity. Like Sir Thomas, Thopas falls in love with a woman of the other world, but he is not, like Thomas, overwhelmed by the spell of an all-consuming, supernatural passion. He accepts his destiny most phlegmatically, remarking, as he rides off in search of his dream lover, that an elf-queen will, after all, make a mate more worthy for him than any of the women in town.

In keeping with the general bathos of his narrative, Chaucer abandons his usual concern for the perfection of his versification and imitates the worst features of ballad and romance. He allows irregular rimes, *soore*, for instance, riming correctly with *goore* in l. 78 but wrongly with *armoure* in l. 108. He fills out lines with empty phrases, such as "The birds sing, there is no denial" (l. 55), and builds his extraordinary array of stanzaic patterns up to mighty anticlimaxes, as when the pagan giant, whose control of English seems appropriately uncertain, warns Thopas: "Unless you ride off out of my preserve / At once I slay your steed/ With mace." (ll. 100–103)

Yet, unlike some parodies, *Sir Thopas* can be appreciated for its fun alone, even though the reader knows nothing of its background.

Listeth,° lordes, in good entent,°	Listen attention
And I wol telle verrayment°	truly
Of myrthe and of solas,°	amusement
Al of a knyght was fair and gent°	refined
In bataille and in tornament —	
His name was Sire Thopas.	
Y-born he was in fer contree,	
In Flaundres° al biyonde the see,	Flanders
At Poperyng in the place.°	Poperinghe right there
His fader was a man ful free,° 10	generous
And lord he was of that contree,	
As it was Goddes grace.	
Sir Thopas wax a doghty swayn.	
Whit was his face as payndemayn,°	the best white bread
His lippes rede as rose.	
His rode° is lyk scarlet in grayn,°	complexion cloth dyed in cochineal
And I yow telle in good certeyn,	
He hadde a semely nose.	
His heer, his berd, was lyk safroun,°	saffron
That to his girdel raughte° adoun; 20	reached
His shoon of cordewane.°	shoes of cordovan
Of Brugges° were his hosen° broun;	Bruges leggings
His robe was of syklatoun°	costly cloth
That coste many a jane.°	half-penny
He koude hunte at wilde deer°	animals
And ride an haukyng for ryver	

With grey goshauk on honde.[1]
Ther-to he was a good archeer.
Of wrastlyng was ther noon his peer
   Ther° any ram° shal stonde.   30   Where prize

Ful many a mayde bright in bour°   bedroom
They moorne for hym paramour°   passionately
   Whan hem were bet° to slepe.   it were better for them
But he was chaast and no lechour°   lecher
And swete as is the brambel° flour   wild-rose
   That bereth the rede hepe.°   fruit

And so bifel upon a day,
For sothe,° as I yow telle may,   Truly
   Sire Thopas wolde out ryde.
He worth° upon his steede gray,   40   mounted
And in his hand a launcegay,°   light lance
   A long swerd by his syde.

He priketh° thurgh a fair forest   spurs
Therinne is many a wilde best —
   Ye,° bothe bukke and hare!   Yes
And as he priketh north and est,
I telle it yow, hym hadde almest
   Bitydde° a sory care.   Happened

There spryngen° herbes grete and smale,   spring
The licorys, and the cetewale,°   50   ginger
   And many a clowe-gylofre,°   clove
And notemuge° to putte in ale,   nutmeg
Wheither it be moyste° or stale,   new
   Or for to leye in cofre.°   chest

The briddes° synge, it is no nay,°   birds   denial
The sparhauk° and the popynjay,°   sparrowhawk   parrot
   That joye it was to here.
The thrustel-cok° made eek° his lay;   male thrush also
The wode-dowve° upon the spray,   wood-pigeon
   She sang ful loude and clere.   60

---

[1] ". . . ride hawking for waterfowl with gray goshawk on hand." The goshawk, which loses its skill after four or five seasons and becomes suitable only for catching rabbits, was considered more suitable for a yeoman than a knight.

Sire Thopas fil in love-longynge,
Al whan he herde the thrustel synge,
  And pryked as he were wood.°   mad
His faire steede in his prikynge
So swatte° that men myghte hym wrynge.   sweated
  His sydes were al blood.

Sire Thopas eek so wery was
For prikyng on the softe gras,
  So fiers was his corage,
That doun he leyde hym in the plas   70
To make his steede som solas°   comfort
  And yaf° hym good forage.°   gave fodder

"O Seinte Marie, *benedicite°!*   blessings!
What eyleth this love at me
  To bynde me so soore?
Me dremed° al this nyght, pardee,°   I dreamt certainly
An elf-queene shal my lemman° be   mistress
  And slepe under my goore.°   clothes

"An elf-queene wol I love, ywys,°   indeed
For in this world no womman is   80
  Worthy to be my make°   mate
          In towne.
Al othere wommen I forsake,
And to an elf-queene I me take
  By dale and eek by downe."

Into his sadel he clamb anoon°   at once
And priketh over stile and stoon
  An elf-queene for t'espye,°   to discover
Til he so longe hath riden and goon
That he foond in a pryvee woon°   90   hidden retreat
  The contree of Fairye°   Fairyland
          So wilde.
For in that contree was ther noon
That to hym dorste ryde or goon,
  Neither wyf ne childe,

Til that ther cam a greet geaunt —
His name was Sire Olifaunt,°   Eliphant

A perilous man of dede.
He seyde, "Child, by Termagaunt! [1]
But if° thow prike out of myn haunt,°   100   Unless   preserve
    Anon I sle thy steede
          With mace.
Heere is the queene of Fairye,
With harpe and pipe and symphonye,°   instrument
    Dwellyng in this place."

The Child seyde, "Also mote I thee,°   As I may thrive
Tomorwe wol I meete thee
    Whan I have myn armoure.
And yet I hope, *par ma fay,*°   by my faith
That thow shalt with this launcegay   110
    Abyen° it ful soure.   Pay for
          Thy mawe°   stomach
Shal I percen, if I may,
Er° it be fully pryme of day,   Before
    For here thow shalt be slawe.°"   slain

Sire Thopas drow abak ful faste.
This geant at hym stones caste
    Out of a fel staf-slynge,°   a fell sling (on a staff)
But faire escapeth Child Thopas,
And al it was thurgh Goddes gras   120
    And thurgh his fair berynge.

Yet listeth, lordes, to my tale!
Murier° than the nyghtyngale   Merrier
    I wol yow rowne°   whisper
How Sire Thopas with sydes smale,°   slender
Prikyng over hill and dale,
    Is come agayn to towne.

His murye° men comanded he   merry
To make hym bothe game and glee,
    For nedes moste° he fighte   130   needs must
With a geaunt with hevedes° thre   heads

[1] The giant addresses Thopas by the archaic word *Child*, meaning "young knight." Like the conventional Saracen villains of romance, he swears by Termagant, a supposed Moslem deity.

For paramour° and jolitee°   love   passion
  Of oon that shoon ful brighte.

"Do° come," he seyde, "my mynstrales   Have
And gestours° for to tellen tales   story-tellers
  Anon in° myn armynge,   At once during
Of romances that been reales°   are regal
Of popes and of cardynales
  And eek of love-likynge."

They fette° hym first the swete wyn,   140   fetched
And mede° eek in a maselyn,°   mead   maple bowl
  And real° spicerye   regal
Of gyngebred° that was ful fyn,   gingerbread
And lycorys, and eek comyn,°   cummin
  With sugre that is trye.°   choice

He dide° next his white leere°   put   flesh
Of clooth of lake° fyn and cleere   linen
  A breech and eek a sherte,
And next his sherte an aketoun,°   padded jacket
And over that an haubergeoun°   150   coat of mail
  For° percyng of his herte,   To avert

And over that a fyn hauberk,°   breastplate
Was al y-wroght of Jewes werk,[1] —
  Ful strong it was of plate —
And over that his cote-armour°   tunic
As whit as is a lilie flour,
  In which he wol debate.°   contend

His sheeld was al of gold so reed,
And therinne was a bores° heed,   boar's
  A charbocle bisyde.°   160   carbuncle (stone) next it
And there he swoor on ale and breed
How that the geaunt shal be deed,
  Bityde what bityde!

Hise jambeux° were of quyrboily,°   leggings   toughened leather
His swerdes shethe° of yvory,   sword's sheath

[1] In the Middle Ages Jews specialized both in the manufacture and the sale of armor and weapons.

His helm of latoun° bright;   copper alloy
His sadel was of rewel bon°;   whalebone
His brydel as the sonne shon
    Or as the moone light.

His spere was of fyn cipres,   170
That bodeth werre and nothyng pes,[1]
    The heed ful sharp y-grounde.
His steede was al dappel gray.
It gooth an ambel in the way
    Ful softely and rounde
            In londe.°   In the country
Lo, lordes myne, here is a fit°!   canto
If ye wole any moore of it,
    To telle it wol I fonde.°   try

Now holde youre mouth, *par charitee*,°   180   out of charity
Bothe knyght and lady free,°   noble
    And herkneth to my spelle.°   story
Of bataille and of chivalry
And of ladyes love-drury°   ladies' passion
    Anon I wol yow telle.

Men speken of romances of pris° —   esteem
Of *Hornchild*, and of *Ypotys*,
    Of *Beves*, and *Sire Gy*,
Of *Sire Lybeux*, and *Pleyndamour*,[2] —
But Sire Thopas, he bereth the flour°   190   bears the flower
    Of real° chivalry!   regal

His goode steede al he bystrood,
And forth upon his wey he glood°   glided
    As sparcle out of the bronde.°   firebrand
Upon his creest he bar a tour,°   wore a tower
And therinne stiked° a lilie flour.   stuck
    God shilde his cors fro shonde°!   body from harm

---

[1] ". . . which portends war and, in no way, peace." From the *Parliament of Birds*, however, we learn that Chaucer really believes the cypress to symbolize the lamentation of death.

[2] A religious legend concerning the young child Ypotys and romances celebrating Child Horn, Sir Beves of Hampton, Sir Guy of Warwick, and Sir Li Beaus Desconus (The Fair Unknown) are still extant. Pleyndamour (Full of Love) has not been positively identified.

And, for he was a knyght auntrous,°		adventurous
He nolde° slepen in noon hous		would not
But liggen° in his hoode.	200	lie
His brighte helm was his wonger°;		pillow
And by hym baiteth° his destrer°		feeds war-horse
Of herbes fyne and goode.		

Hymself drank water of the well,	
As dide the knyght Sire Percyvell ¹	
So worthy under wede,°	clothes
Til, on a day, —	

LINK

[B 2109–2156. Here translated.]

"No more of this, for the worship of God," said our Host, "for you make me so weary of your very stupidity that, God so wisely bless my soul, my ears ache from your filthy recital. Now such a rime I commit to the Devil. This could well be doggerel rime," said he.

"Why so?" said I. "Why do you stop me in my tale any more than any other man, since this is the best rime I know?"

"By God," said he, "plainly, in short, because your filthy riming isn't worth a turd. You're doing nothing but wasting time. Sir, in a word, you're not to rime any longer. Let's see whether you can tell a story or something in prose, at least, in which there may be some amusement or instruction."

"Gladly," said I, "by God's precious suffering! I will tell you a little thing in prose that ought to please you, I should think, or else you're certainly too demanding. It's a virtuous moral tale, although it's told from time to time in sundry ways by sundry people, as I must explain to you. Thus, for example, you know that not every Evangelist who tells us the suffering of Jesus Christ narrates everything as his fellow does; but nevertheless their intention is entirely true, and all concur as far as their intention is concerned although there may be difference in their telling. For some of them say more, and some say less when they declare his piteous passion — I mean Matthew, Mark, Luke, and John — but undoubtedly

¹ The pure and innocent Sir Perceval was brought up in ignorance of warfare.

their intention is all one. Therefore, gentlemen all, I beseech you, if you think I deviate in what I say and, for instance, relate somewhat more proverbs than you have heard included in this little treatise before, in order to reinforce the effect of my subject matter — and if I do not speak the same words you have heard —, yet I pray you all, don't blame me; for, as far as my intention is concerned, you will find no difference anywhere from the intention of the little treatise according to which I write [1] this merry tale. And therefore listen to what I am to say, and let me tell *all* my tale, I pray."

CHAUCER'S TALE OF MELIBEUS

[B 2157–3078. Here omitted.]

In *Sir Thopas* Chaucer has playfully demonstrated that, of all the pilgrims whom he has created, he himself is the least capable of composing original poetry, and now he proves that he is even incapable of inventing a prose narrative, for he doggedly translates, almost word for word, a French prose version of the moral tale of Melibeus, conscientiously resisting the impulse to introduce any of those vitalizing changes which he must have felt tempted to make.

The basis of the tale is a thirteenth-century Latin tractate which attained sufficient popularity to be translated into at least four different French versions and into Italian, Dutch, and German. Its theme provides a striking proof of the wisdom of women, which must have pleased the Wife of Bath, but Chaucer does not introduce any allusion to her. The contents consist primarily of an exhaustive scholastic debate concerning the justifiability of revenge, in which the wise Prudence persuades her husband Melibeus to show mercy to his enemies. The tale is highly schematic and, as a consequence, sadly deficient in characterization, but Chaucer's translation probably satisfied contemporary taste. At least no one interrupts Chaucer's attempt this time; and actually any of his listeners who were familiar with the contemporary feuds waged by England's nobility, and particularly by Chaucer's powerful kinsman John of Gaunt, would be compelled to admit that the topic, though old, was still timely.

LINK

[B 3079–3180. Here translated.]

When my tale of Melibeus and of Prudence and her goodness was ended, our Host said, "Upon my faith as a Christian, and by the precious body of Madrian, I'd sooner than a barrel of ale that Godelief my wife had heard this tale, for she has no such patience as had Prudence, this wife of Melibeus. By God's bones! When I beat my helpers, she brings me

---

[1] The word *write* is evidently an oversight.

great club-shaped sticks and shouts, 'Slay the dogs, every one of them!
And break their backs and every bone!'

"And if one of my neighbors won't bow to my wife in church, or is so
bold as to do her any wrong, when she comes home she ramps in my
face and cries, 'Heavenly bones! I'll take your knife, and you take my dis-
taff and go spin.' She'll start up in this same way, from day till night.
'Alas,' she says, 'that I was ever fated to marry a milksop or a cowardly
ape who'll let himself be browbeaten by everyone. You don't dare stand
up for the rights of your wife.'

"This is my life, unless I want to fight. And I have to hurry out of doors
at once, or else I'm lost, unless I'm as foolhardy as a savage lion. I know well
that some day she's going to make me kill some neighbor and then pay the
price. For I'm dangerous with a knife in hand, even if I don't dare stand
up to her, for by my faith she's big in arms. Whoever does or says the
wrong thing to her will find out that! But let's leave aside this subject.

"My lord the Monk," said he, "put on a cheerful face, for truly you're
to tell a tale. Look. Rochester stands close by.[1] Ride up, my good lord.
Don't hold up our fun. But, in truth, I don't know your name. Am I to
call you my lord sir John, or sir Thomas, or else sir Albon? What house
do you belong to? By your father's kin, I vow to God, your skin is certainly fair. It is a noble pasture where you go. You're not like a penitent
or a ghost. Upon my faith, you are some office-holder, some sacristan
of worth or some cellar-keeper.[2] For, by my father's soul, I'd judge that
you're a master when you're at home — no poor cloisterer or novice, but
a governor shrewd and wise, and one with brawn and bones besides, who
fares exceptionally well. I pray that God may bring confusion upon him
who first introduced you to religion. You'd have been a fine rooster,
indeed! If you'd had as much freedom as you might have to carry out all
your pleasure in engendering, you'd have begotten many a creature.
Alas, why do you wear so wide a cope? If I were pope, God grant me
sorrow if not only you but every other man of might, even though he
were shaven to the top of his head, should have a wife. For all the world
is lost. Religion has taken up all the best of the begetters, and we laymen
are mere shrimps. From feeble trees come feeble shoots. Thus our heirs
are so slight and feeble that they can't engender well. Thus our wives
will try out religious folk because they can pay Venus's payment better
than can we. God knows, you don't pay out mere Luxemburgers.[3] But

---

[1] Rochester is thirty miles east of London, about half way to Canterbury.
[2] The sacristan in a religious house is in charge of the building and the ecclesiastical
vessels and ornaments. The cellar-keeper is in charge of provisions in the kitchen and cellar.
[3] False, underweight coins brought from Luxemburg into England.

don't be angry, my lord, if I jest. The truth quite often I've heard spoken in game."

The worthy Monk took all in patience and said, "I'll do all my diligence, as far as is in keeping with morality, to tell you a tale, or two or three. And if you care to listen, I'll tell you the life of St. Edward, or else first of all I'll tell some tragedies, of which I have a hundred in my cell.

"By tragedy is meant a certain story, which old books hold in memory for us, of one that stood in great prosperity and then fell from high degree into misery and ended wretchedly. And they are commonly versified in six feet, called hexameter. Many are composed in prose also, and in meters of many various kinds, too. Well now, this explanation ought to suffice enough.[1]

"Now listen, if you care to hear. But first, in this matter, I beg you excuse me for my ignorance if I don't tell these things in order, whether it be of popes, emperors, or kings, in accordance with the dates which are found written, but tell them, some before and some behind, as they come to my memory."

THE MONK'S TALE

[B 3181–3956. (B 3189–3564, 3653–3948 here omitted.)]

The Monk models his tale after a once well-known and popular genre of writing in which the author supports a central argument by the recital of a series of miscellaneous examples. Having asserted that tragedy is produced by the unpredictable turning of blind Fortune's wheel, the Monk illustrates the fact by seventeen examples, which include such diverse figures as Lucifer, Adam, Croesus, Alexander the Great, and four relatively recent rulers.

The general plan and at least four of the examples were obviously suggested by Boccaccio's Latin prose work, *The Fall of Illustrious Men*, which in turn derives its concept of Fortune's role in the fate of man from Boethius's *Consolation of Philosophy*, with which, as a translator, Chaucer was also thoroughly familiar. But Boc-

---

[1] The medieval and renaissance definition of tragedy does not apply primarily to drama but to prose and verse epics such as Vergil's *Aeneid*, Lucan's *Pharsalia*, and Statius's *Thebaid*, which are composed in Latin hexameters; medieval Latin epics, usually composed in elegiac meter; and *Famous Women* and *The Fall of Illustrious Men* by the fourteenth-century Italian writer Boccaccio, composed in Latin prose. The theme of the epic is here interpreted in the light of Fortune's remark, contained in the *Consolation of Philosophy*, written by Chaucer's favorite philosopher, Boethius: "I turn the whirling wheel with the turning circle; I am pleased to change the lowest to the highest, and the highest to the lowest. . . . What else do the lamentations of tragedy bewail than the deeds of Fortune, who with unforseen stroke overturns the realms of great nobility?"

caccio is much more positive in his moral teaching than the Monk, who ignores the fact that Philosophy had proved to Boethius that even adverse Fortune is good.

Thirteen of the examples are omitted from the present selection, for, as the Host clearly implies, the over-all effect of the Monk's melancholy catalogue is decidedly soporific; but the four modern instances deserve inclusion. Of these, the first three reveal Chaucer's personal knowledge of contemporary events in such remote countries as Spain, Italy, and Cyprus and are almost unique among his writings in that they contain his own direct comments upon the complicated intrigues which affected England's diplomacy abroad.

The longer passage dealing with the unfortunate Ugolino of Pisa is derived from Dante and provides an excellent illustration of the complete difference between the spirit of the two authors. For, while Dante views Ugolino's fate in relationship to the great scheme of the *Divine Comedy* (1307–21), Chaucer allows the Monk to add the tale unreflectingly to his list of incomprehensible tragedies. Dante, moreover, concludes his treatment of the incident by berating the citizens of Pisa for countenancing the cruel starvation of Ugolino's children, a protest which Chaucer naturally omits as not germane to the *Monk's Tale*. But Chaucer cannot remain indifferent to the fate of the victims and succeeds even better than Dante in breathing life into his portrait of the children, just as he does in the *Prioress's Tale*.

All readers regret that the graceful *Squire's Tale* and even the improper *Cook's Tale* were left unfinished, because both show real literary promise; some avid readers would prefer that Chaucer had concluded his *Tale of Sir Thopas*, self-sufficient though the fragment is; but no critic has wished that the Monk had been allowed to recite all of the hundred or more tragedies known to him. Chaucer himself obviously approved of the Knight's interruption of the tale, for the Monk's pessimistic fatalism is incompatible with the warm sympathy for mankind and underlying faith in divine providence which Chaucer displays elsewhere. Yet the occasional distinction of the narration and the fundamental clash between the points of view of Monk and Knight redeem what would otherwise have been an unfruitful literary exercise, so that no one would wish that the *Monk's Tale* had been omitted in its entirety.

I wol biwaille in manere of tragedie	
The harm of hem° that stoode in heigh degree	them
And fillen° so that ther nas° no remedie	fell was
To brynge hem out of hire° adversitee.	their
For, certeyn, whan that° Fortune list° to flee,	when (*whan that*) wishes
Ther may no man the cours of hire withholde.	
Lat no man truste on blynd prosperitee.	
Be war° by thise ensamples° trewe and olde.	warned examples

[B 3189–3564 here omitted.]

King Peter of Spain

O noble, O worthy Petro, glorie of Spayne,[1]
Whom Fortune heeld so heighe in magestee,   10
Wel oghten° men thy pitous deeth complayne!   ought
Out of thy land thy brother made thee flee;
And after at a sege by subtiltee
Thow were bitraysed° and lad° unto his tente,   betrayed led
Where-as° he with his owene hand slow° thee,   Where slew
Succedynge in thy regne and in thy rente.°   revenue
The feeld of snow with th'egle of blak therinne
Caught with the lyme-rod coloured as the glede,°   glowing coal
He brew this cursednesse and al this synne.[2]
The Wikked Nest[3] was werkere of this nede.   20
Noght Charles° Olyver, that took ay° hede   Charles's alway
Of trouthe and honour, but of Armorike°   Brittany
Genyloun-Olyver, corrupt for mede,°   bribery
Broghte this worthy kyng in swich a brike.°   such a trap

King Peter of Cyprus

O worthy Petro, Kyng of Cipre, also,
That Alisaundre° wan by heigh maistrie,°   Alexandria skill
Ful many an hethen° wroghtestow° ful wo!   heathen you worked
Of° which thyne owene liges hadde envie,[4]   For

---

[1] In 1369, with the help of the French knight Bertrand du Guesclin and of Oliver Mauny of Brittany, Don Enrique killed his own brother Peter, King of Castile and Leon, whom the English had supported. Two years later Chaucer's patron John of Gaunt married the late King Peter's daughter Constance and laid claim to the kingship. (See Genealogical Table.) Chaucer at first wrote in l. 12, "Thy bastard brother made thee to flee" but tactfully omitted the reference to Enrique's illegitimacy after the reconciliation in 1386 of the disputed claim.

[2] Bertrand du Guesclin is here identified by his coat of arms, a black eagle against a background of white, restrained, as it were, by a diagonal bar like a limed rod used to catch birds.

[3] The "Wicked Nest," a literal translation of Old French *mau ni*, is the conspirator Mauny. Mauny's first name was Oliver, but he was not like Charlemagne's Oliver (l. 21), the faithful comrade of Roland, but an Oliver more like Ganelon (l. 23), the infamous traitor in the Old French *Song of Roland*.

[4] Peter of Lusignan, King of Cyprus, was the last Western ruler to organize a crusade for the recovery of Jerusalem. Some English volunteers served under him in his indecisive victories at Attalia (1361), Alexandria (1365), and Ayas (1367). Chaucer's Knight, according to the *General Prologue*, had served in all three campaigns; and Chaucer himself

And for no thyng but for thy chivalrie
They in thy bed han° slayn thee by the morwe.° 30   have morning
Thus kan Fortune hire wheel governe and gye°   control
And out of joye brynge men to sorwe.

Bernabo of Lombardy

Of Melan grete Barnabo Viscounte,[1]
God of delit, and scourge of Lumbardye,
Why sholde I noght thyn infortune acounte,°   misfortune recount
Sith° in estat thow clombe were° so hye?   Since had climbed
Thy brother° sone, that was thy double allye,°   brother's relation
For he thy nevew was and son-in-lawe,
Withinne his prisoun made thee to dye.
But why ne how noot° I that thow were slawe.° 40   don't know slain

Ugolino of Pisa

Of the Erl Hugelyn of Pize [2] the langour°   languishing
Ther may no tonge° telle for pitee.   tongue
But litel out of Pize stant° a tour,   stands
In which tour in prisoun put was he,
And with hym been hise litel children thre.
The eldeste scarsly fyve yeer was of age.

---

may well have seen King Peter in 1363 when he visited the English court in search of re-
cruits. The King was murdered in 1369 by one of his own lieges, probably not, as Chaucer
says, out of jealousy but out of resentment of his personal behavior.

[1] Bernabo Visconti, the tyrannical lord of Milan, was captured in 1385 by the ruthless
diplomat Gian Galeazzo Visconti and died in prison — having, according to rumor, been
poisoned. Gian was the son of Bernabo's brother and had been induced to marry his own
cousin, Caterina, Bernabo's daughter; but he allowed no scruples over family ties to inter-
fere with his ambition to attain control of Lombardy (northern Italy). Chaucer knew something of the power of the Viscontis. In 1368 Chaucer's employer, Lionel, Duke of Clarence,
had married Gian's sister, Violante, after the death of his first wife, Elizabeth of Ulster.
(See Genealogical Table.) Chaucer had visited Genoa in 1373 while it was in control
of Bernabo and Gian's father Galeazzo II; and he had visited Bernabo at Milan in 1378
on a diplomatic mission. Bernabo's chief military aide, moreover, was an English acquaintance of Chaucer's, Sir John Hawkwood, who had married an illegitimate daughter
of Bernabo and, after his lord's death, continued to resist Gian.

[2] In 1288 Count Ugolino, in collusion with the Archbishop Ruggieri, attempted to gain
exclusive control of Pisa. Later he attacked the Archbishop but was captured, and he and
his sons and grandsons were imprisoned without food in what became known as the
Tower of Famine. In the *Divine Comedy* Dante reports a sympathetic version of the story
from the lips of Ugolino in Hell (Canto XXXIII), which Chaucer adapts to his own
purpose.

Allas, Fortune, it was greet crueltee
Swiche briddes° for to putte in swich a cage!   birds

Dampned° was he to dyen in that prisoun,   Condemned
For Roger, which that bisshop was of Pize,   50
Hadde on hym maad a fals suggestioun°   accusation
Thurgh which the peple gan upon hym rise°   rose (*gan . . . rise*)
And putten hym to prisoun in swich wise
As ye han herd; and mete and drynke he hadde
So smal that wel unnethe° it may suffise,   hardly
And ther-with-al it was ful poure and badde.

And on a day bifel that, in that hour
Whan that his mete wont° was to be broght,   accustomed
The gayler° shette the dores of the tour.   jailer
He herde it wel, but he spak right noght;   60
And in his herte anon ther fil° a thoght   occurred
That they for hunger wolde doon hym dyen.°   have him die
"Allas," quod he, "allas, that I was wroght°!"   made
Therwith the teeris fillen from hise eyen.°   eyes

His yonge sone, that thre yeer was of age,
Unto hym seyde, "Fader, why do ye wepe?
Whanne wol the gayler bryngen oure potage?
Is ther no morsel breed that ye do kepe?
I am so hungry that I may nat slepe.
Now wolde God that I myghte slepen evere,   70
Thanne sholde noght hunger in my wombe° crepe.   belly
Ther is no thyng but breed that me were levere.°"   I'd rather have

Thus day by day this child bigan to crye,
Til in his fadres barm° adoun it lay   father's bosom
And seyde, "Farewel, Fader. I moot° dye!"   must
And kiste his fader, and deyde the same day.
And whan the woful fader deed it say,°   saw him dead
For wo hise armes two he gan° to byte   began
And seyde, "Allas, Fortune, and weylaway°!   alack
Thy false wheel my wo al may I wyte.°"   80   blame (for all my woe)

Hise children wende° that it for hunger was   believed
That he hise armes gnow,° and nat for wo,   gnawed
And seyden, "Fader, do nat so, allas,

But rather ete the flessh upon us two.
Oure flessh thow yaf° us; taak oure flessh us fro°   gave   from us
And ete ynow.°" Right thus they to hym seyde,   enough
And, after that, withinne a day or two
They leyde hem in his lappe adoun and deyde.

Hymself, despeired, eek° for hunger starf.°   also   died
Thus ended is this myghty Erl of Pize.   90
From heigh estat Fortune awey hym carf.°   cut
Of this tragedie it oghte ynogh suffise.
Who so wole heere it in a lenger wise,
Redeth° the grete poete of Ytaille°   Read   Italy
That highte Dant,° for he kan al devyse°   is called Dante   tell
Fro point to point. Nat o° word wol he faille.   one

[B 3653–3948 omitted.]

An-hanged was Cresus,° the proude kyng.   Croesus
His roial trone myghte hym nat availle.
Tragedies noon oother manere thyng
Ne kan in syngyng crye ne biwaille [1]   100
But that Fortune alwey° wole assaille   always
With unwar strook° the regnes that been proude.   unexpected stroke
For, whan men° trusteth hire, thanne wol she faille   one
And covere hire brighte face with a clowde.

LINK

[B 3957–4010. Here translated.]

"Whoa!" said the Knight. "Good sir, no more of this! Indeed, you've
certainly said enough, and far more. For a little gloom is quite enough
for most people, I think. For my part it's a great discomfort, when men
have been in great wealth and ease, to hear of their sudden fall, alas! And
the opposite is a joy and great comfort, when a man has been in poor
estate, and climbs up and becomes fortunate, and there stays in prosperity. It seems to me that such a thing is cheering and would be well
worth telling about."

[1] "Tragedies can in singing (that is, even though they sing) lament and bewail no other
sort of thing . . ."

"Yes," said our Host. "By St. Paul's bell, you're quite right. This Monk chatters loudly. He told how Fortune covered something or other with a cloud,[1] and also you've heard about a tragedy just now, and, by Heaven, it's no use bewailing or complaining over something that is done. And, besides, it's painful, as you've said, to hear of gloom.

"Sir Monk, no more of this, God bless you. Your tale depresses all this company. Such talk isn't worth a butterfly, for there's no fun or game in it.

"Therefore, sir Monk — by name, sir Piers —, I heartily beg you, tell us something else. For certainly, if it weren't for the jingling of the bells that hang on your bridle on every side, by the King of Heaven, who died for us all, I'd have fallen down for sleep before this, no matter how deep the mire had been. Then your tale would have been all told in vain, for certainly, as the scholars say, where a man can have no audience, there's no profit for him to deliver his opinion, and I well know the substance is in me if anything is well narrated. Sir, tell something about hunting, I beg you."

"No," said the Monk. "I have no desire to play. Let another tell, for I have told."

Then our Host spoke with blunt and bold speech and said at once to the Nun's Priest, "Come here, you, sir John. Tell us something such as may cheer our hearts. Be happy, even if you do ride on a jade. What though your horse be both foul and lean! If he serves you, care not one straw. See that your heart continues to be gay."

"Yes, indeed," said he. "Yes, Host, as I may thrive, if I'm not gay, certainly I'll be to blame." And immediately he broached his tale. And this fine priest, this goodly man, sir John, spoke as follows to us one and all.

THE NUN'S PRIEST'S TALE

[B 4011–4636]

The reader may be somewhat disappointed that the opulent Monk has not turned out to be more talented as a story-teller, but in the next tale Chaucer more than makes up for the relapse by allowing the hitherto unnoticed Priest to emerge from obscurity and narrate one of the most brilliant of the *Canterbury Tales*. In the *General Prologue* the Priest is not described, and although some critics have suggested that Chaucer intended eventually to insert a portrait of him in the *Prologue*, the omission may have been deliberate and can certainly be justified

---

[1] The Monk had just said concerning Fortune: "When men trust her, then she will fail and cover her bright face with a cloud."

on artistic grounds, for it lends a striking emphasis to the aristocratic stateliness of the Prioress in whose retinue he rode, apparently in silence. His reticence is again suggested here by the self-effacing manner in which he acquiesces with the Host's demand for a tale and begins his narration without any of the usual preliminary remarks.

The tale which he tells is derived from an amusing though essentially trivial folktale, but the narrator transforms it under the impress of his own character, for the Priest is both learned and witty, even if he carries his learning lightly and conveys his humor effortlessly.

The hero, Chauntecleer the cock, and the heroine, Pertelote the hen, in most versions of the tale are little more than stock characters in an animal fable, but the Priest converts them into genial caricatures of human beings. The fate of Chauntecleer is treated in mock-heroic style, supported by ludicrously incongruous parallels with the deeds of famous heroes and villains of world literature. The Priest innocently explains that he would not dare to criticize women in the present company; and, although he presumably serves as the confessor in the Prioress's convent, he even goes so far as to claim that he cannot imagine there could be any harm in women; but he manages to satirize them, just the same, in the person of the opinionative Pertelote. Dreams, she maintains, are caused by the humors and the complexions of the human body, and it is therefore ridiculous to believe, as her superstitious husband does, that dreams may foreshadow the future. Her theory is modishly new, for although the ancient concepts of the humors and the complexions had long been familiar to the scholars in England who wrote in Latin, Chaucer is the first writer known to have employed these two terms in English. But, as often happens in human affairs, Pertelote's theory, though new and though apparently logical, turns out to be fallible, and Chauntecleer's illogical forebodings are vindicated.

Satire can, of course, recoil upon the satirist if he appears to value his own opinions too highly, but the Priest avoids this pitfall, in the same way that Chaucer himself does when he plays the role of social critic in the *General Prologue*, by belittling his own intelligence. The Priest regrets, for instance, that he does not possess the poetic skill of Geoffrey de Vinsauf, a twelfth-century rhetorician, although he obviously derides Geoffrey's pedestrian style. He confesses that he cannot solve that difficult theological problem, the relation between God's foreknowledge of events and man's freedom of action, but he is so well acquainted with the authorities on the subject that he can summarize their views most adroitly.

Thus, though he belittles his own abilities, the Nun's Priest does not represent himself as a mere buffoon. He jestingly alludes to the contemporary slaying of immigrant Flemish artisans by their English-born competitors, but his tone suggests that he does not intend to condone their unjustifiable action. And when he comes to the end of his story, he takes the opportunity to direct its moral implications against the folly of trusting in flattery, and even if he has made no pretensions to eloquence as a preacher, as the Pardoner does, his sermon is none the less effective.

A poure widwe,° somdel stape° in age,   widow   somewhat advanced
Was whilom° dwellynge in a narwe° cotage   once   small
Biside a grove, stondyng° in a dale.   standing
This widwe of which I telle yow my tale,
Syn thilke° day that she was last a wyf,   Since that same
In pacience ladde a ful symple lyf,
For litel was hire catel° and hire rente.°   property   income
By housbondrye of swich° as God hire sente   such
She foond hireself and eek° hire doghtren° two. supported   also   daughters
Thre large sowes hadde she and namo,°   10   no more
Thre kyn,° and eek a sheep that highte° Malle. cows   was called
Ful sooty was hire bour° and eek hire halle,   bedroom
In which she eet ful many a sklendre° meel.   slender
Of poynaunt° sauce hir neded° never a deel.°   pungent   she needed   bit
No deyntee morsel passed thurgh hir throte;
Hir diete was acordant to hir cote.°   means
Repleccioun ne made hire nevere syk;
Attempree° diete was al hir phisyk,   Temperate
And excercise, and hertes suffisaunce.°   sufficiency
The goute lette° hire no thyng° for to daunce, 20   hindered   in no way
N'apoplexie shente nat° hir heed.   Nor did apoplexy trouble
                                                    head
No wyn ne drank she, neither whit ne reed.
Hir bord° was served moost with whit and blak, table
Milk and broun breed, in which she foond no lak,° found no fault
Seynd° bacoun, and som tyme an ey or tweye,°   Broiled   egg or two
For she was, as it were, a maner deye.°   sort of dairy-woman

    A yeerd she hadde, enclosed al aboute
With stikkes, and a drye dych° withoute,   ditch
In which she hadde a cok heet° Chauntecleer.   named
In al the land of crowyng nas° his peer.   30   (there) was not
His voys was murier° than the myrie orgon   merrier
On massedayes that in the chirche gon.°   plays
Wel sikerer° was his crowyng in his logge°   Much more accurate   lodge
Than is a clokke or any abbey orlogge.°   horologe (clock)
By nature he knew ech ascensioun
Of the equinoxial in thilke toun,
For whan degrees fiftene were ascended,[1]
Thanne krew he that it myghte nat ben amended.° so that it couldn't be bettered

___

[1] According to ancient astronomy the heavens were thought of as rotating 360° daily around the earth's equator in what was called the "equinoctial circle." Thus a new sector of 15° "ascended" at each of the twenty-four hours of the day.

His comb was redder than the fyn coral
And batailled as° it were a castel wal.   40   battlemented as if
His byle° was blak, and as the jeet° it shoon.   bill   jet
Lyk asure were hise legges and his toon,°   toes
Hise nayles whitter than the lylye flour,
And lyk the burned° gold was his colour.   burnished
This gentil cok hadde in his governaunce°   control
Sevene hennes for to doon° al his plesaunce,°   do pleasure
Whiche were hise sustres° and his paramours,°   sisters (sweethearts)
                                                                     mistresses
And wonder° lyke to hym as of colours,   wonderfully
Of whiche the faireste hewed on hire throte
Was cleped° faire damoysele Pertelote.   50   called
Curteys she was, discreet, and debonaire,
And compaignable, and bar° hirself so faire   conducted
Syn thilke° day that she was seven nyght oold   Since that same
That, trewely, she hath the herte in hoold
Of Chauntecleer, loken° in every lith.°   locked   limb
He loved hire so that wel was hym ther-with.°   he was well contented
But swich a joye was it to here hem° synge,   them
Whan that the brighte sonne gan to sprynge,°   began to rise
In swete acord "My leef is faren in londe.°"   sweetheart has gone to the
                                                                     country
For thilke° tyme, as I have understonde,   60   (at) that
Beestes and briddes° koude speke and synge.   birds

   And so bifel that in a dawenynge,°   one dawn
As Chauntecleer among hise wyves alle
Sat on his perche, that was in the halle,
And next hym sat this faire Pertelote,
This Chauntecleer gan gronen° in his throte   began to groan
As man that in his dreem is drecched° soore.   tormented

   And whan that° Pertelote thus herde hym rore,   when (whan that)
She was agast and seyde, "Herte deere,
What eyleth yow to grone in this manere?   70
Ye ben a verray° slepere. Fy, for shame!"   sound

   And he answerde and seyde thus: "Madame,
I prey yow that ye take it nat agrief.°   ill
By God, me mette° I was in swich meschief   I dreamed
Right now that yet° myn herte is soore afright.   still
Now God," quod° he, "my swevene recche° aright,   said may my dream work
                                                                     out
And kepe my body out of foul prisoun.
Me mette how that° I romed up and doun   I dreamed that
Withinne oure yeerd, where-as I say° a beest,   where I saw

Was lyk an hound and wolde han maad areest° 80	have seized
Upon my body and han° had me deed.	have
His colour was bitwixe yelow and reed,	
And tipped was his tayl and bothe hise erys°	ears
With blak unlik the remenaunt° of hise herys,°	rest hair
His snowte smal, with glowyng eyen tweye.°	eyes two
Yet of his look for fere almoost I deye.	
This caused me my gronyng, doutelees."	
"Avoy!°" quod she. "Fy on yow, herteless!	Shame
Allas," quod she, "for, by that God above,	
Now han° ye lost myn herte and al my love. 90	have
I kan nat love a coward, by my feith!	
For, certes,° what so° any womman seith,	certainly whatever
We alle desiren, if it myghte be,	
To han housbondes hardy, wise, and fre,°	generous
And secree,° and no nygard, ne no fool,	discreet
Ne hym that is agast of every tool,°	weapon
Ne noon avauntour,° by that God above.	boaster
How dorste° ye seyn, for shame, unto youre love	dared
That any thyng myghte make yow aferd?	
Have ye no mannes herte and han a berd°? 100	beard
"Allas, and konne ye ben agast of swevenys.°	be afraid of dreams
No thyng, God woot,° but vanytee in swevene is.[1]	knows
Swevenes engendren of replexions,°	are engendered from repletion
And ofte of fume° and of complexions,°	vapor temperaments
Whan humours ben to° habundant in a wight.°	are too person
"Certes, this dreem which ye han met to-nyght°	have dreamt this night
Comth of the grete superfluytee	
Of youre rede colera,° pardee,°	choler certainly
Which causeth folk to dreden° in hir° dremes	be frightened their
Of arwes,° and of fyr with rede lemes,° 110	arrows flames
Of rede bestes that they wol hem byte,	
Of contek,° and of whelpes grete and lyte	strife
Right° as the humour of malencolie°	Just melancholy

[1] Pertelote dismisses Chauntecleer's *swevene* or dream as a "natural dream" of physiological and not of supernatural origin, presumably produced by a superabundance in his "complexion" (l. 104) of one of the four "humors" or bodily fluids — choler, melancholy, phlegm, or blood. The colors involved in the dream suggest that the excess humor in his case is choler; she therefore prescribes a laxative (l. 123, ll. 142–145) to be preceded by a digestive of worms (l. 141) in order to absorb the choler, and warns him against ague and the tertian fever (ll. 139–140), a fever recurring every other day, which was associated with both choler and melancholy.

Causeth ful many a man in sleep to crie
For fere of blake beres,° or boles° blake,   bears bulls
Or elles blake develes, wol hem° take.   (which) will them
Of othere humours koude I telle also
That werken° many a man in sleep ful wo,°   make woeful
But I wol passe as lightly as I kan.
Lo Catoun,° which that was so wys a man,   120   (Dionysius) Cato
Seyde he nat thus: 'Ne do no fors of° dremes'?   Pay no attention to
  "Now sire," quod she, "whan we fle fro° the   fly down from
     bemes,
For Goddes love, as taak° som laxatif.   take (*as taak*)
Up° peril of my soule and of my lif,   Upon
I conseille yow the beste, I wol nat lye,
That bothe of colere and of malencolye
Ye purge yow. And, for° ye shal nat tarye,   in order that
Thogh in this toun is noon° apothecarye,   no
I shal myself to herbes techen° yow   direct
That shul ben for youre heele° and for youre   cure
     prow.°   130   well-being
And in oure yerd tho° herbes shal I fynde   those
The whiche han° of hire propretee by kynde°   Which have nature
To purge yow bynethe and eek° above.   also
Foryet° nat this, for Goddes owene love: Forget
Ye ben ful colerik of complexioun.
Ware° the sonne in his ascensioun   Beware that
Ne fynde yow nat replet of° humours hote,   overfilled with
And, if it do, I dar wel leye a grote°   groat (4*d.*)
That ye shul have a fevere terciane°   tertian
Or an agu that may be youre bane.°   140   destruction
A day or two ye shul have digestyves
Of wormes er° ye take youre laxatyves   before
Of lauriol,° centaure,° and fumetere,°   spurge-laurel centaury fumitory
Or elles° of ellebor° that groweth there,   else hellebore
Of katapuce,° or of gaitrys beryis,°   caper-spurge gay-tree berries
Of herbe yve° growyng in oure yerd, ther merye is.°   ground-ivy where it is pleasant
Pekke hem up right as they growe, and ete hem in.
Be myrie, housbonde, for youre fader kyn°!   father's kin
Dredeth° no dreem. I kan sey yow namoore."   Dread
  "Madame," quod he, "graunt mercy of° youre   much thanks for
     loore.°   150   instruction
But nathelees, as touchyng daun Catoun,°   as for sir Cato

That hath of wisdom swich° a gret renoun,   such
Thogh that he bad no dremes for to drede,
By God, men may in olde bokes rede
Of many a man moore of auctoritee
Than evere Catoun was, so mote I thee,°   may I prosper
That al the revers° seyn of his sentence° contrary opinion
And han wel founden° by experience   found
That dremes ben° significaciouns   are
As wel of joye as of tribulaciouns   160
That folk enduren in this lyf present.
Ther nedeth° make of this noon argument; There is (no) need to
The verray preeve° sheweth it in dede.   very proof
 "Oon° of the gretteste auctor° that men rede One author(s)
Seith thus, that whilom° two felawes° wente once companions
On pilgrymage in a ful good entente,
And happed° so they coomen° in a toun   it happened came
Where-as ther was swich° congregacioun such
Of peple and eek so streit of herbergage° short of lodgings
That they ne founde° as muche as a cotage 170 didn't find
In which they bothe myghte y-logged° be. lodged
Wherfore they mosten° of necessitee,   must
As for° that nyght, departen° compaignye, For part
And ech of hem gooth to his hostelrye
And took his loggyng as it wolde falle.
That oon of hem° was logged in a stalle The one of them
Fer in a yeerd° with oxen of the plow.   Far off in a courtyard
That oother man was logged wel ynow°   enough
As was his aventure° or his fortune,   lot
That us governeth alle as in commune.° 180 all in common
 "And so bifel that, longe er it were day,
This man mette° in his bed ther-as° he lay dreamt where
How that his felawe gan° upon hym calle began to
And seyde. 'Allas, for in an oxes stalle
This nyght I shal be mordred ther° I lye. murdered where
Now help me, deere brother, or I dye.
In alle haste com to me,' he sayde.
 "This man out of his sleep for feere abrayde,° awoke
But whan that he was wakned of his sleep,
He turned hym and took of this no keep.° 190 heed
Hym thoughte° his dreem nas but° a vanytee. It seemed to him was only
Thus twies° in his slepyng dremed he, twice

And atte thridde tyme yet his felawe
Cam, as hym thoughte, and seyde, 'I am now
   slawe.°   slain
Bihoold my blody woundes, depe and wyde.
Arys up erly in the morwe tyde,°   morning time
And at the west gate of the toun,' quod he,
'A carte ful of donge° ther shaltow se,°   dung   you will see
In which my body is hid ful pryvely.°   very secretly
Do thilke° carte aresten° boldely.   200   Have that same   stopped
My gold caused my mordre, sooth to seyn°';   truth to tell
And tolde hym every poynt how he was slayn
With a ful pitous° face pale of hewe.   piteous
And truste wel his dreem he fond° ful trewe,   found
For on the morwe, as soone as it was day,
To his felawes in° he took the way,   companion's lodging
And whan that he cam to this oxes stalle,
After° his felawe he bigan to calle.   For
    "The hostiler answerde hym anon°   at once
And seyde, 'Sire, youre felawe is agon.°   210   gone
As soone as day he wente out of the toun.'
    "This man gan fallen° in suspecioun,   began to fall
Remembrynge on hise dremes that he mette,°   dreamt
And forth he gooth, no lenger wolde he lette,°   stay
Unto the west gate of the toun and fond
A dong carte, wente° as it were to donge° lond,   (which) went   manure
That was arrayed in the same wise
As ye han herd the dede man devyse,°   describe
And with an hardy herte he gan to crye
Vengeaunce and justice of this felonye.   220
'My felawe mordred is this same nyght,
And in this carte heere he lyth° gapyng upright.°   lies face-upward
I crye out on the mynystres,' quod he,
'That sholden kepe and reulen this citee.
Harrow,° allas! Heere lyth my felawe slayn!'   Help
What sholde I moore unto this tale sayn?
The peple out sterte° and caste the cart to grounde, sprang
And in the myddel of the dong they founde
The dede man, that mordred was al newe.°   just recently
    "O blisful God, that art so just and trewe,   230
Lo how that thow biwreyest mordre alway°   reveal murder always
Mordre wol out, that se° we day by day.   see

Mordre is so wlatsom° and abhomynable   foul
To God, that is so just and resonable,
That he ne wol nat suffre it heled° be,   concealed
Thogh it abyde° a yeer, or two, or thre.   await
Mordre wol out, this is my conclusioun.
And right anon ministres of that toun
Han hent° the cartere and so soore hym pyned°   Have seized tortured
And eek° the hostiler so soore engyned°   240   also racked
That they biknewe hir° wikkednesse anon   confessed their
And were an-hanged by the nekke bon.°   bone
     "Heere may men seen that dremes ben to drede.°   are to be feared
And, certes,° in the same book I rede,   certainly
Right in the nexte chapitre after this —
I gabbe° nat, so have I° joye or blys —   exaggerate may I have
Two men that wolde° han passed over see   wished to
For certeyn cause into a fer contree,
If that the wynd ne hadde ben contrarie,
That made hem in a citee for to tarie,   250
That stood ful myrie° upon an haven° syde.   pleasant harbor
But on a day, agayn the even tyde,°   towards evening time
The wynd gan chaunge and blew right as hem
     leste.°   they wished
Jolif° and glad they wente unto hir° reste   Jolly their
And casten hem° ful erly for to saille.   decided
     "But herkneth! To that o° man fil° a greet   one befell
     mervaille,
That oon of hem, in slepyng as he lay,
Hym mette° a wonder° dreem agayn° the day. Dreamt wonderful before
Hym thoughte° a man stood by his beddes syde, It seemed to him
And hym comanded that he sholde abyde,   260
And seyde hym thus: 'If thow tomorwe wende,°   travel
Thow shalt be dreynt.° My tale is at an ende.'   drowned
He wook, and tolde his felawe what he mette,°   dreamt
And preyde hym his viage° to lette.°   voyage delay
As for that day, he preyde hym to abyde.
His felawe, that lay by his beddes syde,
Gan for to laughe and scorned hym ful faste.
'No dreem,' quod he, 'may so myn herte agaste°   frighten
That I wol lette for to do my thynges.°   stop doing my business
I sette nat a straw by thy dremynges,   270
For swevenes ben° but vanytees and japes.°   dreams are follies

Men dreme alday° of owles and of apes   *everyday*
And of many a maze° therwithal;   *wonder*
Men dreme of thyng that nevere was ne shal.°   *nor shall (be)*
But, sith° I see that thow wolt here abyde,   *since*
And thus forslewthen wilfully° thy tyde,°   *squander willingly*   **time**
God woot,° it reweth me,° and have good day!'   *knows*   *I rue it*
And thus he took his leve and wente his way,
But er that° he hadde half his cours y-seyled,   *before*
Noot I° nat why ne° what meschaunce it eyled,° 280   *I don't know*   **nor**   **ailed**
But casuelly° the shippes botme rente,°   *by chance*   **burst**
And ship and man under the water wente
In sighte of othere shippes it bisyde°   *beside it*
That with hem seyled at the same tyde.
And therfore, faire Pertelote so deere,
By swiche ensamples° olde maystow leere°   *such examples*   **you may** *learn*
That no man sholde been to recchelees°   *too heedless*
Of dremes, for I sey° thee, doutelees,   *tell*
That many a dreem ful soore is for to dred.°   *to be dreaded*

    "Lo, in the lyf of Seint Kenelm I rede, 290
That was Kenulphus sone,° the noble kyng   *Kenulphus's son*
Of Mercenrike,° how Kenelm mette° a thyng.[1]   *Mercia*   **dreamt**
A lite er° he was mordred on a day,   *little before*
His mordre° in his avysioun° he say.°   *murder*   *vision*   **saw**
His norice° hym expowned every del°   *nurse*   *expounded* **completely**
His swevene,° and bad hym for to kepe hym° wel   *dream*   *to guard himself*
For° traisoun, but he nas but° sevene yeer old,   *Against*   *was only*
And therfore litel tale° hath he told°   *heed*   *paid*
Of any dreem, so holy was his herte.
By God, I hadde levere° than my sherte 300   *rather*
That ye hadde rad° his legende as have I.   *read*
Dame Pertelote, I sey yow trewely,
Macrobeus,° that writ° the avysioun°   *Macrobius* *writes* **vision**
In Affrike° of the worthy Cipioun,°   *Africa*   *Scipio*
Affermeth dremes and seith that they ben
Warnynge of thynges that men after sen.° [2]   *afterwards see*

[1] After the death of his father Kenulphus in 821, seven-year-old Kenelm became heir to Mercia but was murdered by his aunt. Shortly before his death he dreamt that he climbed a tree, a friend cut it down, and he flew to heaven in the shape of a bird.

[2] The Latin author Macrobius wrote, at the end of the fourth century, a commentary on Cicero's account of the dream of Scipio Africanus Minor, which became a standard authority on dreams in the Middle Ages.

And forther-moore, I pray yow, looketh wel
In the Olde Testament,[1] of Daniel,
If he heeld dremes any vanytee.

Rede eek of Joseph, and there shul ye see   310
Wher° dremes be somtyme, I sey nat alle,   **Whether**
Warnynge of thynges that shul after falle.
Looke of Egipte° the kyng, daun Pharao,°   Egypt lord Pharaoh
His bakere, and his butiller also,
Wher° they ne felte noon effect in dremes.   Whether
Who-so° wol seke actes of sondry remes°   Whoever various realms
May rede of dremes many a wonder° thyng.   wondrous
Lo Cresus,° which that was of Lyde° kyng,   Croesus Lydia
Mette° he nat° that he sat upon a tree,   Dreamt not
Which signified he sholde an-hanged be?   320
Lo heere Andromacha,° Ectores° wyf,   Andromache Hector's
That day that Ector sholde lese° his lyf,   lose
She dremed on the same nyght biforn°   before
How that the lyf of Ector sholde be lorn°   lost
If thilke° day he wente in to bataille.   that same
She warned hym, but it myghte nat availle;
He wente for to fighte, nathelees.°   nevertheless
But he was slayn anon of° Achilles.   immediately by
But thilke° tale is al to° long to telle,   that same too
And eek it is ny° day. I may nat dwelle.   330 near
    "Shortly I seye, as for conclusioun,
That I shal han of this avysioun
Adversitee, and I seye forther-moor
That I ne telle of laxatyves no stoor,°   set no store on laxatives
For they ben venymes,° I woot° it wel.   are venomous know
I hem deffye! I love hem never a del.°   them not at all
    "Now lat us speke of myrthe and stynte° al this.   stop
Madame Pertelote, so have I° blis,   may I have
Of o° thyng God hath sent me large grace,   one
For whan I se the beautee of youre face,   340
Ye ben° so scarlet reed° aboute youre eyen,°   are red eyes
It maketh al my drede for to dyen,
For, also siker° as *In principio,*   as sure

---

[1] Daniel (according to the book of *Daniel*) and Joseph (*Gen.*, xxxvii, xl, and xli) are both typical of the Old Testament seers who prophesy the future by their own dreams and the dreams of others. Joseph correctly predicted the meaning of dreams for Pharaoh and for Pharaoh's butler and baker.

'*Mulier est hominis confusio.*' [1]

"Madame, the sentence° of this Latyn is,   meaning
'Womman is mannes joye and al his blis.'
For whan I feele a-nyght youre softe syde,
Al be it that I may nat on yow ryde
For that° oure perche is maad° so narwe,° allas,   Because made narrow
I am so ful of joye and of solas°   350   pleasure
That I deffye bothe swevene° and dreem."   vision
     And with that word he fley° doun fro the beem,   flew
For it was day, and eke° hise hennes alle.   also
And with a chuk he gan° hem for to calle,   began
For he hadde founde a corn,° lay° in the yerd.   corn-grain (which) lay
Real° he was; he was na moore aferd.°   Regal no more afraid
He fethered Pertelote twenty tyme
And trad° as ofte er that it was pryme.°   trod (her) prime (9 A.M.)
He looketh as it were° a grym leoun,°   looks like lion
And on hise toos he rometh up and doun.   360
Hym deyned° nat to sette his foot to grounde.   He deigned
He chukketh whan he hath a corn y-founde,
And to hym rennen thanne° hise wyves alle.   run then
Thus real° as a prince is in his halle   regal
Leve I this Chauntecleer in his pasture,
And after wol I telle his aventure.
     Whan that the monthe in which the world bigan,
That highte° March, whan God first maked° man,[2]   is called made
Was complet, and passed were also,
Syn° March bigan, thritty dayes and two,   370   Since
Bifel° that Chauntecler in al his pryde,   It befell
Hise sevene wyves walkyng hym bisyde,
Caste up hise eyen to the brighte sonne,
That in the signe of Taurus hadde y-ronne
Twenty degrees and oon, and som-what moore,
And knew by kynde° and by noon oother loore   nature
That it was pryme,° and krew with blisful stevene.° prime (9 A.M.) voice
"The sonne," he seyde, "is clomben° upon hevene   has climbed

[1] The phrase *In principio*, "In the beginning (was the Word)," with which the Latin
version of *John* commences, was esteemed in Chaucer's time as a formula of almost magical
efficacy. The Friar, according to the *General Prologue* (l. 254), used it as a preliminary greet-
ing to his victims. The widely used Latin proverb, which Chauntecleer carefully mis-
translates, means "Woman is man's ruin."
[2] It was believed in the Middle Ages that the creation of the world occurred in March
during the spring equinox.

Fourty degrees and oon, and moore ywis.°   indeed
Madame Pertelote, my worldes blis,   380
Herkneth° thise blisful briddes,° how they synge,   Listen to   birds
And se the fresshe floures how they sprynge.
Ful is myn herte of revel and solas.°"   pleasure
But sodeynly hym fil° a sorweful cas,°   befell him happening
For evere the latter ende of joye is wo.
God woot° that worldly joye is soone ago,°   knows gone
And if a rethor° koude faire endite,°   rhetorician compose
He in a cronycle saufly myghte it write
As for a sovereyn notabilitee.°   As a supreme observation
Now every wys man, lat hym herkne° me;   390 listen to
This storie is also° trewe, I undertake,°   as vow
As is the book of *Launcelot de Lake*,[1]
That wommen holde in ful gret reverence.
Now wol I torne agayn to my sentence.°   subject
  A colfox° ful of sly iniquitee,   coal-fox
That in the grove hadde woned° yeres three,   lived
By heigh ymaginacioun forncast,°   divine knowledge fore-
                                ordained
The same nyght thurgh-out the hegges brast°   hedges burst
Into the yerd ther° Chauntecleer the faire   where
Was wont,° and eek hise wyves, to repaire,   400 accustomed
And in a bed of wortes° stille he lay   plants
Til it was passed undren° of the day,   mid-morning
Waitynge his tyme on Chauntecleer to falle,
As gladly doon° thise homycides° alle   usually do murderers
That in awayt liggen° to mordre men.   waiting lie
O false mordrour, lurkynge in thy den,
O newe Scariot,° newe Genyloun,°   Iscariot Ganelon
False dissimilour,° O Greek Synoun,°   deceiver Sinon
That broghtest Troye al outrely° to sorwe![2]   utterly
O Chauntecleer, acursed be that morwe°   410 morning
That thow into the yerd flaugh° fro the bemes.   flew
Thow were ful wel y-warned by thy dremes
That thilke° day was perilous to thee.   that same
But what that God forwoot moot nedes° be   foreknows must needs

[1] An entirely fictitious romance concerning Lancelot, the lover of Guinevere, King Arthur's wife.

[2] Judas Iscariot, the disciple, betrayed Christ. Ganelon betrayed Charlemagne's nephew Roland. Sinon, in conspiracy with the Greeks besieging Troy, persuaded the Trojans to take the Greeks' Wooden Horse into their city.

After° the opynyoun of certeyn clerkis.°   According to scholars
Witnesse on hym that any parfit clerk is,
That in scole is greet altercacioun
In this matere and greet disputisoun,°   disputation
And hath ben of an hundred thousand men.
But I ne kan nat bulte° it to the bren°   420   sift bran
As kan the holy doctour Augustyn°   Augustine
Or Boece,° or the bisshop Bradwardyn,°   Boethius Bradwardine
Wheither that Goddes worthy forewityng°   excellent foreknowing
Streyneth° me nedely° for to doon a thyng — Constrains necessarily
"Nedely" clepe° I symple necessitee —   call
Or ellis° if fre choys be graunted me   else
To do that same thyng or do it noght,
Though God forwoot° it er that° it was wroght; foreknows before
Or if his wityng streyneth never a del°   knowing constrains not at
But° by necessitee condicionel.[1]   430   all
I wol nat han° to do of swich° matere.   Except
My tale is of a cok, as ye may heere,   have (anything) with such
That took his conseil of his wyf with sorwe
To walken in the yerd upon that morwe°   morning
That he hadde met° the dreem that I yow tolde. dreamt
Wommens conseils ben° ful ofte colde.°   are fatal
Wommanes conseil broghte us first to wo
And made Adam fro Paradys to go,
Ther-as° he was ful myrie and wel at ese.   Where
But, for I noot° to whom it myghte displese 440 since I don't know
If I conseil of wommen wolde blame,
Passe over, for I seyde it in my game.°   in jest
Rede auctours° where they trete of swich matere, authors
And what they seyn° of wommen ye may heere. say
Thise ben the cokkes wordes and nat myne;
I kan noon° harm of no womman devyne.°   no imagine
    Faire in the sond° to bathe hire myrily°   sand happily
Lith° Pertelote, and alle hir sustres° by,   Lies sisters

---

[1] God, being omniscient, must at all times have a correct foreknowledge of man's choice of action. Has man, therefore, "free choice" (l. 426) of action; and, if not, to what extent is he responsible for his own good or bad actions? Among the many philosophers and theologians who have discussed this complex problem, St. Augustine of Hippo (354–430) elaborated the concept of "free choice"; Boethius in his *Consolation of Philosophy* (sixth century), translated by Chaucer, distinguished between simple (l. 425) and conditional (l. 430) necessity; and Thomas Bradwardine (l. 422), Archbishop of Canterbury, who died in 1349, delivered notable lectures at Oxford on the subject.

Agayn the sonne°; and Chauntecleer so free   In the sun
Song° myrier than the mermayde in the see,   450   Sang
For Phisiologus seith sikerly°   says certainly
How that° they syngen wel and myrily.[1]   That
    And so bifel that, as he caste his eye
Among the wortes° on a boterflye,°   plants butterfly
He was war° of this fox that lay ful lowe.   aware
No thyng ne liste hym thanne° for to crowe,   Not at all did he wish then
But cryde anon° "Cok, cok," and up he sterte°   at once sprang
As man° that was affrayed° in his herte,   Like someone frightened
For naturelly° a beest desireth flee°   by nature to flee
Fro his contrarie,° if he may it see,   460   opposite
Though he nevere erst° hadde syn° it with his eye.   before seen
    This Chauntecleer, whan he gan hym espye,°   noticed him
He wolde han fled but° that the fox anon   except
Seyde, "Gentil sire, allas! Wher wol ye gon?
Be ye affrayed of me that am youre freend?
Now, certes,° I were worse than a feend   certainly
If I to yow wolde° harm or vileynye.   intended
I am nat come youre conseil for t'espye,°   secret to discover
But trewely the cause of my comynge
Was oonly for to herkne how that° ye synge,   470   hear how
For trewely ye han as myrie a stevene°   voice
As any aungel hath that is in hevene.
Ther-with ye han in musyk moore feelynge
Than hadde Boece [2] or any that kan synge.
My lord, youre fader — God his soule blesse! —
And eek youre moder, of hire gentillesse,°   gentility
Han in myn hous y-ben° to my greet ese.°   been satisfaction
And, certes, sire, ful fayn° wolde I yow plese.   gladly
    "But, for° men speke of syngynge, I wol seye —   since
So mote I brouke° wel myne eyen tweye! —   480   may I use
Save° yow I herde nevere man so synge   Except for
As dide youre fader in the morwenynge.
Certes, it was of herte,° al that he song.   hearty
And for to make his voys the moore strong,

---

[1] Physiologus was the reputed author of a Greek work on natural history, composed in the second century, which gave rise to numerous later imitations known as *Bestiaries*. These notoriously unscientific works provided entertaining lore about animals and fabulous creatures, and instructive allegorical interpretations.

[2] Boethius, besides writing on philosophy, was the author of a work entitled *On Music*.

He wolde so peyne hym° that with bothe hise eyen   strive
He moste wynke,° so loude he wolde cryen,   must shut (his eyes)
And stonden° on his tiptoon° ther-with-al,   stand   tiptoes
And strecche forth his nekke long and smal.
And eek he was of swich discrecioun
That ther nas no° man in no regioun   490   was no
That hym in song or wisdom myghte passe.
I have wel rad° in *Daun*° *Burnel the Asse*,   read   *Sir*
Among his vers, how that ther was a cok,
For° a preestes sone yaf° hym a knok   Because   gave
Upon his leg, whil he was yong and nyce,°   foolish
He made hym for to lese° his benefice.[1]   lose
But, certeyn, ther nys no comparisoun
Bitwix the wisdom and discrecioun
Of youre fader and of his subtiltee.
Now syngeth, sire, for seinte° charitee!   500   holy
Lat se, konne ye youre fader countrefete?°"   imitate
    This Chauntecleer hise wynges gan° to bete   began
As man that koude his traysoun nat espie,°   perceive
So was he ravysshed with° his flaterie.   overwhelmed by
    Allas, ye lordes, many a fals flatour°   flatterer
Is in youre court, and many a losengeour,°   deceiver
That plesen° yow wel moore, by my feith,   please
Than he that soothfastnesse° unto yow seith.   truth
Redeth Ecclesiaste of° flaterye.   Ecclesiasticus on
Beth war,° ye lordes, of hir° trecherye.   510   Beware   their
This Chauntecler stood hye upon his toos,
Strecchynge his nekke, and heeld hise eyen cloos,°   closed
And gan to crowe loude for the nones.°   occasion
And daun° Russell the fox stirte up atones,°   sir   sprang up at once
And by the gargat hente° Chauntecleer,   throat seized
And on his bak toward the wode hym beer,°   carried
For yet ne was ther no man that hym sewed.°   pursued
    O destynee, that mayst nat ben eschewed°!   be avoided
Allas that Chauntecler fleigh° fro the bemes!   flew
Allas, his wif ne roghte nat° of dremes!   520   took no heed
And on a Friday fil al this meschaunce.

---

[1] According to the tale in Nigel Wireker's twelfth-century Latin poem *Burnellus the Ass*, a young man named Gundulf threw a stone at a cock and broke its leg. Later, when Gundulf was to have been appointed as priest to a benefice, the cock avenged himself by failing to awaken Gundulf with his crowing in time for the ordination.

O Venus, that art goddesse of plesaunce,°   pleasure
Syn that° thy servant was this Chauntecleer,   Since
And in thy servyce dide al his power
Moore for delit° than world to multiplie,   delight
Why woldestow suffre° hym on thy day to dye?   would you allow
  O Gaufred,° deere maister soverayn,   Geoffrey
That, whan thy worthy kyng Richard was slayn
With shot, compleynedest° his deth so soore, lamented
Why ne hadde I now thy sentence° and thy loore° erudition learning
The Friday for to chide, as diden ye?   531
For on a Friday, soothly,° slayn was he.[1]   truly
Thanne wolde I shewe yow how that I koude
    pleyne°   lament
For Chauntecleres drede and for his peyne.
  Certes, swich cry ne° lamentacioun   or
Was nevere of ladyes maad° whan Ylioun° made Ilium (Troy)
Was wonne, and Pirrus° with his streite swerd° Pyrrhus drawn sword
Whanne he hadde hent° kyng Priam by the berd seized
And slayn hym, as seith us *Eneydos*,° (the) *Aeneid* tells us
As maden° alle the hennes in the cloos° 540 made enclosure
Whan they hadde seyn° of Chauntecleer the sighte. seen
But sovereynly° dame Pertelote shrighte° especially shrieked
Ful louder than dide Hasdrubales wyf [2]
Whan that° hire housbonde hadde lost his lyf When
And that the Romayns hadden brend Cartage.° burned Carthage
She was so ful of torment and of rage
That wilfully° into the fyr she sterte° voluntarily leapt
And brende hirselven° with a stedefast herte. burned herself
  O woful hennes, right so cryden ye
As, whan that Nero brende the citee   550
Of Rome, cryden senatours wyves

---

[1] Friday, as the French word *vendredi* indicates, is the day of Venus. In his Latin verse treatise on the composition of poetry, entitled *The New Poetry* and composed at the end of the twelfth century, Geoffrey de Vinsauf offers as a sample of his highly rhetorical techniques an elegy for King Richard I, who was mortally wounded (in 1199) on a Friday. It begins: "O tearful day of Venus! O sorry star! That day was your night, and that Venus was venomous." Although Geoffrey's rhetoric was still imitated by students in Chaucer's age, Chaucer himself obviously intends the Priest's homage to be ironical.

[2] Chaucer uses the same reference to Hasdrubal's wife in the *Franklin's Tale*, 691–696. (See also p. 145, n. 1.) A comparison between the two passages well illustrates the difference between Chaucer's serious use of exemplification in a conventional medieval lament and his present mock-heroic tone.

For that° hir housbondes losten alle hire° lyves.   Because all lost their
Withouten° gilt this Nero hath hem slayn.   Without
Now wol I turne to my tale agayn.

   The sely widwe° and eek hire doghtres two   poor widow
Herden thise hennes crye and maken wo,
And out atte dores stirten° they anon,°   out of doors rushed at once
And syen° the fox toward the grove gon,°   saw go
And bar° upon his bak the cok away,   carry (*lit.* carried)
And criden "Out! Harrow!" and "Weilaway°! 560   Alas
Ha, ha, the fox!" And after hym they ran,
And eek with staves° many another man.   sticks
Ran Colle oure dogge, and Talbot, and Gerland,
And Malkyn, with a distaf in hire hand.¹
Ran cow, and calf, and eek the verray hogges,
So fered for the berkyng° of the dogges   frightened by the barking
And showtynge° of the men and wommen eek.   shouting
They ronne° so, hem thoughte hir° herte breek.°   ran they thought their / would break
They yelleden as fendes doon° in helle.   fiends do
The dokes° cryden as° men wolde hem quelle.° 570   ducks as if kill
The gees for feere flowen° over the trees.   flew
Out of the hyve cam the swarm of bees.
So hydous° was the noyse, A, *benedicitee,*°   hideous blessings
Certes, he Jakke Straw and his meynee°   company
Ne made nevere shoutes half so shrille
Whan that° they wolden° any Flemyng kille   When would
As thilke° day was maad upon the fox.²   that same
Of bras they broghten bemes,° and of box,°   brought trumpets box-wood
Of horn, of boon,° in whiche they blewe and   bone
   powped,°   puffed
And ther-with-al they skryked,° and they howped.°   shrieked whooped
It semed as that° hevene sholde falle. 581   as if
Now goode men, I prey yow, herkneth alle.
   Lo, how Fortune turneth sodeynly°   overturns suddenly

---

¹ *Talbot* and *Gerland* (modern *Garland*) are presumably, like *Colle*, customary names for dogs. *Malkyn* was the name typifying a country girl and is so used by the Man of Law in the link (translated above) introducing his tale.

² During a widespread revolt of English workers (in 1381) against the leaders of state, church, and commerce, an otherwise unknown rebel named Jack Straw, who was later executed, led a group of Kentishmen into London. There they destroyed property and murdered those whom they considered to be their exploiters, including a large number of clothmakers, recently arrived from Flanders, who had kept their superior technique secret from the native English workmen.

The hope and pryde eek of hire enemy.
This cok that lay upon the foxes bak
In al his drede unto the fox he spak
And seyde, "Sire, if(that) I were as ye,
Yit sholde I seyn,° as wys God helpe me,   say
'Turneth agayn,° ye proude cherles alle.   Turn back
A verray pestilence upon yow falle.   590
Now I am come unto this wodes° syde,   wood's
Maugree youre heed,° the cok shal here abyde.   Despite all you can do
I wol hym ete, in feith, and that anon.' "
    The fox answerde, "In feith, it shal be don."
And as he spak that word, al sodeynly
This cok brak° from his mouth delyverly,°   broke   nimbly
And hye° upon a tree he fley° anon.   high   flew
And whan the fox say° that he was gon,   saw
"Allas," quod he, "O Chauntecleer, allas!
I have to yow," quod he, "y-doon trespas°   600   offence
In as muche as I maked yow aferd
Whan I yow hente° and broghte out of the yerd.   seized
But, sire, I dide it in no wikke° entente.   evil
Com doun, and I shal telle yow what I mente.
I shal seye sooth° to yow, God help me so."   truth
    "Nay thanne," quod he, "I shrewe° us bothe two.   curse
And first I shrewe myself, bothe blood and bones,
If thow bigile me any ofter° than ones.   more often
Thow shalt namoore thurgh° thy flaterye   no more through
Do° me to synge and wynke with° myn eye,   610   Persuade close
For he that wynketh, whan he sholde see,
Al wilfully,° God lat hym nevere thee.° "   voluntarily prosper
    "Nay," quod the fox, "but God yeve° hym   give
        meschaunce°   misfortune
That is so undiscreet of governaunce°   self-control
That jangleth° whan he sholde holde his pees.° "   chatters peace
    Lo, swich it is for to be recchelees,°   careless
And necligent, and truste on flaterye.
    But ye that holden this tale a folye
As of° a fox, or of a cok and hen,   Concerning
Taketh the moralitee, goode men.   620
For seint Poul° seith that al that writen is,   Paul
To oure doctryne° it is y-write,° ywis.°   instruction written indeed
Taketh the fruyt, and lat the chaf be stille.

Now goode God, if that it be thy wille,
As seith my lord, so make us alle goode men,
And brynge us to his heye° blisse. Amen.   high

THE WIFE OF BATH'S PROLOGUE

[D 1–856]

It is clear that Chaucer planned the arrangement of the unattached series of seven tales (D 1–2294, E 1–2440, F 1–1624) initiated by the Wife of Bath and concluded by the Franklin. They are connected by the conversation within the links and are so completely dominated by the provocative views of the Wife concerning the proper status of women in marriage that the unit has been labeled the Marriage Group.

Chaucer's amplification of the Wife of Bath's character is exceptionally copious. Her prologue is the only one in the *Canterbury Tales* which exceeds in length the tale which follows it; and from it we learn that she has married opportunistically in her youth, has won financial independence as owner of a weaving business, and now remains a childless widow, who though aging is still insatiably addicted to love. The portrait is highly individual and peculiarly reflective of the society of Chaucer's own day, but there is much within the delineation that is universally human.

Chaucer's technique is deceptively subtle. The volubility of the Wife of Bath, for instance, does more than reveal her views; it reflects her neurotic restlessness and often hints at emotions which even she would prefer to conceal but which the reader can sense. Thus, although she classifies her first three husbands as "good" and her next two as "bad," we suspect that the only genuine delight which she has derived from marriage has been gained from the troublesome fourth and fifth husbands. In fact, the first three are in her eyes so insignificant that she does not even bother to individualize them.

Moreover, as is often the case in successful comic characterizations, the comicality of the Wife of Bath borders upon the tragic. Her fifth husband, whom she had loved, is now dead, and she evidently does not trust herself to mention the fact explicitly; and although she cheerfully boasts that she has had her world in her time, she retains from her lively past little to comfort her declining years except her memories and her eternal buoyancy.

Much of the material included in the portrait is reminiscent of, or even derivative from, the satirical attacks directed against women by such writers as the French poet, Jean de Meun, who in the latter half of the thirteenth century composed the second part of the *Romance of the Rose*, a work with which Chaucer was well acquainted. But Chaucer's treatment of the "arch-wife" is notably sympathetic. She disarms criticism by willingly confessing her own guilt and simultaneously counterattacking the opponents of women.

The medieval church endorsed the precept of St. Paul: "Wives, submit yourselves unto your own husbands, as unto the Lord. For the husband is the head of the wife, even as Christ is the head of the church" (*Eph.*, v, 22–23). But, though the Wife of Bath can quote scripture to her own purpose, she ignores this doctrine, just as she ignores the medieval assumption that women are essentially evil because they are the daughters of Eve, the agent of man's fall from Paradise. The Wife of Bath's defiant sense of emancipation may be contrasted, for instance, with the pious sentiments of Queen Constance, the heroine of the *Man of Law's Tale*. When the grievously maltreated Constance prays for aid from the Virgin Mary, her very first words contain a humble confession of woman's inferiority and guilt:

> "Mother," said she, "and bright maiden Mary, true it is that through woman's instigation mankind was lost and condemned to eternal death, for which your child was torn upon the cross."

Although the Wife's fifth husband had rashly mentioned the same argument on the night when she finally quelled him, the Wife does not even deign to dispute a doctrine so repugnant.

With one doctrine of the church she in part agrees, namely, that there is woe in marriage; here her own experience for once confirms academic authority. But the conclusions she draws from this premise are not those of the orthodox church fathers. St. Jerome in the fifth century had painted a melancholy portrait of the married state, but his purpose had been to refute the heretical Jovinian, who held that marriage was not inferior to celibacy. Later writers, even in England, had attempted to sustain Jerome's argument. An anonymous English writer at the beginning of the thirteenth century, for instance, in a lurid homily entitled *Holy Maidenhood*, asks his female listeners what worldly pleasure they can expect to gain from a husband:

> When he is away, you have sore care and worry for his home-coming. When he is at home, all your wide walls seem to you to be too narrow. His looking at you makes you aghast. His loathsome behavior and his conduct towards you set you to shuddering. He chides you and checks you and shamefully maltreats you. He mocks you as a lecher does his mistress. He beats you and bangs you as his purchased thrall and humble servant. Your bones ache; your flesh smarts; and your heart within swells with sore mortification; and your face without reveals your suffering.

The Wife's unacademic contribution to the problem is two-fold. Celibacy is admirable; but marriage is, she holds, also honorable and is, besides, better suited to people of her temperament. Marriage may be woeful, she admits; but a sensible wife will see to it that she is not the one who suffers. Chaucer has so contrived her argument that the reader is compelled to admire it even if he does not agree.

"Experience, thogh noon auctoritee°	no (scholarly) authority
Were in this world, is right ynogh for me	
To speke of wo that is in mariage,	
For, lordynges, sith° I twelve yeer was of age,	since
Thonked be God, that is eterne on lyve,°	eternally alive

Housbondes at chirche dore I have had fyve,
If I so ofte myghte han wedded be,[1]
And alle were worthy men in hir° degree.   their
But me was told, certeyn, noght longe agon° is,   ago
That, sith that° Crist ne wente nevere but onys° 10   since once
To weddyng in the Cane° of Galilee,   Cana
That by the same ensemple taughte he me
That I ne sholde wedded be but ones.[2]
Herke eek,° lo, which° a sharp word for the nones°   also what occasion
Bisyde a welle Jesus, God and man,
Spak in repreeve° of the Samaritan.   reproof
    'Thow hast y-had fyve housbondes,' quod he,
'And that ilke° man that now hath thee   same
Is nat thyn housbonde.' Thus he seyde, certeyn.
What that he mente ther-by, I kan nat seyn,   20
But° that I axe° why that the fifthe man   Except ask
Was noon housbonde to the Samaritan.
How manye myghte she have in mariage?
Yet herde I nevere tellen in myn age
Upon this nombre diffinicioun.
Men may dyvyne° and glosen° up and doun,   guess interpret
But wel I woot,° expres,° withouten lye,   know expressly
God bad us for to wexe° and multiplye.   increase
That gentil text kan I wel understonde.
Eek° wel I woot, he seyde myn housbonde   30   Also
Sholde lete° fader and moder and take to me,   leave
But of no nombre mencioun made he,
Of bigamye° or of octogamye.°   second marriage eighth
                                                                   marriage
Why sholde men thanne° speke of it vileynye°?   then reproach
    Lo, here the wise kyng daun Salomon,[3]
I trowe° he hadde wyves mo° than oon.°   believe more one
As wolde° God it leveful° were to me   Would to allowable
To be refresshed half so ofte as he!

[1] "If I might (lawfully) have been married so often." The Wife, who has been married five times "at the church door" (see *General Prologue*, l. 460, and note), here raises the disputed question whether remarriage (technically known as *bigamy*, as in ll. 33, 92, 102) is canonically lawful.

[2] The Wife has learned, presumably through her fifth husband, of an argument advanced by St. Jerome (see ll. 675, 680, and n. 1) that, since the New Testament (*John*, ii, 1) only mentions Christ's attendance at one wedding, only one marriage was therefore lawful.

[3] *Daun Salomon* or "lord Solomon," according to I *Kings*, xi, 3, "had seven hundred wives . . . and three hundred concubines."

Which yifte° of God hadde he for alle his wyvys!	What a gift
No man hath swich° that in this world alyve is. 40	such
God woot,° this noble kyng, as to my wit,°	knows judgment
The firste nyght had many a murye° fit	merry
With ech of hem, so wel° was hym on lyve.°	well off he in his time
Blessed be God that I have wedded fyve,	
Of whiche I have pyked out the beste	
Bothe of here nether° purs and of here cheste.°	their lower money-chest
Diverse scoles maken parfyt clerkes,	
And diverse practyk° in many sondry werkes	practice
Maken° the werkman parfit, sekirly.°	Make(s) certainly
Of fyve husbondes scoleiyng° am I. 50	schooling
Welcome the sixte whan that evere he shal;	
For sith° I wol nat kepe me chaast° in al,	since chaste
Whan myn housbonde is fro the world y-gon,	
Som Cristen man shal wedde me anon,°	forthwith
For thanne th'apostle [1] seith that I am free	
To wedde, a Goddes half,° wher it liketh me.	in God's name
He seith that to be wedded is no synne;	
Bet° is to be wedded than to brynne.°	Better burn
What rekketh me theigh° folk seye vileynye	care I though
Of shrewed Lameth° and his bigamye? 60	cursed Lamech (*Gen.,* iv, 19)
I woot° wel Abraham was an holy man,	know
And Jacob eek,° as fer as evere I kan,°	also know
And ech of hem hadde wyves mo than two,	
And many another holy man also.	
Where kan ye seye,° in any maner° age,	say kind of
That heighe God defended° mariage	forbade
By expres word? I pray yow, telleth me.	
Or where comanded he virginitee?	
I woot as wel as ye, it is no drede,°	doubt
Th'apostle, whan he speketh of maydenhede,° 70	virginity
He seyde that precept therof hadde he noon.	
Men may conseille a womman to be oon,°	one (a virgin)
But conseillyng is no comandement.	
He put it in oure owene juggement,	

[1] The apostle is St. Paul, from whose discussion of marriage (in I *Cor.*, vii) the Wife ingeniously derives scriptural authority (ll. 55–58, 70–71, 109–110, 135–136, 160–165) to support her own views. She also quotes his views (*Eph.*, v, 25) enthusiastically in ll. 166–167, although later in ll. 348–351 she repudiates the text from I *Tim.*, ii, 9, quoted against her.

For hadde God comanded maydenhede,
Thanne hadde he dampned° weddyng with the   condemned
   dede.°   deed
And certes, if ther were no seed y-sowe,°   sown
Virginitee thanne, wherof sholde it growe?
Poul dorste° nat comanden, at the leeste,   Paul dared
A thyng of which his maister yaf noon heeste.°   80   gave no order
The dart° is set up for virginitee.   race-prize
Cacche who so may, who renneth best lat se.
   But this word is noght take of° every wight°   applied to   person
But ther-as° God list yeve° it, of his myght.   where   wishes to give
I woot° wel that th'apostle was a mayde°;   know   virgin
But nathelees,° thogh that he wroot and sayde   nevertheless
He wolde° that every wight were swich as he,   wished
Al nys but° conseil to virginitee;   is no more than
And for to been a wyf he yaf° me leve   gave
Of indulgence. So is it no repreve   90
To wedde me, if that my make dye,
Withoute excepcioun of bigamye.[1]
Al° were it good no womman for to touche, —   Although
He mente as in his bed or in his couche,
For peril is bothe fyr and tow t'assemble°;   tow to bring together
Ye knowe what this ensample may resemble.
This al and som,° he heeld virginitee   All in all
Moore parfit° than weddyng in freletee.°   perfect   frailty
Freletee clepe° I but if that° he and she   call   unless
Wolde leden al hir° lyf in chastitee.   100   lead all their
   I graunte it wel I have noon envye
Thogh maydenhede preferre° bigamye.   be exalted over
It liketh hem° to be clene in body and goost.°   pleases them   spirit
Of myn estat ne wol I make no boost.
For wel ye knowe, a lord in his houshold
Ne hath nat every vessel al of gold;
Somme been° of tree° and doon hir° lord servyse.   are   wood   their
God clepeth° folk to hym in sondry wyse,°   calls   various ways
And everich° hath of God a propre yifte,°   each   individual gift
Som this, som that, as hym liketh shifte.°   110   to ordain
   Virginitee is greet perfeccioun,
And continence eek° with devocioun;   also

[1] "So there is no reproach in marrying (again), if my mate die, not excepting the reproach directed against remarriage (bigamy)."

But Crist, that of perfeccioun is welle,°   the source
Bad nat every wight he sholde go selle
Al that he hadde, and yeve° it to the poore,   give
And in swich wise folwe° hym and his foore°;   follow   way
He spak to hem° that wolde lyve parfitly.   those
And, lordynges, by youre leve, that am nat I!
I wol bistowe the flour of al myn age
In th'actes and in fruyt of mariage.   120
    Telle me also, to what conclusioun°   purpose
Were membres maad° of generacioun   made
And of so parfit wys a wight y-wrought°?   a manner a person constructed
Trusteth right wel, they were nat maad for noght.
Glose° who so wole, and seye bothe up and doun   Interpret
That they were maad for purgacioun
Of uryne, and oure bothe thynges° smale   the things of us both
Were eek to knowe a femele from a male,
And for noon oother cause! Sey ye no?
Th'experience woot° wel it is noght so.   130   knows
So that° the clerkes° be nat with me wrothe,   As long as   scholars
I sey this, that they maked been° for bothe,   are made
That is to seye, for office,° and for ese°   function   assistance
Of engendrure,° ther° we nat God displese.   procreation   wherein
Why sholde men ellis° in hir° bokes sette   otherwise   their
That man shal yelde° to his wyf hir dette°?   pay   debt
Now, wher-with sholde he make his paiement,
If he ne° used his sely° instrument?   not   good
Thanne° were they maad upon a creature   Therefore
To purge uryne and eek for engendrure.   140
    But I seye noght that every wight is holde,°   required
That hath swich harneys° as I to yow tolde,   such equipment
To goon° and usen hem° in engendrure.   go   them (it)
Thanne sholde men take of chastitee no cure.°   heed
Crist was a mayde° and shapen as a man,   virgin
And many a seynt sith that° the world bigan,   since
Yet lyved they evere in parfit chastitee.
I nyl° envye no virginitee.   will (not)
Lat hem° be breed° of pured whete° seed,   them (virgins)   bread
                                                 finest wheat
And lat us wyves hote° barly breed.   150   be called
And yet with barly breed, Mark telle kan,[1]

---

[1] The miracle of the loaves and fishes is told by Mark (vi, 38), but John (vi, 9) is the only writer to mention *barley* loaves specifically.

Oure lord Jesu refresshed many a man.
In swich estat as God hath cleped° us   called
I wol persevere. I nam nat precius.°   am not fastidious
In wyfhode wol I use myn instrument
As frely as my makere hath it sent.
If I be daungerous,° God yeve° me sorwe.   unyielding give
Myn housbonde shal it have bothe eve and morwe°   morning
Whan that hym list° com forth and paye his dette.   it pleases him to
An housbonde wol I have, I wol nat lette,°   160   desist
Which° shal be bothe my dettour and my thral°   Who slave
And have his tribulacioun withal°   besides
Upon his flessh while that I am his wyf.
I have the power duryng al my lyf
Upon his propre° body, and nat he.   own
Right thus th'apostle tolde it unto me
And bad oure housbondes for to love us wel.
Al this sentence° me liketh° every del.°"   verdict pleases part
    Up stirte° the Pardoner, and that anon.°   started immediately
"Now dame," quod he, "by God and by seint
    John,   170
Ye been° a noble prechour in this cas.   are
I was aboute to wedde a wyf. Allas,
What° sholde I bye° it on my flessh so deere°?   Why pay for dearly
Yet hadde I levere° wedde no wyf to-yeere.°"   rather this year
    "Abyde," quod she. "My tale is nat bigonne.
Nay, thow shalt drynken on another tonne,°   cask
Er that° I go, shal savoure° wors than ale.   Before (which) will taste
And whan that I have toold thee forth my tale
Of tribulacioun in mariage,
Of which I am expert in al myn age, —   180
This is to seye, myself hath been the whippe, —
Thanne maystow chese° whether thow wolt sippe   may you choose
Of thilke° tonne that I shal abroche.°   that same broach
Be war of it er° thow to neigh° approche,   before too near
For I shal telle ensamples mo than ten.
'Who so that nyl° be war° by othere men,   will not warned
By hym shal othere men corrected be.'
Thise same wordes writeth Ptholome.[1]

---

[1] In the Middle Ages various wise sayings, including those quoted in ll. 186–187 and 332–333, were unauthoritatively ascribed to Ptolemy of Alexandria, the celebrated second-century Greek astronomer and geographer.

Rede in his *Almageste,* and take it there."

"Dame, I wolde praye yow, if youre wil were,"
Seyde this Pardoner, "as ye bigan,   191
Telle forth youre tale, spareth° for no man,   hold back
And teche us yonge men of youre praktyke.°"   practice

"Gladly," quod she, "sith° it may yow lyke.°   since please
But that I praye to al this compaignye,
If that I speke after my fantasye,°   according to my notions
As taketh nat agrief of that° I seye,   Take no offence at what
For myn entente nys but° for to pleye.   is only

Now, sire, thanne wol I telle yow forth my tale.
As evere moot° I drynke wyn and ale,   200   may
I shal seye sooth,° tho° housbondes that I hadde,   truly those
As three° of hem were goode, and two were badde.   Three
The thre were goode men, and riche, and olde.
Unnethe myghte° they the statut holde°   Hardly could obey
In which that they were bounden unto me.
Ye woot° wel what I mene of this, pardee.°   know certainly
As help me God, I laughe whan I thynke
How pitously° a° nyght I made hem swynke°   pitifully at toil
And, by my fey,° I tolde° of it no stoor.°   faith took account
They hadde me yeven hir° land and hir tresoor. 210   given me their
Me neded nat do lenger diligence
To wynne hir love or doon hem reverence.
They loved me so wel, by God above,
That I ne tolde no deyntee of hir° love.   set no value on their
A wys womman wol bisye hire evere in oon°   exert herself continually
To gete hir love, ye,° ther-as° she hath noon.   certainly where
But sith I hadde hem hoolly in myn hond,°   control
And sith they hadde yeven me al hir lond,
What° sholde I take kepe° hem for to plese   Why heed
But it were° for my profit and myn ese?   220   Except
I sette hem so awerke,° by my fey,°   to work faith
That many a nyght they songen 'Weylawey!'°   sang 'Alas!'
The bacon was nat fet° for hem, I trowe,°   fat believe
That som men han° in Essex at Donmowe.¹   have
I governed hem so wel after° my lawe   according to
That ech of hem ful blisful was and fawe°   glad

¹ By an old custom sporadically revived the Dunmow Priory awarded a flitch of bacon to any married couple who could swear that they had enjoyed a whole year of marriage in complete contentment.

To brynge me gaye thynges fro the feyre.°　　　　fair
They were ful glad whan I spak to hem feyre,°　　　graciously
For, God it woot, I chidde° hem spitously.°　　　scolded　spitefully
　　Now herkneth how I bar° me proprely,　　230　　conducted
Ye wise wyves that konne° understonde.　　　　can
　　Thus sholde ye speke and bere hem wrong on
　　　honde,°　　　　deceive them
For half so boldely kan ther no man
Swere and lyen° as a womman kan.　　　　lie
I sey nat this by° wyves that ben wyse　　　about
But if it be° whan they hem mysavyse.°　　　Except　fall in error
A wys wyf, it that she kan hir° good,　　　knows her own
Shal beren hym on hond° the cow [1] is wood°　Will maintain to him that
　　　　mad
And take witnesse of hir owene mayde
Of hir assent.° But herkneth how I sayde [2]:　240　agreement
　　'Sire olde kaynard,° is this thyn array?　　　dotard
Why is my neighebores wyf so gay?
She is honoured over al ther° she goth.　　　everywhere
I sitte at hoom, I have no thrifty cloth.°　　　good dress
What dostow° at my neighebores hous?　　　do you do
Is she so fair? Artow so amorous?
What rowne° ye with oure mayde? *Benedicite,*°　whisper　Blessings
Sire olde lechour, lat thy japes° be!　　　tricks
And if I have a gossib° or a freend　　　companion
Withouten gilt,° ye chiden as a feend　　250　Innocently
If that I walke or pleye unto his hous.
Thow comest hoom as dronken as a mous
And prechest on thy bench, with yvel preef°!　　bad luck to you!
Thow seyst to me it is a greet meschief
To wedde a poure womman, for costage°;　　　because of expense
And if that she be riche, of heigh parage,°　　noble extraction
Thanne seistow° that it is a tormentrye°　　　you say　tribulation
To suffre hir pryde and hir malencolye;
And if that she be fair, thow verray knave,
Thow seist that every holour° wol hire have;　260　adulterer
She may no while in chastitee abyde

---

[1] According to a widespread folktale, the chough (*cow*, a bird of the crow family) told its master that his wife was unfaithful, but the wife was able to persuade him that the bird was insane, and so the husband killed it.

[2] In lines 241–384 the Wife of Bath provides a typical sample of the kind of argument which she had employed in order to quell all of her first three old husbands.

That is assayled upon ech a° syde.   every
   'Thow seyst som folk desire us for richesse,
Somme for oure shap,° and somme for oure fair-   shape
    nesse,
And somme for° she kan either synge or daunce,   because
And somme for gentillesse° and daliaunce,°   gentleness amusement
Somme for hir handes and hir armes smale.°   slender
Thus goth° al to the devel, by thy tale.°   goes account
Thow seyst men may nat kepe a castel wal,
It may so longe assailled been over al.°   270   at all points
   'And if that she be foul, thow seyst that she
Coveiteth every man that she may se,
For as a spanyel she wol on hym lepe
Til that she fynde som man hir to chepe.°   to traffic with her
Ne noon so grey goos° goth ther in the lake   And no goose so gray
As, seistow,° wol be withoute make,°   you say mate
And seyst° it is an hard thyng for to welde°   (you) say control
A thyng that no man wol, his thankes,° helde.°   willingly hold
Thus seistow, lorel,° whan thow goost to bedde,   wretch
And that no wys man nedeth for to wedde   280
Ne no man that entendeth° unto hevene.   aims
With wilde thonder dynt° and firy levene°   stroke lightning
Moote° thy welked° nekke be to-broke.°   May withered broken
   'Thow seyst that droppyng° houses, and eek   leaking
    smoke,
And chidyng wyves maken men to flee
Out of hir° owene houses. A! *benedicitee!*   their
What eyleth° swich an old man for to chide?   ails
   'Thow seyst we wyves wil oure vices hide
Til we be fast,° and thanne we wol hem shewe°!   wed show
Wel may that be a proverbe of a shrewe!   290
   'Thow seist that oxen, asses, hors,° and houndes,   horses
They been assayed° at diverse stoundes,°   tested times
Bacynes,° lavours,° er that° men hem bye,°   Basins washbowls before
                                    buy
Spoones, stooles, and al swich housbondrye,
And so be pottes, clothes, and array;
But folk of wyves maken noon assay
Til they be wedded, olde dotard shrewe!
And thanne, seistow, we wil oure vices shewe!
   'Thow seist also that it displeseth me
But if that° thow wolt preise my beautee,   300   Unless

And but thow poure° alwey upon my face   pore
And clepe° me "faire dame" in every place,   call
And but thow make a feeste° on thilke° day   celebration the same
That I was born, and make me fressh and gay,
And but thow do to my norice° honour,   nurse
And to my chambrere° withinne my bour,°   chambermaid room
And to my fadres° folk and his allyes.°   father's connections
Thus seistow, olde barel ful of lyes!
   'And yet of oure apprentice Jankyn,
For° his crisp heer° shynyng as gold so fyn,   310   Because of curly hair
And for he squyereth me bothe up and doun,
Yet hastow caught a fals suspecioun.
I wil° hym nat, thogh thow were deed tomorwe.   wish
   'But tel me this. Why hidestow,° with sorwe,°   do you hide grief upon it
The keyes of thy cheste awey fro me?
It is my good° as wel as thyn, pardee.°   property certainly
What? Wenestow° make an ydiot of oure dame°?   Do you expect to of me
Now, by that lord that called is seint Jame,°   James (of Compostela)
Thou shalt noght bothe, thogh thow were wood,°   mad
Be maister of my body and of my good.°   320   wealth
That oon° thow shalt forgo, maugree° thyne eyen.°   The one (or other) despite eyes
What helpeth it of me enquere° and spyen°?   to enquire spy
I trowe° thow woldest loke° me in thy chiste.°   believe lock chest
Thow sholdest seye, "Wyf, go wher thee liste.°   it pleases
Taak youre disport. I nyl nat leve no talys.°   will believe no tales
I knowe yow for a trewe wyf, dame Alys."
We love no man that taketh kepe° or charge°   note heed
Wher that we goon. We wol been at oure large.°   wish to be at large
   'Of alle men y-blessed moot° he be,   may
The wise astrologen,° daun Ptholome,°   330   astrologer master Ptolemy
That seith this proverbe in his *Almageste:*
"Of alle men his wisdom is hyeste
That rekketh° nat who hath the world in honde.°"   cares owns (*hath . . . in honde*)
By this proverbe thow shalt understonde,
"Have thow ynogh. What thar thee° rekke or care   Why need you
How myrily that othere folkes fare?"
For certes,° olde dotard, by youre leve,   certainly
Ye shal han queynte° right ynogh at eve.   have intercourse
He is to° greet a nygard that wil werne°   too refuse
A man to lighte a candel at his lanterne;   340
He shal han never the lasse light, pardee.°   certainly

Have thow ynogh! Thee thar nat pleyne thee.°   You need not complain
  'Thow seist also that if we make us gay
With clothyng and with precious array,
That it is peril of oure chastitee;
And yet, with sorwe,° thow most enforce thee°   grief upon it   yourself
And seye thise wordes in th'apostles name:
"In habit° maad with chastitee and shame°   clothing   modesty
Ye wommen shal apparaille yow," quod he,
"And nat in tressed heer° and gay perree°   350   hair   jewelry
As° perles, ne° with gold, ne clothes riche."   Such as   nor
After° thy text, ne after thy rubriche,°   According to   rubric
                                                             (direction)
I wol nat werke as muchel° as a gnat.   much
  'Thow seydest this, that I was lyk a cat.
For who so wolde senge° a cattes skyn,   singe
Than wolde the cat wel dwellen in his in°;   willingly stay in its home
And if the cattes skyn be slyk and gay,
She wol nat dwelle in house half a day,
But forth she wole er° any day be dawed°   before   dawned
To shewe hir skyn and goon a-caterwawed.°   360   go caterwauling
This is to seye, if I be gay, sire shrewe,
I wol renne° out, my borel° for to shewe.   run   clothing
  'Sire olde fool, what helpeth° thee t'espyen°?   does it help   to spy
Thogh thow preye Argus with his hundred eyen
To be my warde-corps,° as he kan best,   guardian
In feith, he shal nat kepe me but me lest.°   unless it pleases me
Yet koude I make his berd,° so moot I thee°!   outwit him   may I prosper
  'Thow seydest eek that ther ben° thynges three,   are
The whiche thynges troublen al this erthe,
And that no wight° may endure the ferthe.°   370   one   fourth
O leeve° sire shrewe, Jesu shorte° thy lyf!   dear   shorten
Yet prechestow and seist° an hateful wyf   say
Y-rekened is for oon of thise myschaunces.[1]
Been° ther noone othere resemblaunces   Are
That ye may likne youre parables to
But if° a sely° wyf be oon of tho°?   Unless   poor   those
  'Thow liknest eek wommanes love to helle,
To bareyne lond ther° water may nat dwelle.   where
  'Thow liknest it also to wilde fyr,

[1] According to *Proverbs*, xxx, 21–23, one of the four intolerable misfortunes here referred to is "an odious woman when she is married." The direct source of this passage and two others ultimately from *Proverbs* in ll. 377–383 is St. Jerome's anti-feminist writing (see p. 104, n. 1).

The moore it brenneth,° the moore it hath desyr 380   burns
To consume every thyng that brent wol be.
Thow seist, right° as wormes shende° a tree,   just   destroy
Right so a wyf destroyeth hir housbonde;
This knowen they that been to wyves bonde.°'   bound
   Lordynges, right thus, as ye han understonde,
Bar° I stifly° myne olde housbondes on honde   Accused (*Bar . . . on honde*)
                                                boldly
That thus they seyden in hir° dronkenesse,   their
And al was fals, but° that I took witnesse   except
On Jankyn, and on my nece also.
O Lord, the peyne I dide hem and the wo   390
Ful giltlees, by Goddes swete pyne°!   precious suffering
For as an hors I koude byte° and whyne.°   bite (crossly)   whinny
                                                (nicely)
I koude pleyne and° I was in the gilt,   complain if
Or elles° often tyme I hadde been spilt.°   else   ruined
Who so that first to mille comth, first grynt.°   grinds
I pleyned first; so was oure werre stynt.°   war stopped
They were ful glad to excusen hem ful blyve°   speedily
Of thyng° of which they nevere agilte hir lyve.°   something   were guilty in
                                              their lives
Of wenches wolde I beren hem on honde°   accuse them
Whan that for syk° they myghte unnethe° stonde.   sickness   could hardly
Yet tikled I his herte, for that he   401
Wende° that I hadde of hym so greet chiertee.°   Believed   affection
I swoor that al my walkyng out by nyghte
Was for to espye wenches that he dighte.°   lay with
Under that colour° hadde I many a myrthe.   pretext
For al swich wit° is yeven° us in oure birthe;   ingenuity   given
Deceite, wepyng, spynnyng God hath yeve
To wommen kyndely° whil they may lyve.   by nature
And thus of o° thyng I avaunte° me: one   boast
Atte° ende I hadde the bet° in ech degree,   410   At the   better
By sleighte, or force, or by som maner° thyng,   sort of
As° by continuel murmur or grucchyng.°   Such as   grumbling
Namely° abedde hadden they meschaunce;   Particularly
Ther wolde I chide and do° hem no plesaunce°;   show   affection
I wolde no lenger in the bed abyde
If that I felte his arm over my syde
Til he hadde maad his raunceon° unto me.   ransom
Thanne wolde I suffre° hym do his nycetee.°   allow   will
And ther-fore every man this tale I telle,
Wynne° who so may, for al is for to selle.°   420   Gain (from it)   for sale

With empty hond men may none° haukes lure.   no
For wynnyng° wolde I al his lust endure   gain
And make me a feyned appetit,
And yet in bacoun° hadde I nevere delit.   old meat
That made me that evere I wolde hem chyde,
For, thogh the Pope had seten hem bisyde,°   sat beside them
I wolde noght spare hem at hir owene bord,
For, by my trouthe, I quytte° hem word for word.   requited
As help me verray God omnipotent,
Thogh I right now sholde make my testament,   430
I ne owe hem nat a word that it nys quyt.°   isn't requited (already)
I broghte it so aboute by my wit
That they moste yeve it up as for the beste,
Or elles° hadde we nevere been in reste.   else
For thogh he looked as a wood leoun,°   savage lion
Yet sholde he faille of his conclusioun.°   purpose
    Thanne wolde I seye, 'Good lief, taak keep°   Dear, take notice
How mekely looketh Wilkyn oure sheep.
Com neer, my spouse. Lat me ba° thy cheke.   kiss
Ye sholden be al pacient and meke   440
And han a swete, spiced° conscience,   scrupulous
Sith° ye so preche of Jobes pacience.   Since
Suffreth alwey, syn° ye so wel kan preche.   since
And, but° ye do, certeyn° we shal yow teche   unless certainly
That it is fair to han a wyf in pees.
Oon of us two moste bowen,° douteless.   yield
And, sith a man is moore resonable
Than womman is, ye mosten° been suffrable.°   must   patient
What eyleth° yow to grucche thus and grone?   ails
Is it for° ye wolde have my queynte° allone?   450   because genitals
Wy°! Taak it al! Lo, have it every del.°   Why   part
Peter°! I shrewe° yow but ye love it wel!   By St. Peter curse
For if I wolde selle my *bele chose*,°   genitals
I koude walke as fressh as is a rose.
But I wol kepe it for youre owene tooth.
Ye be to blame, by God. I sey yow sooth.°'   truth
    Swiche manere° wordes hadde we on honde.   kind of
Now wol I speke of my ferthe° housbonde.   fourth
    My ferthe housbonde was a revelour,° —   playboy
This is to seyn, he hadde a paramour° —   460   mistress
And I was yong and ful of ragerye,°   wildness

Stibourne and strong, and joly as a pye.°   magpie
How koude I daunce to an harpe smale
And syng, ywys,° as any nyghtyngale   indeed
Whan I had dronke a draughte of swete wyn!
Metellius, the foule cherl, the swyn,
That with a staf birafte° his wyf hir lyf   bereft
For she drank wyn, though° I hadde been his wyf,   if
Ne sholde nat han daunted me fro drynke!
And after wyn, on Venus moste° I thynke,   470   must
For also siker° as coold engendreth hayl,   as surely
A likerous° mouth moste han a likerous tayl.   lecherous
In womman vynolent° is no defence° —   wine-filled   resistance
This knowen° lechours by experience.   know
     But, Lord Crist, whan that it remembreth me°   when I look back
Upon my youthe and on my jolytee,
It tikeleth me aboute myn herte roote.°   heart's root
Unto this day it dooth myn herte boote°   good
That I have had my world as in my tyme.
But age, allas, that al wole envenyme,°   480   will envenom all
Hath me biraft my beautee and my pith.
Lat go! Far wel! the devel go ther-with.
The flour° is goon; ther is namoore to telle.   flower
The bren° as I best kan now moste I selle.   bran
But yet to be right murye wol I fonde.°   try
Now wol I tellen of my ferthe housbonde.
     I seye, I hadde in herte gret despit°   spite
That he of any oother had delit.
But he was quyt,° by God and by seint Joce!   paid back
I made hym of the same wode° a croce.°   490   wood   stick
Nat of my body, in no foul manere,
But certeynly I made folk swich cheere°   behaved to people so
That in his owene grece I made hym frye
For angre and for verray jalousye.
By God, in erthe I was his purgatorie,
For which I hope his soule be in glorie.
For God it woot, he sat ful ofte and song°   sang
Whan that his shoo ful bitterly hym wrong.°   pinched
Ther was no wight save God and he that wiste,°   knew
In many wise,° how soore I hym twiste.°   500   ways   tortured
He deyde whan I cam from Jerusalem
And lyth y-grave° under the roode beem,°   lies buried   crucifix beam

Al° is his toumbe noght so curyous°   Even if   intricate
As was the sepulcre of hym Daryus°   (King) Darius
Which that Appelles wroghte subtilly.
It nys but wast° to burye hym preciously.°   is only a waste   expensively
Lat hym fare wel, God gyve his soule reste.
He is now in his grave and in his cheste.
   Now of my fifthe housbonde wol I telle,
God lat his soule nevere come in helle!   510
And yet was he to me the mooste shrewe.°   greatest scold
That feele I on my ribbes al by rewe°   each in order
And evere shal unto myn endyng day.
But in oure bed he was so fressh and gay,
And ther-with-al so wel koude he me glose,°   interpret
Whan that he wolde han my *bele chose*,
That, thogh he hadde me bet° on every bon,°   beaten   bone
He koude wynne agayn my love anon.°   immediately
I trowe° I loved hym best for that° he   believe   because
Was of his love daungerous° to me.   520 reticent
We wommen han, if that I shal nat lye,
In this matere a queynte fantasye.°   quaint fancy
Wayte what° thyng we may nat lightly° have,   Whatever (*Wayte what*)
Ther-after wol we crye al day and crave.   easily
Forbede us thyng,° and that desiren we.   something
Preesse on us faste, and thanne wol we fle.°   flee
With daunger oute° we al oure chaffare°;   (apparent) reluctance offer
Greet prees° at market maketh deere ware,   wares
And to° greet cheep° is holde° at litel prys.°   demand
This knoweth every womman that is wys.   530 too   cheapness   held
                                                                esteem
   My fifthe housbonde, God his soule blesse,
Which that° I took for love and no richesse,   Whom
He som tyme was a clerk of Oxenford°   Oxford student
And hadde laft scole and wente at hom° to bord   in a private home
With my gossyb° dwellyng in oure toun;   friend
God have hir soule, hir name was Alisoun.
She knew myn herte and eek my pryvetee°   secrets
Bet° than oure parissh preest, so mote I thee°!   Better   may I prosper
To hire biwreyed° I my conseil al,   revealed
For hadde myn housbonde pissed on a wal   540
Or doon a thyng that sholde have cost his lyf,
To hire and to another worthy wyf
And to my nece, which that° I loved wel,   whom

I wolde han toold his conseil every del°   part
And so I dide ful often, God it woot,°   knows
That made his face often reed° and hoot   red
For verray shame, and blamed° hymself for° he   (he) blamed because
Hadde toold to me so greet a pryvetee.
    And so bifel that ones in a Lente —
So often tymes I to my gossyb wente,   550
For evere yet I loved to be gay
And for to walke in March, Aprill, and May
From hous to hous to here° sondry tales —   hear
That Jankyn clerk, and my gossyb dame Alys,
And I myself into the feeldes wente.
Myn housbonde was at Londoun al that Lente;
I hadde the bettre leyser° for to pleye,   leisure
And for to se, and eek for to be seye,°   seen
Of lusty° folk. What wiste° I wher my grace°   By pleasure-loving How
      knew favor
Was shapen for to be,° or in what place?   560   destined to be granted
Ther-fore I made my visitacions
To vigilies° and to processions,   festivals on eves of saints' days
To prechyng eek, and to thise pilgrymages,
To pleyes of myracles and mariages,
And wered upon° my gaye scarlet gytes°   wore gowns
Thise wormes, ne thise moththes, ne thise mytes,
Upon° my peril, frete° hem nevere a del.°   At ate` bit
And wostow° why? For° they were used wel!   do you know Because
    Now wol I tellen forth what happed° me.   happened to
I seye that in the feeldes walked we   570
Til trewely we hadde swich daliaunce,°   intimate conversation
This clerk and I, that, of my purveiaunce,°   out of foresight
I spak to hym and seyde hym how that he,
If I were wydewe,° sholde wedde me.   widow
For certeynly, I seye for no bobaunce,°   boast
Yet was I nevere withouten purveiaunce
Of mariage n'of° othere thynges eek.   nor of
I holde a mouses herte° nat worth a leek   heart
That hath but oon hole for to sterte° to,   run
And if that faille, thanne is al y-do.°   580   done
    I bar hym on honde° he hadde enchanted me, —   made him think
My dame taughte me that soutiltee —
And eek I seyde I mette° of hym al nyght,   dreamed
He wolde han slayn me as I lay upright,°   face-up

And al my bed was ful of verray° blood: real
'But yet I hope that ye shal do me good,
For blood bitokeneth° gold, as me was taught.'   signifies (in dreams)
And al was fals. I dremed of it right naught,
But as I folwed ay° my dames loore°   always teaching
As wel of that as of othere thynges moore.   590
     But now, sire, lat me se. What shal I seyn°?   am I about to say
A ha, by God, I have my tale ageyn!
     Whan that my fourthe housbonde was on beere,°   his bier
I weep algate° and made sory cheere,   wept constantly
As wyves mooten,° for it is usage,°   must the custom
And with my coverchief° covered my visage.   kerchief
But, for that° I was purveyed° of a make,°   because provided **mate**
I wepte but smal, and that I undertake.°   vouch for
     To chirche was myn housbonde born amorwe°   the next morning
With neghebores that for hym maden sorwe,   600
And Jankyn oure clerk was oon of tho.°   those
As help me God, whan that I saw hym go
After the beere, me thoughte he hadde a paire
Of legges and of feet so clene and faire
That al myn herte I yaf° unto his hoold.   gave
He was, I trowe, twenty wynter oold,
And I was fourty, if I shal seye sooth°;   truth
But yet I hadde alwey a coltes° tooth.   colt's
Gat-tothed° I was, and that bicam° me weel.   Gap-toothed suited
I hadde the preente° of seynt Venus seel.°   610   imprint birthmark
As help me God, I was a lusty oon,
And fair and riche and yong and wel bigoon,°   contented
And trewely, as myne housbondes tolde me,
I hadde the beste *quonyam* mighte° be.   genitals that could
For certes° I am al Venerien°   certainly influenced by Venus
In feelyng, and myn herte is Marcien.°   influenced by Mars
Venus me yaf my lust, my likerousnesse,°   lecherousness
And Mars yaf me my sturdy hardynesse.°   boldness
Myn ascendent° was Taur,° and Mars ther-inne.   sign at birth Taurus (Venus' mansion)
Allas, allas, that evere love was synne!   620
I folwed ay° myn inclinacioun   always
By vertu° of my constellacioun,   influence
That made me I koude noght withdrawe
My chambre of Venus from a good felawe;
Yet have I Martes° mark upon my face   Mars's

And also in another pryvee° place.   private
For God so wysely be my savacioun,°   salvation
I loved nevere by no° discrecioun   according to any
But evere folwed myn appetit
Al were he° short, long, blak, or whit. 630 Whether he were
I took no kepe,° so that° he liked° me,   heed as long as pleased
How poure he was, ne eek° of what degree.° nor also rank
 What sholde I seye, but at the monthes ende
This joly clerk Jankyn that was so hende° fine
Hath wedded me with greet solempnytee°! splendor
And to hym yaf I al the lond and fee°   property
That evere was me yeven° ther bifore,   given
But afterward repented me ful sore.
He nolde suffre° no thyng of my list.°   would (not) allow pleasure
By God, he smoot me ones° on the lyst,° 640 once ear
For that° I rente out of his book a leef,   Because
That of the strook myn ere wex° al deef.   grew
Stibourne° I was as is a leonesse   Stubborn
And of my tonge a verray jangleresse,°   real prattler
And walke I wolde as I hadde doon biforn
From hous to hous, al thogh he hadde it sworn°; sworn against it
For which he often tymes wolde preche,
And me of olde Romayn gestes° teche,   Roman stories
How he Symplicius° Gallus lafte his wif   Simplicius
And hire forsook for terme° of al his lif 650 the remainder
Noght but for open-heveded° he hir say°   Only because bare-headed
Lokyng out at his dore upon a day.   saw
 Another Romayn tolde he me by name
That, for° his wyf was at a someres° game because summer's
Withouten his wityng,° he forsook hire eke. knowledge
And thanne wolde he upon his Bible seke
That ilke° proverbe of *Ecclesiaste*°   same *Ecclesiasticus*
                  (xxv, 25)
Where he comandeth, and forbedeth faste,° strictly
Man shal nat suffre his wyf go roule° aboute. gad
Thanne wolde he seye right thus, withouten doute,
 'Who so that buyldeth his hous al of salwes,° 661 willow-twigs
And priketh° his blynde hors over the falwes,° spurs fallow ground
And suffreth his wyf to go seken halwes° seeking pilgrim shrines
Is worthy to ben hanged on the galwes.°' gallows
But al for noght. I sette° noght an hawe° cared hawthorn fruit
Of° his proverbes n'of his olde sawe,°   For lore

Ne I wolde nat of° hym corrected be.   by
I hate hym that my vices telleth me,
And so doo mo,° God woot,° of us than I.   more knows
This made hym with me wood al outrely.°   670   utterly furious
I nolde noght forbere° hym in no cas.   would not forgive
   Now wol I sey yow sooth, by Seint Thomas,
Why that I rente° out of his book a leef,   tore
For which he smoot me so that I was deef.
   He hadde a book ¹ that gladly nyght and day
For his disport° he wolde rede alway;   amusement
He cleped° it *Valerie and Theofraste*,   called
At which book he lough° alwey ful faste.°   laughed hard
And eek ther was som tyme a clerk at Rome,
A cardynal that highte° Seint Jerome,   680   was called
That made a book agayn Jovinian,
In which book eek ther was Tertulan,
Crisippus, Trotula, and Helowys,
That was abbesse nat fer fro Parys,
And eek the *Parables*° of Salomon,   *Proverbs*
Ovydes *Art*, and bokes many on°;   a one
And alle thise were bounden in o° volume.   one
And every nyght and day was his custume,
Whan he hadde leyser and vacacioun,
From oother worldly occupacioun,   690
To reden in this book of wikked wyves.
He knew of hem mo° legendes and lyves   more
Than been of goode wyves in the Bible.
For trusteth wel, it is an inpossible°   impossibility
That any clerk wol speke good of wyves
But if° it be of holy seintes lyves,   Unless
N'of noon° oother womman never the mo.°   Nor of any more
Who peynted the leoun? Tel me who? ²

---

¹ Like many medieval volumes, Jankin's book was evidently a manuscript collection of miscellaneous texts and excerpts. The title is derived from Walter Map's *Letter of Valerius against Marriage* (twelfth century) and Theophrastus's *Golden Book on Marriage* (third century B.C., known only in later translation). It also included, at least in part, treatments of marriage by the author of *Proverbs;* by the Latin poet Ovid's *Art of Love;* by the church fathers Tertullian (third century), St. Jerome (fifth century), and his adversary, Jovinian; by Abelard's mistress, Héloïse (twelfth century); and by two writers, Chrysippus and Trotula, who have not been positively identified.

² According to fable, a lion reminded an artist, who had portrayed a man overcoming a lion, that lions had also overcome men.

By God, if wommen hadde writen stories
As clerkes han withinne hir oratories,　　700
They wolde han writen of men moore wikkednesse
Than al the mark° of Adam may redresse.　　(male) descendants
The children of Mercurie and Venus
Been in hir wirkyng° ful contrarius.°　　their behavior　contrary
Mercurie loveth wysdam and science,°　　knowledge
And Venus loveth riot and dispence.°　　extravagance
And, for hir diverse disposicioun,
Ech falleth in otheres exaltacioun;
And thus, God woot,° Mercurie is desolat　　knows
In Pisces, wher Venus is exaltat,[1]　　710
And Venus falleth ther° Mercurie is reysed.　　where
Ther-fore no womman of no clerk is preysed.
The clerk, whan he is old and may noght do
Of Venus werkes worth his olde sho,
Thanne sit° he doun and writ° in his dotage　　sits　writes
That wommen kan nat kepe hir mariage.
　　But now, to purpos why I tolde thee
That I was beten for a book, pardee.°　　certainly
Upon a nyght Jankyn, that was oure sire,°　　my husband
Redde on his book as he sat by the fire　　720
Of Eva° first, that for hir° wikkednesse　　Eve　because of whose
Was al mankynde broght to wrecchednesse,
For which that Jesu Crist hymself was slayn,
That boghte us with his herte blood agayn.
Lo, here expres of wymmen may ye fynde
That womman was the los of al mankynde.
　　Tho° redde he me how Sampson loste his heres°;　　Then　hair
Slepynge, his lemman kitte° it with hir sheres,　　lover cut
Thurgh which tresoun loste he bothe his eyen.
　　Tho redde he me, if that I shal nat lyen,°　　730　lie
Of Hercules and of his Dianyre,°　　Dejanira
That caused hym to sette hymself afyre.°　　afire (with a poisoned shirt)
　　No thyng° forgat he the care and the wo　　In no way
That Socrates hadde with his wyves two,
How Xantippa° caste pisse upon his heed.　　Xantippe

---

[1] "And, because of their contrary positions (as planets), each falls (in the heavens) during the rising of the other. And thus . . . Mercury is desolate in Pisces (a sign of the zodiac), where Venus reaches the highest ascendance." Hence a scholar, influenced astrologically by Mercury, cannot sympathize with anyone who, like the Wife, is influenced by Venus.

This sely° man sat stille as he were deed;   innocent
He wipte his heed; namoore dorste° he seyn   no more dared
But 'Er that° thonder stynte,° comth a reyn.'   Before stops
   Of Phasipha,° that was the queene of Crete,   Pasiphaë
For shrewednesse hym thoughte° the tale swete. 740   seemed to him
Fy! Spek namoore — it is a grisly thyng —
Of hir horrible lust and hir likyng.
   Of Clitermystra,° for hir lecherye,   Clytemnestra
That falsly made hir housbonde for to dye,
He redde it with ful good devocioun.
   He tolde me eek for what occasioun
Amphiorax° at Thebes loste his lyf.   Amphiaraus
Myn housbonde hadde a legende of his wyf,
Eriphilem,° that for an ouche° of gold   Eriphyle brooch
Hath pryvely° unto the Grekes told   750   secretly
Wher that hir housbonde hidde hym in a place,
For which he hadde at Thebes sory grace.
   Of Lyvia° tolde he me and of Lucye.°   Livia Lucilia
They bothe made hir housbondes for to dye;
That oon for love, that oother was for hate.
Lyvia hir housbonde on an even late
Empoysoned hath, for that she was his fo.
Lucya, likerous,° loved hir housbonde so   lustful
That, for he sholde alwey upon hir thynke,
She yaf hym swich a maner° love-drynke   760   kind of
That he was deed er it were by the morwe.
And thus algates° housbondes han sorwe.   always
   Thanne tolde he me how oon Latumyus
Compleyned unto his felawe° Arrius   friend
That in his gardyn growed° swich a tree   grew
On which he seyde how that his wyves thre
Honged hemself for° herte despitus.°   Hung themselves out of
                                                                  angry
'O leeve° brother,' quod° this Arrius,   dear said
'Yif° me a plante of thilke° blessed tree,   Give that same
And in my gardyn planted shal it be.'   770
   Of latter date of wyves hath he red
That somme han slayn hir housbondes in hir bed,
And lete hir lechour dighte° hire al the nyght   lie with
Whan that the corps lay in the floor upright.°   face-up
And somme han dryven nayles in hir° brayn   their
Whil that they sleep, and thus they han hem slayn.

Somme han hem yeven° poysoun in hir drynke.	given
He spak moore harm than herte may bithynke,°	imagine
And ther-with-al he knew of mo° proverbes [1]	more
Than in this world ther growen gras or herbes. 780	
'Bet° is,' quod he, 'thyn habitacioun	Better
Be with a leoun or a foul dragoun	
Than with a womman usyng° for to chide.'	accustomed
'Bet is,' quod he, 'hye in the roof abyde°	to stay
Than with an angry wyf doun in the hous.	
They been so wikked and contrarious,	
They haten that° hir housbondes loveth ay.°'	hate what always
He seyde, 'A womman cast° hir shame away	casts
Whan she cast of° hir smok'; and forther mo,	casts off
'A fair womman, but° she be chaast° also, 790	unless chaste
Is lyk a gold ryng in a sowes nose.'	
Who wolde wene° or who wolde suppose	guess
The wo that in myn herte was and pyne°?	pain
And whan I say° he wolde nevere fyne°	saw finish
To reden on this cursed book al nyght,	
Al sodeynly thre leves have I plyght°	plucked
Out of his book right as he radde,° and eke	was reading
I with my fist so took hym on the cheke	
That in oure fyr he fil bakward adoun.	
And he up stirte° as dooth a wood° leoun, 800	jumped mad
And with his fest he smoot me on the heed	
That in the floor I lay as I were deed.	
And whan he saugh how stille that I lay,	
He was agast and wolde han fled his way,	
Til atte laste out of my swough° I brayde.°	swoon revived
'O hastow° slayn me, false theef,' I sayde,	have you
'And for my land thus hastow mordred° me?	murdered
Er I be deed, yet wol I kisse thee.'	
And neer he cam and kneled faire adoun	
And seyde, 'Deere suster° Alisoun, 810	sweetheart
As help me God, I shal thee nevere smyte.	
That° I have doon, it is thyself to wyte.°	What blame
Foryeve° it me, and that I thee biseke.°'	Forgive beseech
And yet eft-soones° I hitte hym on the cheke	once again
And seyde, 'Theef, thus muchel° am I wreke.°	much avenged

[1] The examples that follow (ll. 781–791) are from the apocryphal *Ecclesiasticus* and from *Proverbs*.

Now wol I dye. I may no lenger speke.'
But at the laste, with muchel care and wo,
We fille acorded° by us-selven° two.   fell into accord ourselves
He yaf me al the brydel in myn hond
To han the governaunce° of hous and lond, 820 control
And of his tonge, and of his hond also,
And made hym brenne° his book anon° right tho°; burn immediately then
And whan that I hadde geten° unto me got
By maistrye al the soveraynetee,
And that° he seyde, 'Myn owene trewe wyf, when
Do as thee lust° the terme of al thy lyf; it pleases
Keep thyn honour, and keep eek myn estaat,' —
After that day we hadden nevere debaat.
God help me so, I was to hym as kynde
As any wyf from Denmark unto Inde° 830 India
And also° trewe, and so was he to me. as
I pray to God, that sit° in magestee, sits
So blesse his soule for his mercy deere.
Now wol I seye my tale, if ye wol here."

    The Frere logh° whan he hadde herd al this. Friar laughed
"Now dame," quod he, "so have I joye or blis,
This is a long preamble of a tale!"
And whan the Somnour herde the Frere gale,° exclaim
"Lo," quod the Somnour, "Goddes armes two!
A frere wol entremette hym evere mo.° 840 meddle always
Loo, goode men, a flye and eek a frere
Wol falle in every dyssh and matere.
What spekestow° of preambulacioun? Why do you speak
What, amble, or trotte, or pees,° or go sit doun! peace
Thow lettest° oure disport in this manere." hinder

    "Ye°! Woltow° so, sir Somnour?" quod the Frere. Yes Will you
"Now, by my feith, I shal, er that° I go, before
Telle of a somnour swich a tale or two
That al the folk shal laughen in this place."

    "Now, elles,° Frere, I wol bishrewe° thy face," otherwise curse
Quod this Somnour, "and I bishrewe me 851
But if° I telle tales two or three Unless
Of freres, er I come to Sydyngborne,° Sittingbourne
That I shal make thyn herte for to morne,
For wel I woot° thy pacience is gon." know
    Oure Hoost cride, "Pees, and that anon,"

And seyde, "Lat the womman telle hir tale.
Ye fare as folk that dronken ben of ale.
Do, dame, tel forth youre tale, and that is best."
    "Al redy, sire," quod she, "right as yow lest,° 860   just as it pleases you
If I have licence of this worthy Frere."
    "Yis,° dame," quod he. "Tel forth, and I wol   Yes indeed
    here.°"   hear

THE WIFE OF BATH'S TALE

[D 857–1264]

    The source of Chaucer's tale is some unidentified version of an internationally disseminated folktale which his friend John Gower also uses in his English poem, the *Lover's Confession*. Both authors use this same plot to illustrate the value of obedience; but, while Gower employs his story schematically in order to demonstrate that a courtly lover's obedience will finally gain him the affections of his loved one, the Wife of Bath applies her story subjectively in support of a two-fold text — first, that all women desire obedience from their husbands, and second, that when they gain it, all the woes of marriage, which she has already enumerated, disappear.

    Chaucer departs from the bare narrative contained in his source, moreover, adapting the story in numerous ways to the individuality of the Wife of Bath. Characteristically, the Wife manages, in the midst of her narration, to relate an almost completely irrelevant tale from Ovid about Midas, without for one minute really losing the thread of her story. She succeeds in depicting the heroine as a debater almost as formidable as herself, and she obviously relishes the indignant manner in which her heroine rebukes the knight for his misconceived pride in ancestry, just as the reader relishes the fact that the knight really objects to his forced marriage with her not merely because she is of low degree but because she appears to be a loathsome and aged hag. The lecture which the hag delivers is ludicrously reminiscent of the same kind of special pleading upon which the Wife of Bath, by her own admission, has always relied; and its topic, true gentility, is ironically at variance with what we have learned from the *General Prologue* about the Wife's own lack of humility in a matter so trivial as her precedence over her neighbors when she makes her offering in church.

    In th'olde dayes of the Kyng Arthour,
Of which that Britons speken greet honour,
Al was this land fulfild of fairye.°   filled with fairy magic
The elf queene with hir joly compaignye
Daunced ful ofte in many a grene mede.°   meadow

This was the olde opynyoun,° as I rede;   belief
I speke of many hundred yeres ago.
But now kan no man se none elves mo,°   more
For now the grete charitee and prayeres
Of lymytours° and othere holy freres,   10   friars begging within a limit
That serchen° every lond and every streem,   search
As thikke as motes in the sonne° beem,   sun
Blessynge halles, chambres, kichenes, boures,°   bedrooms
Citees, burghes, castels, hye° toures,   high
Thropes,° bernes,° shipnes,° dayeryes —   Villages barns stables
This maketh° that ther been no fairyes.   brings it about
For, ther-as wont° to walken was an elf,   where accustomed
Ther walketh now the lymytour hymself
In undermeles° and in morwenynges,   afternoons
And seith his matyns and his holy thynges   20
As he gooth° in his lymytacioun.   walks
Wommen may go saufly up and doun
In every bussh or under every tree.
Ther is noon oother incubus° but he,   impregnating demon
And he ne wol doon hem but° dishonour.   do them nothing worse than
   And so bifel that this kyng Arthour
Hadde in his hous a lusty bacheler
That on a day cam ridyng fro ryver°;   from hawking
And happed° that, allone as he was born,   it happened
He say° a mayde walkynge hym biforn   30   saw
Of which mayde anoon,° maugree hir hed,°   immediately despite her resistance
By verray force he rafte° hir maydenhed°;   took away maidenhood
For which oppressioun was swich° clamour   such
And swich pursuyte unto the kyng Arthour
That dampned° was this knyght for to be deed   condemned
By cours of lawe and sholde han° lost his heed —   was to have
Paraventure° swich was the statut tho° —   Perchance then
But° that the queene and othere ladyes mo°   Except more
So longe preyden° the kyng of° grace   begged for
Til he his lyf hym graunted in the place   40
And yaf° hym to the queene, al at hir wille,   gave
To chese° wheither she wolde hym save or spille.°   choose destroy
   The queene thanked the kyng with al hir myght,
And after this thus spak she to the knyght
Whan that she saugh° hir tyme upon a day: saw
"Thow standest yet," quod° she, "in swich array   said

That of thy lyf yet hastow° no suretee.   *you have*
I graunte thee lyf if thow kanst tellen me
What thyng is it that wommen moost° desiren.   *most*
Be war,° and keep thy nekke boon° from iren.° 50   *Beware bone **iron***
And if thow kanst nat tellen it me anon,°   *right away*
Yet wol I yeve° thee leve for to gon°   *give go*
A twelf monthe and a day to seche° and lere°   *seek learn*
An answere suffisant in this matere.
And suretee wol I han er that° thow pace,°   *have before go*
Thy body for to yelden° in this place."   *to surrender*
    Wo° was this knyght, and sorwefully he siketh,°   *Woeful sighs*
But what! He may nat doon° al as hym liketh.°   *do it pleases*
And atte laste he chees hym for to wende°   *chose to go*
And come agayn right at the yeres ende   60
With swich° answere as God wolde hym purveye,°   *such provide*
And taketh his leve and wendeth forth his weye.
    He seketh every hous and every place
Where-as° he hopeth for to fynde grace   *Where*
To lerne what thyng wommen loven moost,
But he ne koude arryven in no coost°   *region*
Where-as he myghte° fynde in this matere   *Where he could*
Two creatures acordyng in feere.°   *agreeing together*
    Somme seyden wommen loven best richesse,°   *riches*
Somme seyde honour, somme seyde jolynesse,   70
Somme riche array, somme seyden lust a-bedde,
And ofte tyme to be wydwe° and wedde.°   *widow wed (again)*
    Somme seyde that oure herte is moost esed°   *satisfied*
Whan that we been° y-flatered and y-plesed.   *are*
    He gooth ful ny° the sothe,° I wol nat lye.   *near truth*
A man shal wynne us best with flaterye;
And with attendaunce and with bisynesse°   *diligence*
Been we y-lymed,° bothe moore° and lesse.°   *snared high low*
And somme seyn° that we loven best   *say*
For to be free and do right as us lest,°   80 *just as we please*
And that no man repreve° us of oure vice   *reprove*
But seye that we be wise and no thyng nyce.°   *in no way foolish*
For trewely ther is noon° of us alle,   *no one*
If any wight° wol clawe° us on the galle,°   *person scratch **sore spot***
That we nyl kike for° he seith us sooth.°   *because truth*
Assay,° and he shal fynde it that so dooth,   *Try*
For, be we nevere so vicious withinne,

We wol be holden° wise and clene° of synne. considered **pure**

And somme seyn° that greet delit han° we say have
For to be holden stable and eek secree,° 90 also secretive
And in o° purpos stedefastly to dwelle, one
And nat biwreye° thyng that men us telle; betray
But that tale is nat worth a rake-stele.° rake-handle
Pardee,° we wommen konne no thyng hele.° Certainly conceal
Witnesse on Mida,° wol ye heere the tale. Midas

Ovyde,° amonges othere thynges smale, Ovid
Seyde Mida hadde under his longe heres° hair
Growynge upon his heed two asses eres,° ears
The whiche vice° he hidde as he best myghte defect
Ful sotilly° from every mannes sighte 100 skillfully
That, save° his wyf, ther wiste° of it namo.° except for knew no other
He loved hire moost and trusted hire also.
He preyed hire that to no creature
She sholde tellen of his disfigure.

She swoor hym, "Nay." For al this world to
wynne,° gain
She nolde° do that vileynye or synne wouldn't
To make hir housbonde han° so foul a name. have
She nolde nat telle it for hir owene shame.
But, nathelees,° hir thoughte° that she dyde° nevertheless it seemed to died
That she so longe sholde a conseil hyde. 110
Hir thoughte it swal° so soore aboute hir herte, swelled
That nedely° som word hir moste asterte°; necessarily escape from
And, sith° she dorste° telle it to no man, since dared
Doun to a marys faste by° she ran. marsh nearby
Til she cam there, hir herte was afyre.
And, as a bitore bombleth° in the myre,° bittern drones swamp
She leyde hir mouth unto the water doun.
"Biwrey° me nat, thow water, with thy soun,°" Betray sound
Quod° she. "To thee I telle it and namo.° Said no other
Myn housbonde hath longe asses erys° two! 120 ears
Now is myn herte al hool.° Now is it oute. whole
I myghte° no lenger kepe° it, out of doute." could conceal
Heere may ye see, thogh we a tyme abyde,° wait
Yet out it moot.° We kan no conseil° hyde. must secret
The remenant of the tale if ye wol heere,
Redeth Ovyde, and ther ye may it leere.° learn

This knyght of which my tale is specially,

Whan that he say° he myghte nat come ther-by,° —   saw discover it
This is to seye, what wommen loven moost —
Withinne his brest ful sorweful was the goost°;   130   spirit
But hom he gooth. He myghte nat sojourne.°   stay
The day was come that homward moste° he torne°;   must turn
And in his wey it happed hym° to ryde,   he happened
In al this care, under a forest syde,
Wher-as° he say° upon a daunce go   Where saw
Of ladyes foure-and-twenty and yet mo,
Toward the whiche daunce he drow° ful yerne°   drew eagerly
In hope that som wisdom sholde he lerne.
But certeynly, er° he cam fully there,   before
Vanysshed was this daunce, he nyste° where.   140   knew not
No creature saugh° he that bar° lyf,   saw bore
Save° on the grene he say sittynge a wyf.   Except that
A fouler wight° ther may no man devyse.°   person imagine
Agayn° the knyght this olde wyf gan ryse°   Towards arose
And seyde, "Sire knyght, heer° forth ne lyth° no   here lies
    wey.
Tel me what that ye seken, by your fey.°   faith
Par aventure,° it may the bettre be.   Perchance
Thise olde folk konne muchel° thyng," quod she.   know many a
    "My leeve moder,°" quod° this knyght, "certeyn   dear mother said
I nam but deed but if that° I kan seyn   150   am but dead unless
What thyng it is that wommen moost desire.
Koude ye me wisse,° I wolde wel quyte° youre   inform reward
    hyre."
    "Plight° me thy trouthe,° here in myn hand,°"   Give promise by hand-
    quod she,   shake
"The nexte thyng that I requere° thee,   require of
Thow shalt it do, if it lye in thy myght,
And I wol telle it yow er° it be nyght."   before
    "Have here my trouthe," quod the knyght, "I
    graunte.°"   consent
    "Thanne," quod she, "I dar me wel avaunte,°   dare well boast
Thy lyf is sauf,° for I wole stonde ther-by,°   safe guarantee
Upon my lyf, the queene wol seye as I.   160
Lat see which is the proudeste of hem alle
That wereth on a coverchief° or a calle°   has on a kerchief cap
That dar seye 'Nay' of that° I shal thee teche.   that which
Lat us go forth withouten lenger speche."

Tho rowned° she a pistel° in his ere	Then whispered lesson
And bad hym to be glad and have no fere.	
Whan they be comen to the court, this knyght	
Seyde he hadde holde° his day as he had hight,°	kept promised
And redy was his answere, as he sayde.	
Ful many a noble wyf, and many a mayde, 170	
And many a widwe,° for that° they ben wise,	widow because
The queene hirself sittyng as justise,	
Assembled been,° his answere for to here.	are
And afterward this knyght was bode° appere.	ordered to
To every wight comanded was silence,	
And that the knyght sholde telle in audience	
What thyng that worldly wommen loven best.	
This knyght ne stood nat stille as dooth a best°	beast
But to his questioun anon° answerde	immediately
With manly voys that° al the court it herde. 180	so that
"My lige lady, generally," quod° he,	said
"Wommen desiren to have sovereyntee	
As wel over hir housbonde as hir love	
And for to been in maistrie° hym above.	mastery
This is youre mooste° desir, thogh ye me kille.	greatest
Dooth as yow list.° I am here at youre wille."	it pleases
In al the court ne was ther wyf, ne mayde,	
Ne wydwe that contraried that° he sayde	contradicted what
But seyden he was worthy han° his lyf.	to have
And with that word up stirte° that olde wyf 190	sprang
Which that° the knyght say° sittyng on the grene.	Whom saw
"Mercy," quod she, "my sovereyn lady queene,	
Er that° youre court departe, do me right.	Before
I taughte this answere unto the knyght,	
For which he plighte° me his trouthe° there,	gave promise
The firste thyng I wolde hym requere,	
He wolde it do, if it laye in his myght.	
Bifore the court thanne preye I thee, sire knyght,"	
Quod she, "that thow me take unto° thy wyf.	to be
For wel thow woost° that I have kept° thy lyf. 200	know protected
If I seye fals, sey 'Nay,' upon thy fey.°"	faith
This knyght answerde, "Allas and weylawey,°	woe
I woot° right wel that swich was my biheste.	know
For Goddes love, as chees° a newe requeste!	choose (as chees)
Taak al my good,° and lat my body go."	substance

"Nay, thanne," quod she. "I shrewe° us bothe   curse
    two.
For, thogh that I be foul, old, and poore,
I nolde,° for al the metal ne for oore°   wouldn't wish (anything else)
    ore
That under erthe is grave° or lith° above,   buried lies
But if thy wyf I were and eek° thy love."   210   also
    "My love!" quod he. "Nay, my dampnacioun°!   ruination
Allas that any of my nacioun°   birth
Sholde evere so foule° disparaged be!"   foully
But al for noght! Th'ende is this that he
Constreyned was, he nedes moste° hir wedde,   needs must
And taketh his olde wyf, and goth to bedde.
    Now wolden som men seye, par aventure,°   perhaps
That for my necligence I do no cure°   take no care
To tellen yow the joye and al th'array
That at the feste was that ilke° day;   220   same
To which thyng shortly answere I shal.
I seye, ther nas° no joye ne° feste at al.   was nor
Ther nas but hevynesse° and muche sorwe,   was nothing but **gloom**
For pryvely° he wedded hire on morwe,°   privately the **morrow**
And al day after hidde hym° as an owle,   himself
So wo was hym,° his wyf looked so foule.   woeful was he
    Greet was the wo the knyght hadde in his thoght
Whan he was with his wyf a-bedde° y-broght.   to bed
He walweth,° and he turneth to and fro.   flounders
His olde wyf lay smylyng evere mo°   230   all the while
And seyde, "O deere housbonde, *benedicite°!*   blessings
Fareth° every knyght thus with his wyf as ye?   Behaves
Is this the lawe of kyng Arthures hous?
Is every knyght of his thus daungerous°?   unyielding
I am youre owene love and youre wyf.
I am she which that° saved hath youre lyf.   who
And certes° yet ne dide I yow nevere unright.   certainly
Why fare ye thus with me this firste nyght?
Ye faren° lyk a man hadde° lost his wit.   act (who) **had**
What is my gilt? For Goddes love, tel it,   240
And it shal ben amended, if I may.°"   can
    "Amended!" quod this knyght. "Allas, nay,
    nay.
It wol nat ben amended nevere mo.°   ever after
Thow art so loothly, and so old also,

And ther-to comen of° so lowe a kynde°   descended from nature
That litel wonder is° thogh I walwe and wynde.° it is twist
So wolde God, myn herte wolde breste°!"   burst
  "Is this," quod she, "the cause of youre unreste?"
"Ye, certeynly," quod he. "No wonder is."
  "Now sire," quod she, "I koude amende al this,
If that me liste,° er° it were dayes thre,   251 it pleased before
So wel ye myghte bere yow unto me.
  "But, for° ye speken of swich gentilesse° since such gentility
As is descended out of old richesse,°   wealth
That therfore sholden ye be gentil men,
Swich arrogance is nat worth an hen.
Looke who that° is moost vertuous alway, Whoever (*Looke who that*)
Pryvee° and apert,° and moost entendeth ay° In private in public
To do the gentil dedes that he kan;   strives always
Taak hym for the gretteste gentil man. 260
Crist wol,° we clayme of hym oure gentillesse, desires (that)
Nat of oure eldres for hir° old richesse, their
For, thogh they yeve° us al hir heritage give
For which we clayme to been of heigh parage,° lineage
Yet may° they nat biquethe, for no thyng, can
To noon of us hir° vertuous lyvyng   their
That made hem gentil men y-called be
And bad° us folwen° hem in swich degree. required to follow
  "Wel kan the wise poete of Florence
That highte Dant° speken in this sentence.° 270 is called Dante opinion
Lo, in swich maner° rym is Dantes tale°: sort of saying
'Ful selde° up riseth by his braunches smale seldom
Prowesse° of man, for God of his prowesse Excellence
Wol° that of hym we clayme oure gentillesse.' Wishes
For of oure eldres may we nothyng clayme
But temporel thyng that man may hurte and
  mayme.
  "Eek° every wight woot° this as wel as I, Also knows
If gentillesse were planted naturelly° implanted by nature
Unto° a certeyn lynage doun the lyne, Within
Pryvee° and apert,° thanne wolde they nevere fyne° Inwardly outwardly cease
To doon of gentilesse the faire office; 281
They myghte° do no vileynye or vice. could
  "Taak fyr, and bere° it in the derkeste° hous bring darkest
Bitwix this and the mount Kaukasous,° Caucasus

And lat men shette° the dores and go thenne,°   shut   thence
Yet wol the fyr as faire lye° and brenne°   blaze   burn
As° twenty thousand men myghte it biholde.   As if
His office° naturel ay° wol it holde,°   Its function **ever retain**
Up° peril of my lyf, til that it dye.   On
   "Here may ye se wel how that genterye°   290   gentility
Is nat annexed to possessioun,
Sith° folk ne doon hir operacioun°   Since   don't **behave**
Alwey as dooth the fyr, lo, in his kynde.°   its nature
For, God it woot,° men may wel often fynde   knows
A lordes sone do shame and vileynye.
And he that wol han prys of° his gentrye,   have esteem **for**
For° he was born of a gentil hous   Because
And hadde his eldres noble and vertuous,
And nyl° hymselven do no gentil dedis°   will (not) **deeds**
Ne folwen° his gentil auncestre that deed° is,   300   follow   dead
He nys° nat gentil, be he duc or erl,   is (not)
For vileyns synful dedes make a cherl.
For gentilesse nys but renomee°   is only renown
Of thyn auncestres for hir hye° bountee,   their high
Which is a straunge° thyng for thy persone.   alien
Thy gentilesse cometh fro God allone.
Thanne comth oure verray° gentilesse of grace;   true
It was no thyng biquethe° us with oure place.   in no way bequeathed to
   "Thenketh how noble, as seith Valerius,°   Valerius Maximus
Was thilke° Tullius Hostillius   310   that same
That out of poverte roos to heigh noblesse.
Redeth Senek,° and redeth eek Boece.°   Seneca   Boethius
Ther shul ye seen° expres that no drede° is   see   doubt
That he is gentil that dooth gentil dedis.
And therfore, leve° housbonde, I thus conclude,   dear
Al° were it that myne auncestres were rude,   Even if
Yet may the hye God, and so hope I,
Graunte me grace to lyven vertuously.
Thanne am I gentil, whan that I bigynne
To lyven vertuously and weyve° synne.   320   shun
   "And ther-as° ye of poverte me repreve,°   whereas   reproach
The hye God, on whom that we bileve,
In wilful° poverte chees° to lyve his lyf.   willing   chose
And certes° every man, mayden, or wyf   certainly
May understonde that Jesus, hevene° Kyng,   heaven's

Ne wolde nat chese° a vicious lyvyng.   choose
Glad° poverte is an honeste thyng, certeyn;   Willing
This wol Senek and othere clerkes° seyn.   scholars
Who so that halt hym payd of° his poverte,   considers himself rewarded by
I holde hym riche, al° hadde he nat a sherte. 330 even if
He that coveiteth is a poure wight,
For he wolde han that° is nat in his myght;   what
But he that noght hath ne° coveiteth to have   nor
Is riche, althogh ye holde° hym but a knave.   consider
    "Verray° poverte, it syngeth proprely.   True
Juvenal seith of poverte myrily°:   merrily
'The poure man, whan he gooth by the weye,
Biforn° the theves he may synge and pleye.'   In front of
Poverte is hateful good and, as I gesse,
A ful greet bryngere out of bisynesse,°   340 care
A greet amendere eek° of sapience,°   improver also wisdom
To hym that taketh° it in pacience.   receives
Poverte is this, althogh it seme alenge,°   miserable
Possessioun that no wight wol chalenge.
Poverte ful often, whan a man is lowe,
Maketh° his God and eek hymself to knowe.   Causes (him)
Poverte a spectacle° is, as thynketh° me,   eye-glass it seems to
Thurgh which he may his verray° freendes se. true
And therfore, sire, syn that° I noght yow greve,° since harm
Of my poverte namoore ye me repreve.°   350 reproach
    "Now, sire, of elde° ye repreve me;   old age
And certes,° sire, thogh noon auctoritee°   certainly authoritative
                                       decision
Were in no book, ye gentils of honour
Seyn° that men sholde an old wight doon favour Say
And clepe° hym fader, for youre gentilesse;   call
And auctours° shal I fynden,° as I gesse.   authors find (as authorities)
    "Now, ther° ye seye that I am foul and old, whereas
Thanne drede yow noght to been a cokewold,° husband of an unfaithful wife
For filthe and elde, also mote I thee,°   as I may prosper
Been grete wardeyns upon chastitee.   360
But, nathelees,° syn° I knowe youre delit,   nevertheless since
I shal fulfille youre worldly appetit.
    "Chees° now," quod she, "oon of thise thynges Choose
        tweye°:   two
To han me foul and old til that I deye,
And be to yow a trewe, humble wyf,

And nevere yow displese in al my lyf;

Or elles° ye wol han me yong and fair   *else*

And take youre aventure° of the repair°   *chance resort*

That shal be to youre hous by cause of me,

Or in som oother place, may wel be.   370

Now chees yourselven wheither that° yow liketh.°"   *whichever pleases*

   This knyght avyseth hym° and soore siketh,°   *ponders sighs*

But atte laste he seyde in this manere:

"My lady, and my love and wyf so deere,

I putte me in youre wise governaunce.

Cheseth° youreself which may be moost plesaunce°   *Choose pleasure*

And moost honour to yow and me also.

I do no fors the wheither° of the two,   *don't care which*

For as yow liketh,° it suffiseth me."   *it pleases*

   "Thanne have I gete° of yow maistrye," quod   *gotten*

    she,   380

"Syn I may chese and governe as me lest°?"   *it pleases*

   "Ye, certes, wyf," quod he. "I holde it best."

   "Kys me," quod she. "We be no lenger wrothe,

For, by my trouthe,° I wol be to yow bothe —   *faith*

This is to seyn, ye,° bothe fair and good.   *indeed*

I pray to God that I mote sterven wood°   *may die mad*

But° I to yow be also° good and trewe   *Unless as*

As evere was wyf syn that° the world was newe.   *since*

And but I be to-morn as fair to sene°   *see*

As any lady, emperice, or queene   390

That is bitwix the est and eek the west,

Do with my lyf and deth right as yow lest.°   *it pleases*

Cast up the curtyn. Looke how that it is."

   And whan the knyght sey° verraily al this,   *saw*

That she so fair was and so yong ther-to,

For joye he hente° hire in his armes two.   *seized*

His herte bathed in a bath of blisse,

A thousand tyme a rewe he gan hir kisse,°   *in turn he kissed her*

And she obeyed hym in every thyng

That myghte do hym plesance° or likyng.   400   *pleasure*

   And thus they lyve unto hir° lyves ende   *their*

In parfit joye, and Jesu Crist us sende

Housbondes meke, yonge, and fressh a-bedde,

And grace t'overbyde hem° that we wedde.   *to overrule them*

And eek I praye Jesu shorte hir° lyves   *shorten their*

That noght wol be governed by hir wyves;
And olde and angry nygardes of dispence,°   niggardly spenders
God sende hem soone verray pestilence.

LINK

[D 1265–1300. Here translated.]

This worthy limiter, this noble Friar, kept making a somewhat glowering face at the Summoner, but with self-control he didn't speak any churlish word to him as yet. But at last he said to the Wife, "Madam, God grant you a right good life. As I may thrive," said he, "you have here touched upon a great problem in scholastic matters, and you have said much very well, I should say. But, madam, here as we ride along the way, we need speak only in jest and can leave the authorities, in God's name, to preaching and the schools of clerics. But if this company is willing, I'll tell you a jest about a summoner. By Heaven, you probably know well from the name that no good can be said about a summoner. I beg that none of you be offended. A summoner is a runner-up-and-down with summonses for fornication and is thrashed at every town's end."

Our Host then said, "Sir, you should be courteous and polite as a man in your rank. We don't want any argument in company. Tell your tale, and let the Summoner be."

"Oh, no," said the Summoner. "Let him say whatever he likes to me. When it comes to my turn, by God, I'll pay him back every jot. I'll tell him what a great honor it is to be a flattering limiter, and many another sin that need not be mentioned at this time, and indeed I'll tell him his function too."

Our Host answered, "Peace! No more of this." And then he said to the Friar, "Go ahead and tell your tale, my dear good sir."

THE FRIAR'S TALE

[D 1301–1664. Here omitted.]

The Friar tells how a summoner through avarice lost his body and soul to the Devil. The plot is derived from a folktale source, but the Devil's victim does not happen, in any of the known analogues, to be a summoner. It is therefore possible that Chaucer himself invented this comic adaptation of the traditional story to suit his development of the feud between the Friar and Summoner. The tale is particularly effective because the narrator's tone is not that of a dispassionate reformer but rather that of an indignant competitor in the ways of avarice. In both this and the following tale, with the usual ironic consequences, the pot calls the kettle black.

LINK

[D 1665–1708. Here translated.]

The Summoner rose high upon his stirrups. His heart was so enraged at the Friar that he shook like an aspen leaf with anger. "My lords," said he, "just one thing I desire. I beg you, since you have heard this false Friar lie, that out of courtesy you will allow me to tell my tale. This Friar boasts that he knows Hell, and, God knows, it's little wonder. Friars and fiends are but little apart. For, by Heaven, you've often heard tell how a friar was carried down to Hell in spirit once by a vision, and as an angel led him up and down to show him the torments there, in the whole place he didn't see a friar. He saw plenty of other people in distress. Then the friar said to the angel, 'Now sir, have friars such grace that none of them is destined to come to this place?'

" 'Oh, yes, yes!' said the angel, 'many a million.' And he led him down to Satan. Now, Satan has a tail broader than a barge's sail. 'Hold up your tail, Satan,' said he. 'Show off your bottom, and let this friar see where the nest of friars is in this place.' And within ninety seconds, like bees swarming from a hive, twenty thousand friars had rushed pell-mell out of the Devil's bottom and swarmed through every part of Hell, and come back as fast as they could go and crept into his bottom again each one. He clapped down his tail and lay quite still again. When the friar had seen his fill of the torments in this sorry place, God in his grace restored his spirit to his body again, and he awoke. But none the less he still was quaking from fear, so well he could remember still the Devil's bottom, which is his proper heritage by nature. God save you all, except for this cursed Friar. And in this manner I will end my prologue."

THE SUMMONER'S TALE

[D 1709–2294. Here omitted.]

The Summoner matches the *Friar's Tale* by narrating a comic tale concerning a friar who, in the manner attributed to his counterpart in the *General Prologue*, enjoys visiting all the prosperous donors living within his "limit." He is at last rudely surprised by an impatient victim. The plot is not original with Chaucer, but, once again, old material transplanted seems new.

LINK

[E 1–56. Here translated.]

"Sir Clerk of Oxford," said our Host, "you ride as shy and quiet as does a girl who's newly wed, sitting at the table. I haven't heard one word from your tongue this day. I suppose you're concentrating on some sophism; but Solomon says 'Everything has its time.' For Heaven's sake, be more cheerful. It's no time to concentrate now. Tell us some merry tale, for goodness's sake. For when anyone has started in a game, he has to agree to the game. But don't preach, as friars do in Lent, to make us weep for our old sins, and don't let your tale make us sleep.

"Tell us of some merry sort of adventure. Keep your terms, your ornaments, and your figures of speech in reserve until it happens that you are inditing in the high style used when men write to kings. Speak so plainly at this time, we beg you, that we can understand what you say."

The worthy Clerk benignly answered: "Host, I'm under your control. You have the direction of us for now, and so I'll do obedience to you, certainly, as far as reason demands. I'll tell you a tale which I learned at Padua from a scholar of worth, proved by his words and his works. He is now dead and nailed in his coffin. I pray God, give rest to his soul.

"Francis Petrarch the poet laureate is the name of this scholar, whose sweet rhetoric has illuminated all Italy with poetry, just as Legnano did with philosophy, with law, and with other special arts.[1] But death, which will not allow us to linger here longer than as it were the twinkling of an eye, has slain them both, and all of us shall die.

"But to continue as I began about this worthy man who taught me this tale, first, I say, before he writes the body of his tale, he indites a preface with high style, in which he describes Piedmont and the country of Saluzzo and speaks of the high hills of the Apennines, which are the boundary of West Lombardy; and in particular of Monte Viso, where out of a small well the Po takes its first spring and its source, which keeps increasing in its flow eastward towards Aemilia, Ferrara, and Venice. This would be lengthy to relate, and indeed, in my judgment, it seems to me irrelevant,

---

[1] Petrarch (1304–1374), best known to posterity for his Italian love poems to Laura, was crowned poet laureate, chiefly for his Latin epic *Africa*, in 1341. He was still alive when Chaucer first visited Italy. He spent the last years of his life in the vicinity of Padua, whose celebrated university would have attracted such a scholar as Chaucer's Clerk. John of Legnano (ca. 1310–1383), professor of canon law at Bologna, wrote not only on law but also on ethics, theology, and astronomy.

except that he wishes to introduce his topic. But this is his tale, which you shall hear."

THE CLERK'S TALE

[E 57–1162, translated on pp. 192–208. E 1163–1212g, here translated.]

It is possible that Chaucer acquired a copy of Petrarch's version of the tale of Griselda when he visited Italy in 1373 or later on a diplomatic mission. But the ironic fact is that he apparently never learned that Petrarch's Latin prose version was a translation of one of the tales in the *Decameron* (1353), which was written in Italian by Boccaccio, the author to whom Chaucer was also indebted for the plot of his *Knight's Tale* and of his romance *Troilus and Criseyde*.

The story deals with the patience maintained by Griselda when her husband undertakes to assess her love for him by testing her submissiveness. In Chaucer's version the insensitivity of the husband and the composure of the wife are both heightened, and the conservative and academic Clerk voices an appropriately scornful condemnation of the fickleness of the vulgar throng; but, apart from such slight changes, Chaucer found little need to alter his material. The story had circulated as an unpretentious folktale before Boccaccio made his adaptation; and Chaucer, by preserving the remoteness and unreality inherent in the folktale, establishes a comic contrast between the incredible submissiveness of Griselda and the entirely credible demands for sovereignty made by the Wife of Bath. The Clerk's whimsical conclusion is included here in translation.

"But hear one word, my lords, before I go. It would be very hard nowadays to find in a whole town Griseldas three or two, for if they were put to such tests, their gold is now so badly alloyed with brass that, although the coin may seem fair to the eye, it would sooner break in two than bend.

"And so now, for the love of the Wife of Bath, whose life and all whose sect may God maintain in high sovereignty — and otherwise it would be a pity — I'm going to recite you with lusty heart, fresh and verdant, a song that will cheer you, I think. And let's lay aside serious matters. Listen to my song, which runs in this manner:

"Griselda is dead and her patience too, and both are buried in Italy together; and therefore in open hearing I beseech that no man be so rash as to tax his wife's patience, expecting to discover a Griselda, for certainly he'll fail.

"O noble wives, full of high prudence, let no humility nail your tongue, and let no clerk have cause or diligence to write about you a story so marvelous as that of Griselda kind and patient, lest Chichevache [1] swallow you up in her entrails.

"Imitate Echo, who never keeps silence but answers always in retort. Don't be outwitted because of your innocence, but sharply take over control for yourself. Imprint this lesson well in your mind since it may avail for common profit.

"You archwives, stand at defense since you are strong as a great camel, and don't allow men to offend you. And you slender wives, feeble in battle, be as fierce as a tiger in distant India. Clatter always, I counsel you, like a mill.

"Neither dread them nor pay them reverence, for even if your husband be armed in mail, the arrows of your crabbed eloquence will pierce his chest and his helmet's face-plate. Bind him in jealousy too, I advise you, and you'll make him cower like a quail.

"If you are fair, show off your face and your clothing where people are present. If you are foul, be free in your spending. Try always to win yourself friends. In appearance be always as light as the leaf on the linden, and leave him to worry and weep and wring and wail."

When this worthy Clerk's tale was ended, the Host said and swore, "By God's bones, I'd sooner than a barrel of ale that my wife at home had some time heard this legend. It's an excellent tale, now, for my purpose, if you knew what I had in mind. But a thing that cannot be, let it stay still."

LINK

[E1213–1244. Here translated]

"Weeping and wailing, care, and other sorrow I know enough of, both morning and night," said the Merchant, "and so do many others that are married. So I assume, for I well know that it's so with me. I have the worst wife that could be, for even if the fiend were coupled to her, she would outmatch him, I'd dare to swear.

"Why should I relate you her high malice in particular? She's a shrew in everything. There's a difference large and long between the great patience of Griselda and my wife's supreme cruelty. As I may prosper, if I were unbound I'd never again come into the snare. We married men live in care and sorrow. Let him try who will, and by St. Thomas of India,

[1] As the name implies in French, Chichevache, a legendary creature who fed only on patient wives, was a lean cow.

he'll find that I tell the truth for the majority. I don't say all, for God forbid that that should come to pass.

"Ah, good sir Host, I've been married these two months and no more, by Heaven, and yet I don't believe that any man who has been without a wife all his life, even though he were torn to the heart, could in any way tell so much sorrow as I could now tell here about my wife's shrewishness."

"Now," said our Host, "God bless you, Merchant, since you know so much of that mystery, I beg you most heartily, tell us some part of it."

"Gladly," said he. "But, from sorrow of heart, I can't say any more about my own suffering."

THE MERCHANT'S TALE

[E 1245–2418. Here omitted.]

It is characteristic of Chaucer not to proceed by formula. The tale told by each pilgrim so far has, in general, confirmed the delineation of that character presented in the *General Prologue*, but the reader is now surprised by an alternative procedure. The apparently reticent and shrewd Merchant cannot refrain from exposing publicly the worst mistake he has ever made in his life, namely, his marriage with a shrew. In keeping with the disillusioned tone of his introductory lament, he then tells a savage tale about a lecherous old man, symbolically called January, who is shamelessly beguiled by his young wife, called, also symbolically, May. The aged lover, as Chaucer realized, is a stock figure ridiculed in Latin literature by Ovid and in medieval French literature by numerous lyric poems dealing with unhappy marriages; and the plot of the story is derived from a widely known folklore motif. But the tone of the narration is unique because of the context. The Merchant and January both sound very much like a reincarnation of any one of the Wife of Bath's first three husbands; and although the reader may smile at their folly, he is also likely to sympathize with the narrator and even with January.

LINK

[E 2419–2440; F 1–8. Here translated.]

"Oh, God's mercy!" said our Host then. "Now such a wife I pray God keep me from. See what wiles and subtleties there are in women, for always busy as bees they are to deceive us silly men, and they'll always turn away from the truth. This Merchant's tale well proves it. But I have a wife, without question, as true as any steel although she's poor. However, she's a tattling shrew with her tongue, and besides she has a pile of vices more. But no matter! Let all such matters drop. But do you know what? Confidentially be it said, I sorely rue the fact that I'm tied to her. For if I should reckon every vice she has, I'd be too foolish, because it would be reported and told to her by some of this gathering — there's no need to mention which one [1] — for women know how to deal in such traffic. Besides, my skill would not suffice to tell all, and so my tale is done.

"Squire, come near if you will, and tell us something about love, for certainly you know as much about that as any man."

"Oh, no, sir," said he, "but I'll tell what I can with good will, for I won't rebel against your wish. I'll tell a tale. Excuse me if I speak amiss. My intentions are good, and now then, this is my tale."

THE SQUIRE'S TALE

[F 9–672. Here omitted.]

The *Squire's Tale* is generally described as an interlude in the so-called Marriage Group which the Wife of Bath's views had inspired. It is appropriate, however, not merely to the character of the Squire as he is portrayed in the *General Prologue*, but also to the present context. The Squire is too young and inexperienced to know the degradation of matrimony revealed by the Merchant. His own remarks to the pilgrims, self-effacing though they are, even suggest that the cynicism and ruthless realism of the Merchant may have repelled him. The kind of love with which his tale is concerned mirrors an idealistic world of romance and courtly love, and the setting is laid in Mongolia, an area so remote that not even his much traveled father can claim to have visited it.

The tale, though promising, stands incomplete in all the existing manuscripts, a fact lamented by two competent judges of poetry — Spenser and Milton. Although many of the individual motifs in the tale are folklore commonplaces, no source for the tale as it stands has been discovered. It is therefore sometimes assumed that on this occasion Chaucer was, for once, inventing his plot without a model before him and that he ran out of ideas. Since Chaucer apparently never went so far as to prepare the existing drafts of the *Canterbury Tales* for publication, however, we may alternatively consider the possibility that he did in fact complete the tale but that, after his death, only the first part reached the hands of the copyists.

In any case, the surviving fragment demonstrates that, if he had wished to, Chaucer could have attained mastery in the genre of what might be called the wonder-romance, which, though popular in his day, he himself did not elsewhere attempt to imitate.

---

[1] Obviously the Wife of Bath.

LINK

[F 673–708. Here translated.]

"Truly, Squire, you've acquitted yourself with great gentility. I praise your intelligence highly," said the Franklin. "Considering your youth, you speak so feelingly, sir, that I applaud you. In my judgment, there's no one here who'll be your equal in eloquence if you live. May God give you good luck and maintain your power, for I find great pleasure in your conversation. I have a son, and, by the Trinity, I'd sooner than land worth twenty pounds a year, even if it fell into my hands right now, that he were a man of such discretion as you are. Fie on property unless a man be talented too. I've scolded my son and shall scold him yet, for he has no desire to attain talent, but his habit is only to play at dice and spend and lose all that he has. And he'd sooner talk with a page-boy than converse with a gentlemanly person, where he might learn gentility properly."

"A straw for your gentility," said our Host. "Why, Franklin, by Heaven, sir, you know well that each of you must tell at least one tale or two, or else break his agreement."

"I know that well, sir," said the Franklin. "Please don't hold me in disdain just because I speak a word or two to this man."

"Tell your tale without any more discussion."

"Gladly, sir Host," said he. "I'll obey your wish. Now listen to what I say. I won't oppose you in any way as far as my wits suffice. Please God that it will satisfy you; then I'll know well that it is good enough."

THE FRANKLIN'S TALE

[F 709–1624]

The *Franklin's Tale* completes a narrative unit within the *Canterbury Tales*, and perhaps Chaucer thought of it as expressing not merely the last word on marriage but also the best solution of the attendant problems. The Franklin is, according to the *General Prologue*, a lover of pleasure; here he turns out to be also a lover of peace and an advocate of middle-class common sense. Although he admires the Squire's eloquence, he protests that he knows little about the "colors of rhetoric," and he entirely ignores the cardinal assumption in the medieval code of courtly love that the lover's highest job is to be found in serving somebody else's wife and that real love cannot exist within marriage.

Although the plot of the tale relies upon a supernatural motif of folktale origin, set in Brittany but probably derived through a courtly Italian tale of Boccaccio's, the Franklin's treatment of it is essentially realistic; and the reader is perhaps justified in inferring that the love between Arveragus and his wife Dorigen is quite similar to that enjoyed by the comfort-loving Franklin and his own wife. The couple whose marriage the Franklin portrays are contented not because either one possesses the sovereignty recommended by the Wife of Bath, nor because either one submits in the manner of the Clerk's Griselda, but because both defer to the dictates of gentility or *gentilesse*.

The fact that Chaucer rests the Franklin's case upon this concept of gentility suggests his personal interest in the settlement of the argument. From the time that Chaucer first used the word *gentilesse* as an equivalent for the Latin term *nobilitas* ("nobility") in his translation of Boethius's *Consolation of Philosophy*, he showed a marked fondness for the concept's various implications; and it is one of the more refined of these which he utilizes here. The heroine of the *Wife of Bath's Tale* introduced the term when she denied the nobility of birth and asserted that "he is gentle who does gentle deeds," but she was using it in somewhat the same revolutionary sense that is implicit in the rime of John Ball, the Wyclifite reformer: "When Adam delved and Eve span, who was then the gentleman?" The Franklin, on the other hand, is not intent upon leveling the existing social order. In fact, he says that he wishes his son knew as much of gentility as the Knight's son does and is snubbed for this aspiration by the unpretentious Host. In contrast, the concept of gentility which dominates his tale is that of a nobility of character bestowed — to use two phrases introduced later by the Parson in his tale — not by "the grace of Fortune" but by "the grace of God."

Thise olde, gentil Britons° in hir° dayes	Bretons their
Of diverse aventures maden layes,°	made lays
Rymeyed° in hir firste Briton tonge,°	Rimed Breton language
Whiche layes with hir instrumentz they songe,°	sang
Or elles redden° hem for hir plesaunce.°	else read pleasure
And oon° of hem have I in remembraunce,	one
Which I shal seyn° with good wyl as° I kan.	tell as best
But, sires, by cause I am a burel° man,	unlearned
At my bigynnyng first I yow biseche,	
Have me excused of my rude speche. 10	
I lerned nevere rethorik,° certeyn.°	rhetoric certainly
Thyng that I speke, it moot° be bare and pleyn.	must
I sleep° nevere on the mount of Parnaso,°	slept Parnassus
Ne lerned Marcus Tullius Scithero.°	Cicero
Colours° ne knowe I none, withouten drede,°	Rhetorical ornaments doubt
But swich° colours as growen in the mede,°	such meadow
Or ellis° swiche as men dye or peynte.	else

Colours of rethoryk ben to queynte°;   are too intricate
My spirit feeleth nat of swich matere.
But, if yow list,° my tale shul ye heere.   20   it pleases
    In Armorik,° that called is Britayne,°   Armorica   Brittany
Ther was a knyght that loved and dide his payne°   took pains
To serve a lady in his beste wise°;   manner
And many a labour, many a gret emprise,°   undertaking
He for his lady wroghte er° she were wonne,   before
For she was oon° the faireste under sonne,°   one of   sun
And eek° ther-to come of so heigh kynrede°   also   such high lineage
That wel unnethes dorste° this knyght for drede°   hardly dared   timidity
Telle hire his wo, his peyne, and his distresse.
But atte laste she for his worthynesse,   30
And namely° for his meke obeysaunce,°   particularly   obedience
Hath swich a pitee caught° of his penaunce°   taken   voluntary suffering
That pryvely° she fel of° his acord   secretly   into
To take hym for hir housbonde and hir lord,
Of swich lordshipe as men han° over hir wyves.   have
And, for to lede the moore in blisse hir° lyves,   their
Of his fre wyl he swoor hire° as a knyght   to her
That nevere in al his lyf he day ne° nyght   or
Ne sholde upon hym take no maistrye°   domination
Agayn° hir wyl, ne kithe° hire jalousye,   40   Against   nor show
But hire obeye, and folwe° hir wyl in al,   follow
As any lovere to his lady shal,°   should
Save° that the name of soveraynetee   Except
That wolde he have for shame of his degree.°   out of regard for his status
    She thanked hym, and with ful gret humblesse
She seyde, "Sire, sith° of youre gentilesse°   since   gentility
Ye profre me to have so large a reyne,°   free a rein
Ne wolde nevere God° bitwix us tweyne,   Would to God that never
As in my gilt,° were outher werre° or stryf.   On my account   either war
Sire, I wol be youre humble, trewe° wyf.   50   faithful
Have heer my trouthe° til that myn herte breste.°" promise   burst
Thus been° they bothe in quiete and in reste.   are
    For o° thyng, sires, saufly° dar I seye,   one   safely
That freendes everich° oother moot° obeye   each   must
If they wol longe holden compaignye.
Love wol nat be constreyned by maistrye.
Whan maistrie comth, the god of love anon
Beteth hise wynges, and farwel, he is gon.

Love is a thyng as any spirit free.
Wommen of kynde° desiren libertee   60   by nature
And nat to been constreyned as a thral,°   slave
And so doon° men, if I sooth seyn° shal.   do   truth say
Looke who that° is moost pacient in love,   Whoever
He is at his avantage al above.
Pacience is an heigh vertu, certeyn,
For it venquysseth,° as thise clerkes seyn,°   vanquishes say
Thynges that rigour sholde° nevere atteyne.   could
For every word men may° nat chide or pleyne.°   can   complain
Lerneth to suffre, or elles, so moot I gon,°   may I prosper
Ye shul it lerne wher° so ye wole or non.°   70   whether not
For in this world, certeyn, ther no wight is
That he ne dooth or seith som tyme amys.°   amiss
Ire, siknesse, or constellacioun,°   astrological combination
Wyn,° wo, or chaungyng of complexioun,°   Wine   temperament
Causeth ful ofte to doon amys or speken.
On every wrong a man may nat be wreken.°   avenged
After the tyme moste be temperaunce
To every wight° that kan on governaunce.°   person   understands self-
                                                       control
And therfore hath this wise worthy knyght
To lyve in ese suffraunce° hire bihight,°   80   permission   promised
And she to hym ful wisly gan to swere°   swore (*gan to swere*)
That nevere sholde ther be defaute in here.
   Here may men seen an humble, wys acord.
Thus hath she take hir servant and hir lord,
Servant in love, and lord in mariage.
Thanne was he bothe in lordshipe and servage.°   servitude
Servage? Nay, but in lordshipe above,
Sith° he hath bothe his lady and his love;   Since
His lady, certes,° and his wyf also,   certainly
The which that lawe of love acordeth to.   90
And whan he was in this prosperitee,
Hom with his wyf he gooth to his contree.
Nat fer fro Pedmark° ther his dwellyng was,   far from Penmarch
                                                       (Brittany)
Wher-as° he lyveth in blisse and in solas.°   Where   happiness
Who koude telle but he° hadde wedded be°   he who   been
The joye, the ese, and the prosperitee
That is bitwix an housbonde and his wyf?
A yeer and moore lasted this blisful lyf,
Til that the knyght of which I speke of thus,

That of Kairrud° was cleped° Arveragus, 100 Kerru (? Brittany) called
Shoop hym° to goon and dwelle a yeer or twayne   Prepared
In Engelond, that cleped was eek° Britayne,   also
To seke in armes worship° and honour,   esteem
For al his lust° he sette in swich labour;   pleasure
And dwelled ther two yeer, the book seith thus.

 Now wol I stynte of° this Arveragus,   leave off about
And speke I wole of Dorigene his wyf,
That loveth hir housbonde as hir hertes lyf.
For his absence wepeth she and siketh,°   sighs
As doon thise noble wyves whan hem liketh.° 110 it pleases
She moorneth, waketh, waileth, fasteth, pleyneth.° complains
Desir of his presence hir so destreyneth°   afflicts
That al this wide world she set° at noght.   sets
Hir freendes, whiche that° knewe hir hevy thoght, who
Conforten hire in al that ever they may.
They prechen° hire, they telle hire nyght and day preach to
That causelees she sleeth° hirself, allas.   slays
And every confort possible in this cas
They doon to hire with al hir bisynesse°   their diligence
Al for to make hire leve° hir hevynesse. 120 lay aside

 By proces, as ye knowen everichoon,°   everyone
Men may so longe graven° in a stoon   carve
Til som figure therinne emprented be;
So longe han° they conforted hire til she   have
Receyved hath by hope and by resoun
The emprentyng of hir° consolacioun,   their
Thurgh which hir grete sorwe gan aswage.° began to assuage
She may nat alwey duren° in swich rage.° remain such passion

 And eek Arveragus in al this care
Hath sent hire lettres hom of his welfare, 130
And that he wol come hastily agayn,
Or ellis° hadde this sorwe hir herte slayn. else

 Hir freendes sawe hir sorwe gan to slake° began to slacken
And preyde hire on knees, for Goddes sake,
To come and romen hire° in compaignye, wander
Awey to dryve hir derke fantasye;
And finally she graunted that requeste,
For wel she saw that it was for the beste.

 Now stood hir castel faste° by the see, close
And often with hir freendes walketh she 140

Hir to disporte° upon the bank an-heigh,°   To amuse herself on high
Wher-as° she many a ship and barge seigh°   Where saw
Seillynge hir cours° wher-as hem liste° go.   their courses it pleased
But thanne was that a parcel of hir wo,
For to hirself ful ofte, "Allas," seith she,
"Is ther no ship, of so manye as I se,
Wol bryngen hom my lord? Thanne were myn herte
Al warisshed° of hise° bittre peynes smerte.°"   healed its smart
   Another tyme there wolde she sitte and thynke,
And caste hir eyen° dounward fro the brynke; 150 eyes
But whan she seigh the grisly rokkes blake,°   black
For verray fere° so wolde hir herte quake   fear
That on hir feet she myghte hir° noght sustene.   herself
Thanne wolde she sitte adoun upon the grene,
And pitously° into the see biholde,   pitifully
And seyn° right thus, with sorweful sikes° colde: say sighs
   "Eterne God, that thurgh thy purveiance°   providence
Ledest the world by certeyn governance,°   sure control
In ydel,° as men seyn,° ye no thyng make.   Without purpose say
But, Lord, thise grisly, feendly° rokkes blake, 160 fiendish
That semen° rather a foul confusioun   seem
Of werk than any fair creacioun
Of swich a parfit, wys God and a stable,
Why han ye wroght this werk unresonable,
For by this werk south, north, ne° west, ne est   nor
Ther nys° y-fostred man, ne bryd,° ne beest?   is not bird
It doth no good, to my wit,° but anoyeth.°   judgment harms
Se ye nat, Lord, how mankynde it destroyeth?
An hundred thousand bodies of mankynde
Han rokkes slayn, al° be they nat in mynde°; 170 though remembered
Which mankynde is so fair part of thy werk
That thow it madest lyk to thyn owene merk.°   image
   "Thanne° semed it ye hadde a greet chiertee°   Then (at creation) love
Toward mankynde, but how thanne may it be
That ye swiche menes° make, it to destroyen,   such means
Whiche menes do no good but evere anoyen.
I woot° wel, clerkes wol seyn as hem leste,°   know it pleases
By argumentz, that al is for the beste,
Thogh I ne kan the causes nat y-knowe.
But thilke° God that made wynd to blowe, 180 that same

As kepe° my lord! This is my conclusioun.   *Guard*
To clerkes lete° I al disputisoun°;   *leave disputation*
But wolde God that alle thise rokkes blake
Were sonken into helle for his sake.
Thise rokkes sleen° myn herte for the feere.°"   *slay for fear*
Thus wolde she seyn with many a pitous° teere.   *pitiful*

    Hir freendes sawe that it was no disport°   *amusement*
To romen° by the see, but disconfort,   *wander*
And shopen° for to pleyen somwher elles.   *decided*
They leden° hire by ryvers, and by welles,   190   *lead*
And eek in othere places delitables.°   *delightful*
They dauncen, and they pleyen at ches and tables.°   *backgammon*

    So on a day, right in the morwe-tyde,°   *morning-time*
Unto a gardyn that was ther bisyde,
In which that they hadde maad hir ordinance°   *their preparation*
Of vitaille° and of oother purveiance,°   *victuals provisions*
They goon and pleye hem al the longe day.
And this was on the sixte° morwe of May,   *sixth*
Which May hadde peynted with his softe shoures°   *showers*
This gardyn ful of leves and of floures;   200
And craft of mannes hond° so curiously°   *hand ingeniously*
Arrayed hadde this gardyn, trewely,
That nevere was ther gardyn of swich prys,°   *excellence*
But if° it were the verray Paradys.   *Unless*
The odour of floures and the fresshe sighte
Wolde han maked any herte lighte
That evere was born, but if to° greet siknesse   *unless too*
Or to greet sorwe helde it in distresse,
So ful it was of beautee with plesaunce.°   *delight*
At after-dyner gonne° they to daunce   210   *began*
And synge also, save Dorigen allone,
Which made alwey hir compleynt and hir mone,°   *moan*
For° she ne saugh° hym on the daunce go   *Because did not see*
That was hir housbonde and hir love also.
But, nathelees,° she moste a tyme abyde°   *nevertheless endure*
And with good hope lete hir sorwe slyde.

    Upon this daunce, amonges othere men,
Daunced a squier bifore Dorigen
That fressher was and jolyer of array,
As to my doom,° than is the monthe of May.   220   *judgment*
He syngeth, daunceth, passyng° any man   *surpassing*

That is, or was, sith that° the world bigan.   since
Ther-with he was, if men sholde hym discryve,°   describe
Oon of the beste farynge man on lyve,°   handsomest men **alive**
Yong, strong, right vertuous, and riche, and wys,
And wel biloved, and holden° in gret prys.°   held   esteem
And shortly, if the sothe° I tellen shal,   truth
Unwityng of this Dorigen at al,
This lusty squier, servant to Venus,
Which that y-cleped° was Aurelius,   230   Who called
Hadde loved hire best of any creature
Two yeer and moore, as was his aventure,°   fate
But nevere dorste° he tellen hire his grevance.   dared
Withouten coppe° he drank al his penance.   Without aid of cup
He was despeyred; no thyng dorste he seye,
Save° in his songes somwhat wolde he wreye°   Except that   reveal
His wo, as in a general compleynyng;
He seyde he lovede, and was biloved no thyng.°   in no way
Of swich matere made he many layes,°   lyrics
Songes, compleyntes,° roundels, virelayes,   240   love-laments
How that he dorste nat his sorwe telle,
But langwissheth as a Furye dooth in helle.
And dye he moste, he seyde, as dide Ekko°   Echo
For Narcisus,° that dorste nat telle hir wo.   Narcissus
In oother manere than ye heere me seye,
Ne dorste he nat to hire his wo biwreye,°   disclose
Save that, paraventure,° som tyme at daunces   perchance
Ther° yong folk kepen hir° observaunces,   Where   hold their
It may wel be he looked on hir face
In swich a wise° as man° that asketh grace.   250   manner   one
But no thyng wiste° she of his entente.   knew
Nathelees,° it happed er they thennes wente,   Nevertheless
By cause that he was hir neighebour
And was a man of worship and honour,
And hadde° y-knowen hym of tyme yoore,°   (she) had   of old
They fille° in speche; and forth,° moore and moore,   fell   forward
Unto his purpos drough° Aurelius.   drew
And whan he saugh° his tyme, he seyde thus: saw
   "Madame," quod° he, "by God that this world   said
      made,
So that I wiste° it myghte youre herte glade,° 260   If I knew that   gladden
I wolde, that day that youre Arveragus

Wente over the see, that I Aurelius
Hadde went ther° nevere I sholde have come agayn,   where
For wel I woot° my servyce is in vayn.   know
My gerdon° is but brestyng° of myn herte.   reward   breaking
Madame, reweth° upon my peynes smerte,   rue
For with a word ye may me sleen° or save.   slay
Here at youre feet, God wolde that I were grave°!   buried
I ne have as now no leyser° moore to seye.   leisure
Have mercy, swete, or ye wol do° me deye."   270   make
   She gan° to looke upon Aurelius.   began
"Is this youre wil," quod she, "and sey ye thus?
Nevere erst,°" quod she, "ne wiste° I what ye   before   knew
   mente,
But now, Aurelie, I knowe youre entente.
By thilke° God that yaf° me soule and lyf,   the same   gave
Ne shal I nevere been untrewe wyf
In word ne werk, as fer° as I have wit.°   far   knowledge
I wol been his to whom that I am knyt.
Taak this for fynal answere as of me."
But after that, in pleye, thus seyde she: 280
   "Aurelie," quod she, "by heighe God above,
Yet wolde I graunte yow to been youre love,
Syn° I yow se so pitously complayne,   Since
Looke what° day that endelong Britayne°   On whatever   all along
                                                       Brittany
Ye remoeve alle the rokkes, stoon by stoon,
That they ne lette° ship ne boot to goon.   prevent neither
I seye, whan ye han maad the coost° so clene   coast
Of rokkes that ther nys no° stoon y-sene,   is not any
Thanne wol I love yow best of any man.   289
Have heer my trouthe° in al that evere I kan."   promise
   "Is ther noon oother grace in yow?" quod he.
   "No, by that Lord," quod she, "that maked me.
For wel I woot that it shal nevere bityde.°   happen
Lat swiche folies out of youre herte slyde.
What deyntee° sholde a man han in his lyf   respect
For to go love another mannes wyf
That° hath hir body whan so that hym liketh°?"   Who (the husband)   it
                                                       pleases
   Aurelius ful ofte soore siketh.°   sorely sighs
Wo was Aurelie whan that he this herde,
And with a sorweful herte he thus answerde: 300
   "Madame," quod he, "this were an inpossible.°   impossibility

Thanne moot° I dye of sodeyn° deth horrible."   Then must   sudden

And with that word he turned hym anon.°   turned away at once

Tho coome hir° othere freendes many oon,°   Then came her   a one

And in the aleyes° romeden up and doun,   paths

And no thyng wiste° of this conclusioun,   knew

But sodeynly bigonne° revel newe   began

Til that the brighte sonne loste his hewe°   its color

For th'orisonte° hath reft° the sonne his light.   horizon   taken away from

This is as muche to seye as° it was nyght!   310   as to say that

And hoom they goon in joye and in solas,

Save oonly wrecched Aurelius, allas.

He to his hous is goon with sorweful herte.

He seeth he may nat from his deeth asterte.°   escape

Hym semed° that he felte his herte colde.°   It seemed to him   grow cold

Up to the hevene his handes he gan holde,°   held (*gan holde*)

And on his knowes° bare he sette hym doun,   knees

And in his ravyng seyde his orisoun.°   prayer

For verray wo out of his wit° he breyde.°   mind   went

He nyste° what he spak, but thus he seyde.   320   didn't know

With pitous herte his pleynt hath he bigonne

Unto the goddes,° and first unto the sonne.°   goddess (Lucina)   sun (Apollo)

He seyde, "Appollo, god and governour

Of every plaunte, herbe, tree, and flour,

That yevest,° after thy declynacioun,°   give   according to your height in the sky

To ech° of hem his° tyme and his sesoun   each   its

As thyn herberwe° chaungeth, lowe or heighe,   position

Lord Phebus,° cast thy merciable eighe°   Phoebus (Apollo)   eye

On wrecche° Aurelie, which that° am but lorn.°   wretched   who   lost

Lo, lord, my lady hath my deeth y-sworn   330

Withouten gilt, but° thy benygnytee   unless

Upon my dedly° herte have som pitee.   dying

For wel I woot,° lord Phebus, if yow lest,°   know   it pleases

Ye may me helpen, save° my lady, best.   apart from

Now voucheth sauf° that I may yow devyse°   vouchsafe   explain to

How that I may been holpen,° and in what wyse.°   helped   manner

"Youre blisful suster, Lucyna° the shene,°   Lucina (the moon)   beautiful

That of the see is chief goddesse and queene, —

Thogh Neptunus have deitee° in the see,   godship

Yet emperesse aboven° hym is she, —   340   over

Ye knowen wel, lord, that right° as hir desir   just

Is to be quyked° and lighted of youre fyr,   enlivened

For which she folweth° yow ful bisily,°   follows diligently
Right° so the see desireth naturelly   Just
To folwen° hire as she that is goddesse   follow (in its ebb and flow)
Bothe in the see and ryvers moore° and lesse.° greater smaller
Wher-fore, lord Phebus, this is my requeste:
Do this myracle, or do° myn herte breste,° make break
That now next at this opposicioun,
Which in the signe shal be of the Leoun,[1] 350
As preyeth° hire so greet a flood to brynge Pray
That fyve fadme° at the leeste it oversprynge fathom
The hyeste rok in Armoryk Britayne;
And lat this flood endure yeres twayne.°   two
Thanne, certes,° to my lady may I seye,   certainly
'Holdeth° youre heste.° The rokkes been aweye.' Keep promise
 "Lord Phebus, dooth this myracle for me.
Prey hire, she go no faster cours than ye.
I seye, thus preyeth youre suster that she go
No faster cours than ye thise yeres two; 360
Thanne shal she been evene at the fulle alway,
And spryng flood lasten bothe nyght and day.
And, but° she vouche sauf in swich manere unless
To graunte me my sovereyn lady deere,
Pray hire to synken every rok adoun
Into hir owene dirke° regioun   dark
Under the ground ther° Pluto dwelleth inne, where
Or nevere mo shal I my lady wynne.
Thy temple in Delphos° wol I barfoot seke. Delphi
Lord Phebus, se the teerys° on my cheke, 370 tears
And of my peyne have som compassioun."
And with that word in swowne° he fil adoun, a swoon
And longe tyme he lay forth in a traunce.
 His brother, which that knew of his penaunce,
Up caughte hym, and to bedde he hath hym
  broght.
Dispeired in this torment and this thoght,
Lete° I this woful creature lye.   Leave
Chese° he, for me,° wher° he wol lyve or dye. Choose as far as I'm concerned whether

[1] ". . . now at this next opposition of the sun and moon, which will occur when you (the sun) are in the zodiacal sign of the Lion . . ." The highest tides or spring floods are produced when the sun and moon are either in conjunction and both pull in a line together from one side of the earth, or are in opposition and pull on opposite sides of the earth.

Arveragus with heele° and greet honour,   prosperity
As he that was of chivalrie the flour,   380
Is comen hom, and othere worthy men.
O blisful artow° now, thow Dorigen,   are you
That hast thy lusty housbonde in thyn armes,
The fresshe knyght, the worthy man of armes,
That loveth thee as his owene hertes lyf.
No thyng list hym° to been ymagynatyf°   In no way does he wish
                                                             curious
If any wight hadde spoke, whil he was oute,
To hire of love. He hadde of it no doute.°   fear
He noght entendeth to no swich° matere,   doesn't care about such a
But daunceth, justeth,° maketh hir good cheere, 390   jousts
And thus in joye and blisse I lete hem dwelle,
And of the syke° Aurelius wol I telle.   sick
      In langour and in torment furyus
Two yeer and moore lay wrecche Aurelius
Er any foot he myghte on erthe gon,°   walk
Ne confort in this tyme hadde he noon,
Save of° his brother, which that was a clerk.   Except from
He knew of al this wo and al this werk,
For to noon oother creature, certeyn,
Of this matere he dorste no word seyn.   400
Under his brest he baar it moore secree°   secretively
Than evere dide Pamphilus ¹ for Galathee.°   Galatea
His brest was hool withoute for to sene,°   whole outwardly to be seen
But in his herte ay° was the arwe kene°   ever arrow sharp
And wel ye knowe that of a sursanure°   wound healed only on the
                                                             surface
In surgerye is perilous the cure,
But° men myghte touche the arwe or come ther-by.°   Unless   reach it
His brother weep° and wayled pryvely°   wept   in private
Til at the laste hym fil in remembraunce°   he remembered
That, whiles he was at Orliens° in Fraunce,   410   Orléans (University)
As yonge clerkes that been lykerous°   eager
To reden° artes that been curious°   study   obscure
Seken in every halke° and every herne°   nook   corner
Particuler sciences for to lerne —
He hym remembred that, upon a day
At Orliens in studie, a book he say°   saw

---

¹ Pamphilus was the hero of a romance which circulated so widely in the Middle Ages
that his name gave rise to the word *pamphlet* as applied to any inexpensive booklet.

Of magyk naturel,[1] which his felawe,°   companion
That was that tyme a bacheler of lawe,
Al° were he ther to lerne another craft,   Though
Hadde pryvely upon his desk y-laft,°   420   left
Which book spak muchel° of the operaciouns   much
Touchynge the eighte-and-twenty mansiouns°   daily stations
That longen° to the moone, and swich folye,   belong
As in oure dayes is nat worth a flye,
For holy chirches feith, in oure bileve,°   belief
Ne suffreth° noon illusioun us to greve.   Allows
And whan this book was in his remembraunce,
Anon° for joye his herte gan° to daunce,   At once   began
And to hymself he seyde pryvely,
"My brother shal be warisshed° hastily,   430   cured
For I am siker° that ther be sciences   sure
By whiche men make diverse apparences,°   apparitions
Swiche as thise subtile tregetours° pleye;   jugglers
For ofte at festes, have I wel herd seye,
That tregetours withinne an halle large
Have maad come in, a water and a barge,
And in the halle rowen° up and doun.   (have) rowed
Som tyme hath semed come a grym leoun,
And som tyme floures sprynge as in a mede,°   meadow
Som tyme a vyne and grapes white and rede,   440
Som tyme a castel al of lym° and stoon;   lime
And whan hem lyked,° voyded° it anoon.   it pleased   (they have) removed
Thus semed it to every mannes sighte.
   "Now thanne, conclude I thus, that, if I myghte
At Orliens som old felawe° y-fynde   companion
That hadde thise moones mansions in mynde,°   in his memory
Or oother magyk naturel above,
He sholde wel make my brother han his love.
For with an apparence a clerk may make
To mannes sighte that alle the rokkes blake   450
Of Britaigne were y-voyded everichon,°   everyone
And shippes by the brynke comen and gon,
And in swich forme enduren a day or two.
Thanne were my brother warisshed° of his wo.   cured

[1] The law student was, for unprofessional reasons, studying natural magic (that is, legitimate and not black magic), a knowledge of which the Doctor (*General Prologue*, 416) required professionally.

Thanne moste she nedes holden hir biheste,
Or ellis he shal shame hire, at the leeste."
    What° sholde I make a lenger tale of this?   Why
Unto his brotheres bed he comen is,
And swich confort° he yaf° hym for to gon   encouragement gave
To Orliens that he up stirte° anon,   460   sprang
And on his wey forthward thanne is he fare°   he has fared
In hope for to been lissed° of his care.   relieved
    Whan they were come almoost to that citee,
But if° it were a two furlong or thre,   Unless
A yong clerk romyng by hymself they mette,
Which that in Latyn thriftily° hem grette,°   fluently greeted
And after that he seyde a wonder thyng.
"I knowe," quod he, "the cause of youre comyng."
And er they ferther any foote wente,
He tolde hem al that was in hir° entente.   470   their
    This Britoun° clerk hym asked of felawes   Breton
The whiche that° he hadde knowe in olde dawes,°   Whom days
And he answerde hym that they dede were,
For which he weep ful ofte many a teere.
    Doun of° his hors Aurelius lighte° anon,   off alit
And with this magicien forth is he gon
Hom to his hous, and maden hem° wel at ese.   themselves
Hem lakked no vitaille° that myghte hem plese;   They lacked no victuals
So wel arrayed hous as ther was oon,
Aurelius in his lyf saw nevere noon.   480
    He shewed hym, er he wente to sopeer,
Forestes, parkes ful of wilde deer.°   animals
Ther saw he hertes° with hir hornes hye,   harts
The gretteste that evere were seyn with eye;
He saw of hem an hundred slayn with houndes,
And somme with arwes blede of bittre woundes.
    He saw, whan voyded were thise wilde deer,
Thise fauconers° upon a fair ryver,°   Some falconers river-bank
That with hir haukes han the heron slayn.
    Tho° saugh he knyghtes justyng° in a playn, 490 Then jousting
And after this he dide hym swich plesaunce
That he hym shewed his lady on a daunce,
On which hymself he daunced, as hym thoughte.°   it seemed to him
And whan this maister that this magyk wroughte
Saugh it was tyme, he clapte his handes two,

And farwel, al oure revel was ago.°   gone
And yet remoeved° they nevere out of the hous   moved
Whil they saugh al this sighte merveillous,
But in his studie, ther-as° his bookes be,   where
They seten° stille, and no wight° but they thre. 500   sat   person
    To hym this maister called his squyer
And seide hym thus, "Is redy oure soper?
Almoost an hour it is, I undertake,°   I am sure
Sith° I yow bad oure soper for to make,   Since
Whan that thise worthy men wenten with me
Into my studie, ther as my bookes be."
    "Sire," quod this squyer, "whan it liketh yow,
It is al redy, thogh ye wol right now."
    "Go we thanne soupe,°" quod he, "as for the   sup
     beste.
This amorous folk som tyme mote han hir° reste."   must have their
    At after-soper fille° they in tretee° 511   fell   into discussion
What somme° sholde this maistres gerdoun° be   amount   reward
To remoeven alle the rokkes of Britayne,
And eek from Geronde° to the mouth of Sayne.°   the Gironde   the Seine
    He made it straunge° and swoor, so God hym   difficult
     save,
Lasse° than a thousand pound he wolde nat have,   Less
Ne gladly for that somme he wolde nat gon.
    Aurelius with blisful herte anon
Answerde thus: "Fy on a thousand pound!
This wyde world, which that men seye is round, 520
I wolde it yeve° if I were lord of it.   give
This bargayn is ful dryve,° for we ben knyt.°   fully driven   **agreed**
Ye shal be payed trewely,° by my trouthe,°   faithfully   promise
But looketh° now, for no necligence or slouthe   see to it
Ye tarie° us heer no lenger than tomorwe."   delay
    "Nay," quod this clerk, "have heer my feith to
     borwe.°"   in pledge
    To bedde is goon Aurelius whan hym leste,°   it pleased
And wel neigh al that nyght he hadde his reste.
What for his labour and his hope of blisse,
His woful herte of penaunce hadde a lisse.° 530   relief
    Upon the morwe, whan that it was day,
To Britayne° tooke they the righte way,   Brittany
Aurelius and this magicien bisyde,

And been descended ther° they wolde abyde.   have dismounted where
And this was, as thise bookes me remembre,°   remind
The colde, frosty seson of Decembre.
  Phebus wax° old and hewed lyk latoun,°   grew   copper-colored
That in his hote declynacioun°   declination
Shoon as the burned° gold with stremes° brighte;   burnished   beams
But now in Capricorn adoun he lighte,°   540   descended
Wher-as° he shoon ful pale, I dar wel seyn.¹   Where
The bittre frostes with the sleet and reyn
Destruyed hath the grene in every yerd.
Janus ² sit° by the fyr with double berd   sits
And drynketh of° his bugle-horn the wyn;   from
Biforn° hym stant brawen° of the tusked swyn;   Before   stands flesh
And "Nowel°" crieth every lusty man.   Noël
  Aurelius, in al that evere he kan,
Dooth to this maister cheere and reverence,
And preyeth hym to doon his diligence   550
To bryngen hym out of his peynes smerte,
Or with a swerd that he wolde slitte his herte.
  This subtil clerk swich routhe° hadde of this man   compassion
That, nyght and day, he spedde hym that° he kan   as best
To wayten° a tyme of° his conclusioun,   find   for
This is to seyn, to make illusioun
By swich an apparence or jogelrye —
I ne kan° no termes of astrologye —   know
That she and every wight sholde wene° and seye   believe
That of Britayne the rokkes were aweye,   560
Or ellis they were sonken under grounde.
So at the laste he hath his tyme y-founde
To maken his japes° and his wrecchednesse°   tricks   mischief
Of swich a supersticious cursednesse.
His tables Tolletanes° forth he broght   Toledo (astronomical) tables
Ful wel corrected, ne ther lakked noght,
Neither his collect° ne his expans yeris,°   collected   expanded yearly tables
Ne hise rootes,° ne hise othere geris,°   data   equipment
As been his centris,° and hise argumentz,°   astrolabe centers   tabular guides

¹ The sun (Phoebus) had been bright in its declination in the fourth zodiacal sign, Cancer (from mid-June to mid-July), but in the tenth sign, Capricorn (from mid-December to mid-January), it became pale.
² Two-faced Janus, the Roman god who looks back on the past year and forward to the new year, represents the month of January.

And hise proporcionels convenientz°   570   relevant proportional tables
For hise equacions° in every thyng.   astrological divisions
And by his eighte speere in his wirkyng,
He knew ful wel how fer Alnath was shove
Fro the heed of thilke fixe Aries above,[1]
That in the nynthe speere considered is.
Ful subtilly he kalkuled° al this.   calculated
   Whan he hadde founde his firste mansioun,°   station (of the moon)
He knew the remenaunt by proporcioun,
And knew the arisyng of his moone wel
And in whos face,° and terme,° and everydel°;   580   zodiacal part section every
And knew ful wel the moones mansioun   bit
Acordaunt to his operacioun,
And knew also hise othere observaunces
For swiche illusiouns and swiche meschaunces°   misdeeds
As hethen folk useden° in thilke° dayes.   practiced   those
For which no lenger maked he delayes,
But thurgh his magyk, for a wyke° or tweye,°   week   two
It semed that alle the rokkes were aweye.
   Aurelius, which that yet despeired is
Wher° he shal han his love or fare amys,°   590   Whether   amiss
Awaiteth nyght and day on this myracle;
And whan he knew that ther was noon obstacle,
That voyded were thise rokkes everichon,°   everyone
Doun to his maistres° feet he fil anon   master's
And seyde, "I, woful wrecche, Aurelius,
Thank yow, lord, and lady myn, Venus,
That me han holpen° fro my cares colde."   helped
And to the temple his wey forth hath he holde,°   held
Wher-as° he knew he sholde his lady se.   Where
And whan he saugh his tyme, anon right he,   600
With dredful° herte and with ful humble cheere,   timid
Salued° hath his soverayn lady deere.   Saluted
   "My righte lady," quod this woful man,
"Whom I moost drede, and love as I best kan,

---

[1] "... by his eighth sphere (of fixed stars) ... he knew ... how far Alnath (a star in the constellation Aries) was removed from the (theoretical) head of that same fixed constellation Aries...." Although the Franklin does not pretend to understand all the technical terms he mentions in ll. 565-571, the specific details in his subsequent description of the magician's calculations are all valid and would have been meaningful to any reader versed in the complexities of medieval astronomical calculations.

And lothest were° of al this world displese, most loath would be . to
Nere it° that I for yow have swich disese° Were it not misery
That I moste° dyen heer at youre foot anon, would have to
Noght wolde I telle how me is° wo bigon, I am
But, certes, outher° moste I dye or pleyne.° either complain
Ye sleen me, giltlees, for verray peyne. 610
But of my deeth thogh that ye have no routhe,° compassion
Avyseth yow er that° ye breke youre trouthe. Consider before
Repenteth yow, for thilke° God above, that
Er ye me sleen by cause that I yow love.
For, madame, wel ye woot° what ye han hight,° know promised
Nat that I chalange° any thyng of° right demand by
Of yow, my sovereyn lady, but youre grace.° undeserved kindness
But in a gardyn yond,° at swich a place, there
Ye woot right wel what ye bihighten° me; promised
And in myn hand youre trouthe plighten° ye 620 pledged
To love me best. God woot, ye seyde so,
Al be that° I unworthy am ther-to. Even if
Madame, I speke it for the honour of yow
Moore than to save myn hertes lyf right now.
I have do° so as ye comaunded me; done
And, if ye vouche sauf, ye may go se.
Dooth as yow list°; have youre biheste in mynde. it pleases
For, quyk° or deed, right ther ye shal me fynde; alive
In yow lyth° al to do° me lyve or deye. lies make
But wel I woot, the rokkes been aweye!" 630
  He taketh his leve, and she astoned° stood; astounded
In al hir face nas° a drope of blood. was not
She wende° nevere have come in swich a trappe. expected
"Allas," quod she, "that evere this sholde happe,
For wende I nevere by possibilitee
That swich a monstre° or merveille myghte be. prodigy
It is agayns the proces of nature."
And hom she gooth a sorweful creature;
For verray feere unnethe° may she go. hardly
She wepeth, wayleth, al a day or two, 640
And swowneth,° that it routhe° was to se. swoons a pity
But why it was, to no wight tolde she,
For out of towne was goon Arveragus.
But to hirself she spak and seyde thus,
With face pale and with ful sorweful cheere,

In hir compleinte, as ye shal after heere.

"Allas," quod she, "on thee, Fortune, I pleyne,°   complain
That, unwar,° wrapped hast me in thy cheyne,   unaware
For which t'escape woot I no socour
Save oonly deeth or dishonour.   650
Oon of thise two bihoveth me to chese.°   choose
But, nathelees,° yet have I levere to lese°   nevertheless   I had sooner lose
My lyf than of my body to have a shame,
Or knowe myselven° fals, or lese° my name.   myself   lose
And with my deeth I may be quyt,° ywis.°   freed   indeed
Hath ther nat many a noble wyf er this,
And many a mayde, y-slayn hirself, allas,
Rather than with hir body doon trespas.°   transgression

"Yis, certes. Lo, thise stories [1] beren witnesse:
Whan thritty tirauntz° ful of cursednesse   660   the Thirty Tyrants (of Athens)
Hadde slayn Phidon in Atthenes atte feste,
They comaunded his doghtren for t'areste°   daughters to be seized
And bryngen hem° biforn hem in despit,   them
Al naked, to fulfille hir° foul delit,   their
And in hir fadres° blood they made hem daunce   their father's
Upon the pavement, God yeve° hem myschaunce!   give
For which thise woful maydens ful of drede,
Rather than they wolde lese hir maydenhede,°   lose their virginity
They pryvely been stirt° into a welle   secretly have leapt
And dreynte hemselven,° as the bokes telle.   670   drowned themselves
They of Mecene leete enquere° and seke   Messene (in Greece) caused to find
Of Lacedomye° fifty maydens, eke,°   Lacedaemonia   also
On whiche they wolden doon hir lecherye,
But was ther noon of al that compaignye
That she nas° slayn, and with a good entente   Who was not
Chees° rather for to dye than assente   Chose
To been oppressed° of hir maydenhede.   violated
Why sholde I, thanne, to dye been in drede?

"Lo, eek, the tiraunt Aristoclides,

---

[1] The examples of chastity defended which Dorigen catalogues (ll. 660–748) are all derived from St. Jerome's *Against Jovinian*, a treatise which, as we have seen, became familiar to the Wife of Bath through her fifth husband's lectures. Though by modern standards Dorigen's enumeration of examples seems inappropriate to her situation and makes much less lively reading than the Wife's account of Jankyn's list of evil women (*Wife of Bath's Prologue*, 719–778), elaborate exemplification was an esteemed rhetorical device in Chaucer's age. (See also *Nun's Priest's Tale*, 543, n. 2.)

That loved a mayden heet Stymphalides°; 680   named Stymphalis
Whan that hir fader slayn was on a nyght,
Unto Dianes° temple gooth she right   Diana's
And hente° the ymage in hir handes two,   seized
Fro which ymage wolde she nevere go;
No wight° ne myghte hir handes of it arace,°   No one from it pull
Til she was slayn right in the selve° place.   that very
Now, sith that° maydens hadden swich despit°   since aversion
To been defouled with mannes foul delit,
Wel oghte a wyf rather hirselven° slee   herself
Than be defouled, as it thynketh me. 690
   "What shal I seyn of Hasdrubales wyf,
That at Cartage birafte° hirself hir lyf?   Carthage bereft
For whan she saw that Romayns wan° the toun,   won
She took hir children alle, and skipte° adoun   leapt
Into the fyr, and chees° rather to dye   chose
Than° any Romayn dide hire vileynye.   Than that
Hath nat Lucresse° y-slayn hirself, allas,   Lucretia
At Rome whan that she oppressed° was   violated
Of° Tarquyn, for hir thoughte° it was a shame   By it seemed to
To lyven whan she hadde lost hir name? 700
The sevene maydens of Milesie° also   Miletus
Han slayn hemself for verray drede and wo
Rather than folk of Gawle° hem sholde oppresse.   Gaul
Mo° than a thousand stories, as I gesse,   More
Koude I now telle as touchyng this matere.
   "Whan Habradate° was slayn, his wyf so deere   Abradates
Hirselven slow,° and leet° hir blood to glyde   slew allowed
In Habradates woundes depe and wyde,
And seyde, 'My body, at the leeste way,°   at least
Ther shal no wight defoulen, if I may.°' 710 can help it
   "What° sholde I mo ensamples herof sayn,°   Why tell
Sith that° so many han hemselven slayn,   Since
Wel rather than they wolde defouled be?
I wol conclude that it is bet° for me   better
To sleen myself than ben defouled thus.
I wol be trewe unto Arveragus,
Or rather sle myself in som manere,
As dide Democionis° doghter deere,   Demotion's
By cause that she wolde nat defouled be.
O Cedasus,° it is ful greet pitee 720 Scedasus

To reden how thy doghtren° deyde, allas, | daughters
That slowe° hemself for swich maner cas.° | slew a case of such kind
As greet a pitee was it, or wel moore,
The Theban mayden that for Nichanore° | Nicanor
Hirselven° slow right for swich manere wo. | Herself
Another Theban mayden dide right so,
For° oon of Macedonye° hadde hire oppressed; | Because Macedonia
She with hir deeth hir maydenhed redressed.° | vindicated
What shal I seyn of Nycerates° wyf, | Nicerates'
That for swich cas birafte hirself hir lyf? 730
How trewe eek was to Alcibiades
His love, that rather for to dyen chees° | chose to die
Than for to suffre his body unburyed be.
Lo, which° a wyf was Alceste,°" quod she. | What Alcestis
"What seith Omer° of goode Penolopee°? | Homer Penelope
Al Grece knoweth of hir chastitee.
Pardee,° of Laodomya° is writen thus | Certainly Laodamia
That, whan at Troye was slayn Protheselaus,° | Protesilaus
No lenger wolde she lyve after his day.
The same of noble Porcia° telle I may; 740 | Portia
Withoute Brutus koude she nat lyve,
To whom she hadde al hool° hir herte yeve.° | wholly given
The parfit wifhod of Arthemesye° | Artemisia
Honoured is thurgh al the barbarye.° | barbarian lands
O Teuta queene, thy wifly chastitee
To alle wyves may a mirour bee.
The same thyng I seye of Bilyea,° | Bilia
Of Rodogone,° and eek Valeria." | Rhodogune
Thus pleyned° Dorigene a day or tweye, | complained
Purposynge evere that she wolde deye. 750
But, nathelees, upon the thridde nyght
Hoom cam Arveragus, this worthy knyght,
And asked hire why that she weep so soore;
And she gan° wepen ever lenger° the moore. | began to the longer
"Allas," quod she, "that evere was I born!
Thus have I seyd," quod she, "thus have I sworn."
And tolde hym al as ye han herd bifore;
It nedeth nat reherce° it yow namoore. | repeat
This housbond with glad cheere, in frendly wise,° | manner
Answerde and seyde, as I shal yow devyse,° 760 | tell
"Is ther oght ellis, Dorigen, but this?"

"Nay, nay," quod she, "God help me so as wys°!   as is certain
This is to° muche, and° it were Goddes wille."   too if
     "Ye,° wyf," quod he. "Lat slepen that° is stille.   Yes what
It may be wel, paraventure,° yet today.   perchance
Ye shul youre trouthe holden, by my fay,°   faith
For, God so wisly have mercy upon me,
I hadde wel levere y-stiked for to be,°   much rather be stabbed
For verray love which that I to yow have,
But if° ye sholde youre trouthe kepe and save.   770   Unless
Trouthe is the hyeste thyng that man may kepe."
But with that word he brast° anon to wepe   burst out
And seyde, "I yow forbede, up° peyne of deeth,   on
That nevere, whil thee lasteth lyf ne breeth,
To no wight tel thow of this aventure.
As I may best, I wol my wo endure
Ne make no contenance° of hevynesse   appearance
That folk of yow may demen° harm or gesse."   judge
     And forth he cleped° a squyer and a mayde.   called
"Goth° forth anon with Dorigen," he sayde,   780   Go
"And bryngeth hire to swich° a place anon."   such and such
They take hir leve, and on hir wey they gon,
But they ne wiste° why she thider wente.   did not know
He nolde° no wight tellen his entente.   would not
     Paraventure an heep° of yow, ywis,°   lot indeed
Wol holden hym a lewed° man in this,   stupid
That he wol putte his wyf in jupartie.°   jeopardy
Herkneth the tale er ye upon hire crie;
She may have bettre fortune than yow semeth°;   it seems to
And, whan that ye han herd the tale, demeth.° 790   judge
     This squyer, which that highte° Aurelius,   who was called
On Dorigen that was so amorus,
Of aventure happed° hir to meete   By chance happened
Amydde the toun, right in the quykkest° strete,   busiest
As she was boun° to goon the wey forth right   bound
Toward the gardyn ther-as° she had hight,°   where promised
And he was to the gardynward° also,   (headed) toward the garden
For wel he spyed whan she wolde go
Out of hir hous to any maner° place.   kind of
But thus they mette of aventure° or grace,   800   by chance
And he salueth° hire with glad entente   greets
And asked of hire whiderward° she wente.   where

And she answerde, half as she were mad,
"Unto the gardyn, as myn housbond bad,°   ordered
My trouthe for to holde, allas, allas."
    Aurelius gan° wondren on this cas,   began to
And in his herte hadde greet compassioun
Of hire and of hir lamentacioun,
And of Arveragus the worthy knyght,
That bad hir holden al that she had hight,   810
So looth hym was° his wyf sholde breke hir trouthe.   loath was he
And in his herte he caughte of° this greet routhe,°   conceived from   pity
Considerynge the beste on every syde,
That fro his lust yet were hym levere abyde°   he would rather desist
Than doon so heigh a cherlyssh wrecchednesse
Agayns franchise° and alle gentillesse.   generosity
For which in fewe wordes seyde he thus:
    "Madame, seyeth to youre lord Arveragus
That, sith° I se his grete gentillesse   since
To yow, and eek I se wel youre distresse,   820
That hym were levere han° shame — and that   he would sooner have
    were routhe° —   a pity
Than ye to me sholde breke thus youre trouthe,
I have wel levere° evere to suffre wo   would much rather
Than I departe° the love bitwix yow two.   Than sever
I yow relesse, madame, into youre hond,
Quyt,° every serement° and every bond   Discharged   oath
That ye han maad to me as heer biforn°   hitherto
Sith thilke tyme which that° ye were born.   Since that time when
My trouthe I plighte, I shal yow nevere repreve°   reproach
Of no biheeste. And here I take my leve   830
As of the treweste and the beste wyf
That evere yet I knew in al my lyf.
    "But every wyf be war of hir biheste.
On Dorigene remembreth,° at the leste.   remember
Thus kan a squyer doon a gentil dede,
As wel as kan a knyght, withouten drede.°"   doubt
    She thonketh hym upon hir knees al bare,
And hom unto hir housbond is she fare,
And tolde hym al as ye han herd me sayd.
And be ye siker,° he was so wel apayd°   840   sure   satisfied
That it were inpossible me° to write.   for me
What sholde I lenger of this cas endite°?   narrate

Arveragus and Dorigene his wyf
In sovereyn blisse leden° forth hir lyf.   lead
Nevere eft° ne was ther angre hem bitwene.   again
He cherisseth hire as thogh she were a queene,
And she was to hym trewe for evere moore.
Of thise two folk ye gete of me namoore.
   Aurelius, that his cost° hath al forlorn,°   expenditure lost
Curseth the tyme that evere he was born.   850
"Allas," quod he, "allas that I bihighte°   promised
Of pured° gold a thousand pound of wighte°   pure weight
Unto this philosophre. How shal I do?
I se namoore but that I am fordo.°   destroyed
Myn heritage moot I nedes° selle   I needs must
And been a beggere. Here may I nat dwelle
And shamen al my kynrede in this place,
But° I of hym may gete bettre grace.   Unless
But, nathelees,° I wol of hym assaye°   nevertheless try
At certeyn dayes yeer by yeer to paye,   860
And thonke° hym of his grete curteisye.   thank
My trouthe wol I kepe. I wol nat lye."
   With herte soor, he gooth unto his cofre°   money-box
And broghte gold unto this philosophre
The value of fyve hundred pound, I gesse,
And hym bisecheth of his gentillesse
To graunte hym dayes of the remenant,°   time for the remainder
And seyde, "Maister, I dar wel make avant,°   boast
I failled nevere of my trouthe as yit,
For sikerly° my dette shal be quyt   870   certainly
Towardes yow, however that I fare,
To goon abegged° in my kirtel° bare.   begging frock
But, wolde ye vouche sauf, upon seuretee,°   surety
Two yeer or thre for to respiten me,
Thanne were I wel, for ellis moot° I selle   otherwise must
Myn heritage. Ther is namoore to telle."
   This philosophre sobrely answerde,
And seyde thus, whan he thise wordes herde:
"Have I nat holden° covenant unto thee?"   held
    "Yis, certes, wel and trewely," quod he.   880
    "Hastow° nat had thy lady as thee liketh°?"   Have you it pleases
    "No, no," quod he, and sorwefully he siketh.° sighs
    "What was the cause? Tel me, if thow kan."

Aurelius his tale anon bigan,
And tolde hym al, as ye han herd bifore.
It nedeth nat to yow reherce it moore.

He seyde Arveragus, of° gentillesse,   *out of*
Hadde levere° dye in sorwe and in distresse   *rather*
Than that his wyf were of hir trouthe fals.
The sorwe° of Dorigen he tolde hym, als,°   890   *sorrow   also*
How looth hir° was to ben a wikked wyf,   *loath she*
And that she levere had° lost that day hir lyf,   *would rather have*
And that hir trouthe° she swoor thurgh innocence; *promise*
She nevere erst° hadde herd speke of apparence.° *before   apparition*
"That made me han of hire so greet pitee;
And right° as freely as he sente hir me,   *just*
As frely sente I hire to hym agayn.
This al and som.° Ther is namoore to sayn."   *This is part and all*

This philosophre answerde, "Leeve° brother,   *Dear*
Everich° of yow dide gentilly til oother.   900   *Each*
Thow art a squyer, and he is a knyght;
But God forbede, for his blisful myght,
But if a clerk° koude doon a gentil dede   *Unless a scholar*
As wel as any of yow, it is no drede.°   *doubt*

"Sire, I relesse° thee thy thousand pound,   *release*
As° thow right now were cropen° out of the ground, *Just as if   only now had crept*
Ne nevere er° now ne haddest knowen me.   *And never before*
For, sire, I wol nat take a peny of thee
For al my craft, ne noght° for my travaille.   *nor anything*
Thow hast y-payed wel for my vitaille.°   910   *victuals*
It is ynogh, and fare wel. Have good day."
And took his hors, and forth he goth his way.

Lordynges, this questioun than wol I aske now,
Which was the mooste free,° as thynketh° yow?   *generous   it seems to*
Now, telleth me, er that ye ferther wende.
I kan° namoore. My tale is at an ende.   *can say*

THE PHYSICIAN'S TALE

[C 1–286. Here omitted.]

The state of medicine in Chaucer's day was such that the Physician could certainly have regaled the company by a disclosure of the ways of his profession as
lively as the later confession made by the Canon's Yeoman concerning the tricks
of alchemy. But the *Physician's Tale* commences without introductory link or narrator's preface. Apparently, like the Man of Law, and perhaps with equally good
reason, the Physician prefers to preserve a complete silence about his own profession and to tell, instead, a safe moral tale.

In keeping with Chaucer's comment in the *General Prologue* that the Physician's
study is but little on the Bible, his tale does not contain quite the same piety as
characterizes the *Man of Law's Tale*, and its plot is derived from a non-Christian
source, the Roman history of Livy. It relates how as a last desperate measure in
order to escape from the lust of an evil judge, a beautiful maiden allows her own
father to kill her. Though the material is melancholy in the extreme, it appealed
also to John Gower, who used it to emphasize the value of chastity; and even the
critical Host seems to be satisfied with it.

LINK

[C 287–328. Here translated.]

Our Host began to swear as if he were mad. "Harrow!" said he. "By the
nails of the Cross and the blood of Christ, this was a false churl and a false
judge. May there come to these judges and their advocates as shameful a
death as the heart can devise! But in any case, alas, the innocent girl is
dead. Alas, too dearly did she pay for her beauty. That's why I always say,
you can see that the gifts of Fortune and of Nature are the cause of many
a person's death. From the two gifts that I'm speaking of just now, we often
get more harm than benefit.

"But truly, my own master dear, this is a pathetic tale to listen to. However, pass on. It's no matter. God save your good self, I pray, and also
your urinals and chambers, your Hippocras and your Galiones too,[1] and
every boxful of your electuaries. May God and Our Lady St. Mary bless

---

[1] *Hippocras* is a wine-cordial named after Hippocrates. The term *Galiones* is completely
unknown. Presumably the Host has heard the Physician mention the fact that he has
studied "old Ypocras . . . and Galyen" (*General Prologue*, 431) and therefore coins the
second word for the occasion.

them. As I may prosper, you're a fine man and like a prelate, by St. Runyan. Didn't I speak well? I can't use technical terms, but I certainly know that you've made my heart so sorry that I've almost caught the cardinacle.[1] By the holy bones, unless I have a remedy, or else a drink of moist and corny ale, or hear a merry tale right away, my heart will be lost out of pity for this maid. You, good friend, you, Pardoner," he said. "Tell us some sport or jokes right now."

"It shall be done," said he, "by St. Runyan, but first," said he, "at this ale house I'll drink and eat some cake."

But immediately the gentry began to cry, "No. Don't let him tell us any ribaldry. Tell us something moral so that we may learn some understanding, and then we'll gladly listen."

"I agree, certainly," said he, "but I must think of something respectable while I drink."

THE PARDONER'S PROLOGUE

[C 329–462]

Unlike the Physician, the Pardoner shows no reticence about his profession; in fact, he rivals the Wife of Bath in his willingness to tell all. But the two self-confessed sinners differ in every other respect. Although some of the pilgrims may disagree with the Wife's opinions, all of them appear to enjoy her personality; but the only person who seems to consider the Pardoner congenial is that most unlovable character, the Summoner, whose very face, as Chaucer says, would frighten children.

The Wife may be sinful, but her sins are healthy. The Pardoner, on the other hand, according to the *General Prologue*, is like "a gelding or a mare." Medieval medical men would have classified him as a eunuch from birth, and Chaucer is perhaps also hinting in the *Prologue* that his friendship with the Summoner may be of a homosexual nature. Understandably, the pilgrims shun their abnormal companion. No one deigns to make any comment when he interrupts the Wife of Bath in order to ask her for advice on marriage, or when he later boasts that he has a jolly wench in every town; and when the Host invites him to tell a tale, the pilgrims instinctively object that he will narrate some distasteful piece of ribaldry. Then, after they have discovered that he is not obsessed in his tale by ribaldry but by the avarice associated with his profession, the Host vituperates him with unusual violence, chiefly on the grounds of his personal disabilities.

In further contrast, the Wife of Bath's dominant characteristic is her candor, whereas the Pardoner's is his hypocrisy. Gifted in mind but alienated from his

---

[1] *Cardinacle* is a blunder for *cardiacle*, "heart disease."

fellows both by his personality and by his profession, which was in Chaucer's
age condemned by pious Catholic and fervent Wyclifite alike, he victimizes society
ruthlessly, cynically, and skillfully. Yet his talents are pathetically wasted. If it is
true to say that, in the portrait of the Wife, the comedy contains tragic under-
tones, then it is equally true to say that, in the portrait of the Pardoner, the comic
elements are almost submerged in the tragic. He may seem to be merry, but his
mirth is of a nervous kind which must be supported by frequent draughts of "corny
ale." He has never attained, and never can attain, the Wife of Bath's wholesome
joie de vivre.

Chaucer's treatment of the Pardoner is complex. He borrows his portrait of
the hypocritical ecclesiastic in part from an allegorical figure, called False Sem-
blance, who is satirized in the *Romance of the Rose.* He transforms this allegorical
prototype into a real individual, but he is not content with the effect until he
has intensified the satire by cruelly adding to the portrait the features of a physical
degenerate. Yet Chaucer still seems prepared to exercise toleration and good
nature, for he allows the courteous Knight to restore peace at the end of the scene
with a request that all should laugh and play as they had before.

"Lordynges," quod° he, "in chirches whan I preche,	said
I peyne me° to han an hauteyn° speche	take pains dominating
And rynge it out as round as gooth a belle,	
For I kan° al by rote that I telle.	know
My theme is alwey oon,° and ever was —	always one
Radix malorum est cupiditas.°	The root of evils is avarice
First I pronounce whennes that° I come,	whence
And thanne my bulles° shewe I alle and some.°	papal documents one and all
Oure lige lordes° seel on my patente,	liege lord's (bishop's)
That shewe I first, my body to warente,°	10	person to safeguard
That no man be so bold, ne° preest ne° clerk,	neither nor
Me to destourbe of Cristes holy werk.	
And after that thanne telle I forth my tales.	
Bulles of popes and of cardynales,	
Of patriarkes and bisshopes I shewe,	
And in Latyn I speke a wordes fewe	
To saffron with my predicacioun,°	flavor my preaching with
And for to stire hem° to devocioun.	stir them
Thanne shewe I forth my longe cristal stones°	glass cases
Y-crammed ful of cloutes° and of bones;	20	rags
Relikes been° they, as wenen° they echon.°	are believe each one
Thanne have I in latoun° a shulder-bon	(set) in copper alloy

Which that was of° an holy Jewes sheep.[1]   Which was taken from
'Goode men,' I seye, 'tak of my wordes keep.°   heed
If that this boon be wasshe° in any welle,   washed
If cow, or calf, or sheep, or oxe swelle,
That any worm hath ete or worm y-stonge,[2]
Taak water of that welle, and wassh his° tonge,   its
And it is hool anoon.° And forther moor,   cured at once
Of pokkes, and of scabbe, and every soor   30
Shal every sheep be hool that of this welle
Drynketh a draughte. Taak kepe, eek, what° I telle: heed, also, of what
If that the goode man that the bestes oweth°   owns
Wol every wyke,° er that the cok hym croweth,°   week before the cock crows
Fastynge, drynken of this welle a draughte,
As thilke° holy Jew oure eldres taughte,   that same
Hise bestes and his stoor° shal multiplie.   stock
   'And, sire, also it heeleth jalousie,
For thogh a man be falle° in jalous rage,   fallen
Lat maken° with this water his potage,   40   Have made
And nevere shal he moore his wyf mystriste,°   mistrust
Thogh he the soothe° of hir defaute wiste,°   truth fault should know
Al° hadde she taken preestes two or thre.   Even if
   'Heere is a miteyn,° eek,° that ye may se.   mitten also
He that his hand wol putte in this mitayn,
He shal have multiplyyng of his grayn
Whan he hath sowen, be it whete or otes,
So that° he offre pens or ellis grotes.°   Provided that else groats (four pennies)
   'Goode men and wommen, o° thyng warne I   one
   yow,
If any wight° be in this chirche now   50   person
That hath doon synne horrible, that he
Dar° nat for shame of it y-shryven° be,   Dare confessed and absolved
Or any womman, be she yong or old,
That hath y-maked hir housbond cokewold,°   deceived her husband
Swich° folk shal have no power, ne° no grace,   Such nor
To offren to my relikes in this place.

---

[1] The sheep's shoulder-bone was used in antiquity and in the Middle Ages for divining the future; and, to the credulous, the Pardoner's relic would have seemed particularly efficacious, for, according to his claims, it had once belonged to some "holy Jew," that is, some Old Testament hero.

[2] ". . . which has eaten any (injurious) worm, or which any worm has stung. . . ." The word *worm* in earlier usage meant "serpent" as well as "garden worm."

And who so° fyndeth hym° out of swich blame,   whoever himself
They wol come up and offre, a° Goddes name,   in
And I assoille° hym by the auctoritee°   absolve authority
Which that by bulle y-graunted was to me.'   60
   By this gaude° have I wonne yeer by yeer   trick
An hundred mark° sith° I was pardoner.   marks (13s.4d.) since
I stonde° lyk a clerk° in my pulpet;   stand ecclesiastical scholar
And whan the lewed° peple is doun y-set,   ignorant
I preche so as ye han° herd bifore,   have
And telle an hundred false japes° more.   frauds
Thanne peyne I me° to strecche forth the nekke,   I take pains
And est and west upon the peple I bekke,°   nod
As dooth a dowve° sittyng on a berne.°   dove barn
Myne handes and my tonge goon° so yerne°   70   go eagerly
That it is joye to se my bisynesse.°   industriousness
Of avarice and of swich cursednesse
Is al my prechyng, for to make hem free
To yeven hir° pens, and namely° unto me.   give their particularly
For myn entente is nat but for to wynne,°   only to gain
And no thyng° for correccioun of synne.   in no way
I rekke° nevere, whan that° they been beryed,°   care when are buried
Thogh that hir soules goon a-blakeberyed.¹
For certes° many a predicacioun°   certainly sermon
Comth ofte tyme of yvel entencioun,   80
Som for plesance° of folk and flaterye,   the satisfying
To been avanced° by ypocrisye,   advanced
And som for veyne glorie, and som for hate.
For whan I dar noon oother weyes debate,°   way contend
Thanne wol I stynge hym with my tonge smerte°   sharp
In prechyng, so that he shal nat asterte°   avoid
To been defamed falsly, if that he
Hath trespased to my bretheren or to me.
For thogh I telle noght his propre name,
Men shal wel knowe that it is the same   90
By signes and by othere circumstances.
Thus quyte° I folk that doon° us displesances;   repay cause
Thus spitte I out my venym under hewe°   pretext
Of holynesse, to seme holy and trewe.
   But shortly myn entente I wol devyse°:   explain

¹ "Though their souls go blackberrying," that is, go wandering without direction.

I preche of no thyng but for coveityse.°   covetousness
Therfore my theme is yet, and evere was,
Radix malorum est cupiditas.
Thus kan I preche agayn° that same vice   against
Which that I use, and that is avarice.   100
But though myself be gilty in that synne,
Yet kan I maken oother folk to twynne°   depart
From avarice, and soore° to repente.   sorely
But that is nat my principal entente.
I preche no thyng but for coveitise.°   covetousness
Of this matere it oghte ynow° suffise.   enough
     Thanne telle I hem ensamples° many oon°   (illustrative) examples   a one
Of olde stories longe tyme agoon,°   past
For lewed° peple loven tales olde.   ignorant
Swiche thynges kan they wel reporte° and holde.°   repeat   remember
What! Trowe° ye that, whiles° I may preche,   111   Believe   while
And wynne gold and silver for° I teche,   for what
That I wol lyve in poverte wilfully°?   willingly
Nay, nay! I thoghte it nevere, trewely.
For I wol preche and begge in sondry landes;
I wol nat do no labour with myne handes,
Ne° make baskettes and lyve ther-by,   Nor
By cause I wol nat beggen ydelly.°   in vain
I wol noon of the apostles countrefete.°   imitate
I wol have moneye, wolle,° chese, and whete,   120   wool
Al° were it yeven° of the pouereste° page,   Though   given   poorest
Or of the pouereste widwe° in a village,   widow
Al° sholde hir children sterve° for famyne.   Though   perish
Nay, I wol drynke licour of the vyne
And have a joly wenche in every toun.
     But herkneth, lordynges, in conclusioun.
Youre likyng is that I shal telle a tale.
Now have I dronke a draghte of corny ale,
By God, I hope I shal yow telle a thyng
That shal by resoun been at youre likyng.   130
For, thogh myself be a ful vicious man,
A moral tale yet I yow telle kan,
Which I am wont° to preche for to wynne.°   accustomed   gain
Now, holde youre pees.° My tale I wol bigynne."   peace

THE PARDONER'S TALE

[C 463-968]

The plot of the moral tale which the Pardoner has promised to tell is derived ultimately from a widely known folktale, versions of which had been employed by pagan and Christian alike for purposes of edification or entertainment long before Chaucer wrote the *Canterbury Tales*. The present narrator, who is, as he has himself confessed, a "vicious man," has ingeniously converted it into a sermon, through which he has evidently reaped profit many times. Ironically, the sermon is based on his favorite text, "The love of money is the root of all evil; which while some coveted after, they have erred from the faith, and pierced themselves through with many sorrows." (I *Tim.*, vi, 10)

Medieval usage normally required that the preacher should interpret his text before he adduced any illustrations or applied its doctrine to the situation of the listeners, but the Pardoner is not concerned with theological subtleties, which would at any rate be unlikely to appeal to the unlearned. Besides, he can hardly afford to encourage his victims to examine his reasoning at all closely. "Money is bad," he argues, in effect, "so give it away to me." But, if given the occasion to reflect, they might ask the embarrassing question, "Why to you?"

He therefore hastens to stir their hearts through the use of the least intellectual device proper to a sermon, namely, the *exemplum* or illustrative anecdote. "Ignorant people love old tales," he has cynically remarked. "They can easily grasp and repeat such things." And his dramatic and alarming narrative is well designed to induce impressionable listeners to abandon their worldly wealth for the sake of their souls' salvation.

An honest preacher might also have felt it desirable to expound the application of his text more exhaustively than the Pardoner does (ll. 442-453). But here again the Pardoner hopes to elicit an unreflecting response, and he is evidently so confident in the power of his preaching that he impudently tests the effect of his sermon on his companions, to whom he has, only a moment before, boasted of his successful deceptions. Perhaps, of course, he is only jesting. Chaucer does not tell us. But Chaucer is always willing to satirize both the deceiver and the deceived, and it is possible that he has seen so many well-meaning but overcredulous people victimized by such practices that he gleefully seizes the occasion to ridicule the gullibility of his contemporaries.

In Flaundres whilom° was a compaignye	Flanders once
Of yonge folk that haunteden° folye,	practiced
As° riot, hasard,° stewes,° and tavernes	Such as dicing brothels
Where-as° with harpes, lutes, and gyternes°	Where guitars
They daunce and pleyen at dees° bothe day and nyght,	dice

And ete also and drynke over hir myght,°   beyond their capacity
Thurgh which they doon° the devel sacrifise do
Withinne that develes temple in cursed wise° manner
By superfluytee abhomynable.
Hir othes been° so grete and so dampnable 10 Their oaths are
That it is grisly for to heere hem swere;
Oure blissed Lordes body they to-tere°;   tear apart
Hem thoughte that Jewes rente hym noght
 ynough! ¹
And ech° of hem at otheres synne lough.°   each laughed
And right anon thanne comen tombesteres,° would come dancing-girls
Fetys° and smale,° and yonge frutesteres,° Trim slender fruit-sellers
Syngeres with harpes, baudes,° wafereres,° bawds confectioners
Whiche been the verray develes officeres,
To kyndle and blowe the fyr of lecherye,
That is annexed unto glotonye.   20
The Holy Writ take I to my witnesse
That luxurie° is in wyn and dronkenesse. excess
 Lo how that dronken Loth° unkyndely° Lot (*Gen.*, xix, 33, 35)
               unnaturally
Lay by his doghtres two unwityngly.°   unknowingly
So dronke he was, he nyste° what he wroghte.° didn't know was doing
Herodes,° whoso° wel the stories soghte, Herod (*Matt.*, xiv) as one
              would know who
Whan he of wyn was replet° at his feste, overfilled
Right at his owene table he yaf° his heste° gave order
To sleen° the Baptist John ful giltelees. slay
Senec° seith a good word, doutelees. 30 Seneca
He seith he kan no difference fynde
Bitwix a man that is out of his mynde
And a man which that is dronkelewe,° drunken
But° that woodnesse y-fallen° in a shrewe Except madness occurring
Persevereth lenger than dooth dronkenesse.
O glotonye, ful of cursednesse,
O cause first of oure confusioun°!   ruin
O original of oure dampnacioun,
Til Crist hadde boght us with his blood agayn°! redeemed (*boght . . . agayn*)
Lo how deere,° shortly for to sayn,° 40 dearly say

¹ "It seemed to them that the Jews did not rend him enough!" In his tale the Parson admonishes his listeners: ". . . swear not so sinfully, dismembering Christ by soul, heart, bones, and body. For certainly it would seem that you think that the cursed Jews did not dismember the precious person of Christ enough, but that you should dismember him more."

Aboght° was thilke° cursed vileynye.   Paid for   that same
Corrupt was al this world for glotonye.
  Adam oure fader, and his wyf also,
Fro° Paradys to labour and to wo   From
Were dryven for that vice, it is no drede.°   doubt
For whil that Adam fasted, as I rede,
He was in Paradys; and whan that he
Eet° of the fruyt defended° on the tree,   Ate   forbidden
Anon° he was out cast to wo and peyne.   At once
O glotonye, on thee wel oghte us pleyne.°   50   should we complain
O, wiste° a man how manye maladies   knew
Folwen of° excesse and of glotonyes,   Follow from
He wolde been the moore mesurable°   moderate
Of his diete, sittyng at his table.
Allas, the shorte throte, the tendre mouth,
Maketh that, est and west and north and south,
In erthe, in eyr, in water, men to swynke ¹
To gete a glotoun deyntee mete and drynke.
Of this matere, O Paul, wel kanstow° trete.   can you
"Mete unto wombe,° and wombe eek° unto mete,   belly   also
Shal God destroyen bothe," as Paulus° seith.   61   Paul (I *Cor.*, vi, **13**)
Allas, a foul thyng is it, by my feith,
To seye this word, and fouler is the dede,
Whan man so drynketh of the white and rede°   red (wine)
That of his throte he maketh his pryvee°   privy
Thurgh thilke° cursed superfluitee.   that same
  The apostle° **wepyng** seith ful pitously,   Paul (*Phil.*, iii, **18, 19**)
"Ther walken manye of whiche yow toold have
    I, —
I seye it now wepyng with pitous voys —
They been° enemys of Cristes croys,   70   are
Of whiche° the ende is deth; wombe is hir° God."   whom   their
O wombe, O bely, O stynkyng cod,°   paunch
Fulfilled of donge and of corrupcioun,
At either ende of thee foul is the soun°!   sound
How greet labour and cost is thee to fynde°!   provide for
Thise cokes,° how they stampe, and streyne, and   cooks
    grynde,

---

¹ Chaucer here mixes two constructions: (1) *maketh that men swynke,* "brings about that
men toil"; and (2) *maketh men to swynke,* "makes men toil."

And turnen substaunce into accident,[1]
To fulfillen° al thy likerous talent.° — *satisfy unrestrained appetite*
Out of the harde bones knokke they
The mary,° for they caste noght awey   80 — *marrow*
That may go thurgh the golet° softe and soote.° — *gullet sweet*
Of spicerie of leef, and bark, and roote
Shal been his sauce y-maked, by delit° — *delight*
To make hym yet a newer appetit.
But, certes,° he that haunteth swiche delices° — *certainly pursues such delights*
Is deed whil that° he lyveth in tho° vices. — *dead while those*
  A lecherous thyng is wyn, and dronkenesse
Is ful of stryvyng° and of wrecchednesse. — *strife*
O dronke man, disfigured is thy face,
Sour is thy breeth, foul artow° to embrace,   90 — *are you*
And thurgh thy dronke nose semeth the soun
As thogh thou seydest ay° "Sampsoun, Sampsoun." — *always*
And yet, God woot,° Sampsoun drank nevere no — *knows*
  wyn.[2]
Thou fallest as it were a stiked swyn,° — *like a stuck pig*
Thy tonge is lost, and al thyn honeste cure.° — *care for honor*
For dronkenesse is verray sepulture° — *the very burial*
Of mannes wit° and his discrecioun. — *understanding*
In whom that° drynke hath dominacioun, — *whom*
He kan no conseil kepe, it is no drede.° — *doubt*
Now kepe yow fro the white and fro the rede,   100
And namely fro° the white wyn of Lepe — *particularly from*
That is to selle in Fisshstrete° or in Chepe.° — *Fish Street (London) Cheapside*
This wyn of Spaigne [3] crepeth subtilly
In othere wynes growynge faste by,° — *near by*
Of which ther riseth swich fumositee° — *such spirituous vapors*
That, whan a man hath dronken draghtes thre,
And weneth° that he be at hoom in Chepe, — *believes*
He is in Spaigne right at the toune of Lepe,
Nat at the Rochel° ne at Burdeux° toun.   109 — *La Rochelle Bordeaux (France)*
And thanne wol he seyn "Sampsoun, Sampsoun."

[1] ". . . turn substance into accident"; that is, convert the essential, "substantial" components which, according to contemporary philosophical teaching, were held to cause things to have appearance, into the temporary, "accidental" appearance of things.

[2] Samson had vowed the vow of a Nazarite never to drink wine.

[3] The strong wines of Lepe and of other Spanish vineyards, which were cheaper in England than the superior wines produced "faste by" in France, were evidently used to adulterate the more expensive vintages.

But herkneth, lordynges, o° word, I yow preye,   one
That alle the sovereyn actes, dar I seye,
Of victories in the Olde Testament,
Thurgh verray God, that is omnipotent,
Were doon in abstinence and in prayere.
Looketh° the Bible, and ther ye may it leere.°   Look at   learn
   Looke, Attila,[1] the grete conquerour,
Deyde in his sleep with shame and dishonour,
Bledyng at his nose in dronkenesse.
A capitayn sholde lyve in sobrenesse.   120
And over al this, avyseth yow° right wel   consider
What was comaunded unto Lamwel° —   Lemuel
Nat Samuel but Lamwel, seye I.
Redeth the Bible, and fynd it expresly
Of wyn-yevyng° to hem that han justise.   wine-giving
Namoore of this, for it may wel suffise.
   And now that I have spoken of glotonye,
Now wol I yow defenden hasardrye.°   forbid dicing
Hasard is verray moder of lesynges,°   the very mother of falsehood
And of deceite, and cursed forswerynges,°   130 perjuries
Blaspheme° of Crist, manslaughtre, and wast° also Blasphemy waste
Of catel° and of tyme; and forther mo°   substance   more
It is repreve° and contrarie of honour   reproach
For to ben holde° a commune hasardour.   To be held
And evere the hyer he is of estaat,
The moore is he holden desolat.
If that a prynce useth hasardrye,
In alle governaunce and policye
He is, as by° commune opynyoun,   by (*as by*)
Y-holde the lasse in reputacioun.   140
   Stilbon, that was a wys embassadour,
Was sent to Corynthe in ful gret honour
Fro Lacedomye° to make hire° alliaunce;   Lacedaemon (in Greece) their
And whan he cam, hym happed° par chaunce   it happened to him
That alle the gretteste that were of that lond
Pleiynge atte hasard he hem fond.°   found
For which, as soone as it myghte be,

---

[1] The Pardoner has here abruptly abandoned his generalization about Old Testament victories without attempting to provide examples. Attila, King of the Huns, died in 453, reputedly through drunkenness on his wedding night. In *Proverbs*, **xxxi**, the otherwise unknown King Lemuel (l. 122) is enjoined to avoid wine.

He stal° hym hoom agayn to his contree,   stole
And seyde, "Ther wol I nat lese° my name,   lose
N' I wol nat° take on me so greet defame   150 Nor will
Yow for to allie unto none hasardours.
Sendeth othere wise embassadours,
For, by my trouthe, me were levere° dye   I would rather
Than I yow sholde to hasardours allye.
For ye that been so glorious in honours
Shal nat allye yow with hasardours
As by° my wyl ne as by my tretee."   By
This wise philosophre thus seyde he.
    Looke eek that to the kyng Demetrius
The kyng of Parthes,° as the book seith us,   160 Parthia
Sente hym a paire of dees° of gold in scorn,   dice
For° he hadde used hasard ther-biforn°;   Because   previously
For which he heeld his glorie or his renoun
At no value or reputacioun.
Lordes may fynden oother manere° pley   sort of
Honeste ynow° to dryve the day awey.   enough
    Now wol I speke of oothes false and grete
A word or two, as olde bokes trete.
Greet sweryng is a thyng abhomynable,
And fals sweryng is yet moore reprevable.°   170 reprovable
The heighe God forbad sweryng at al.
Witnesse on Mathew°; but in special   *Matthew*, v, 34
Of sweryng seith the holy Jeremye,°   *Jeremiah*, iv, 2
"Thow shalt swere sooth° thyne othes and nat lye, truthfully
And swere in doom° and eek in rightwisnesse.°"   judgment   righteousness
But ydel° sweryng is a cursednesse.   vain
Bihoold and se that, in the firste table
Of heighe Goddes Hestes° honurable,   (Ten) Commandments
How that the Seconde Heste of hym is this:
"Take nat my name in ydel° or amys."   180 vain
Lo, rather he forbedeth swich sweryng
Than homycide or many a cursed thyng.
I seye that, as by ordre,° thus it standeth;   in order
This knowen, that hise Hestes understandeth,
How that the Seconde Heste of God is that.
And forther over, I wol thee telle al plat°   plainly
That vengeance shal nat parten° from his hous   depart (*Ecclesiasticus*, xxiii,
That of hise othes is to° outrageous.   11)
                      too

"By Goddes precious herte," and "By his nayles,"
And "By the blood of Crist that is in Hayles,°   190   (preserved) **at Hayles** (Gloucestershire)
Sevene is my chaunce, and thyn is cynk° and   five
    treye,°"   three
"By Goddes armes, if thow falsly pleye,
This daggere shal thurgh out thyn herte go," —
This fruyt cometh of the bicched bones° two,   cursed dice
Forsweryng, ire, falsnesse, homycide.
Now, for the love of Crist, that for us dyde,
Lete° youre othes, bothe grete and smale.   Restrain
But, sires, now wol I telle forth my tale.
    Thise riotoures° thre of whiche I telle,   profligates
Longe erst er pryme rong° of any belle,   200   before prime (9 A.M.) rang
Were set hem° in a taverne to drynke;   seated
And, as they sat, they herde a belle clynke°   clang
Biforn a cors° was caried to his° grave.   corpse (which) its
That oon° of hem gan° callen to his knave°:   One began to boy
"Go bet,°" quod° he, "and axe° redily   faster said ask
What cors is this that passeth heer forby.
And looke that thow reporte his name wel."
    "Sire," quod this boy, "it nedeth° never a del.°   is necessary one bit
It was me told er ye cam heer two houres.
He was, pardee,° an old felawe° of youres,   210   certainly companion
And sodeynly he was y-slayn to-nyght,°   last night
Fordronke,° as he sat on his bench upright.   Very drunk
Ther cam a pryvee° theef, men clepeth° Deeth,   secretive (whom) men call
That in this contree al the peple sleeth,°   slays
And with his spere he smoot his herte a-two,°   in two
And wente his wey withouten wordes mo.
He hath a thousand slayn, this pestilence.
And, maister, er ye come in his presence,
Me thynketh that it were necessarie
For to be war of swich an adversarie.   220
Beth° redy for to meete hym evere moore.°   Be always
Thus taughte me my dame.° I sey namoore."   mother
    "By seinte Marie," seyde this taverner,°   innkeeper
"The child seith sooth, for he hath slayn this yer,
Henne° over a myle, withinne a greet village,   Hence
Bothe man and womman, child, and hyne,° and   servant
    page.
I trowe° his habitacioun be there.   believe

To been avysed° greet wisdom it were,   *be prepared*
Er that he dide a man a dishonour."
    "Ye,° Goddes armes!" quod this riotour.   230   *Yes*
"Is it swich peril with hym for to meete?
I shal hym seke by wey and eek by strete,
I make avow to Goddes digne° bones.   *worthy*
Herkneth, felawes. We thre been al ones.°   *one*
Lat ech of us holde up his hand til° oother,   *to*
And ech of us bicome otheres brother,°   *the other's sworn brother*
And we wol sleen° this false traytour Deeth.   *slay*
He shal be slayn, he that so manye sleeth,
By Goddes dignytee, er it be nyght."
    Togidres° han thise thre hir trouthes plight° 240   *Together pledged their faith*
To lyve and dyen ech of hem for oother,
As thogh he were his owene y-bore° brother.   *born*
And up they stirte,° al dronken in this rage,   *sprang*
And forth they goon towardes that village
Of which the taverner hadde spoke biforn.
And many a grisly ooth thanne han they sworn,
And Cristes blessed body they to-rente.°   *tore to pieces*
Deeth shal be deed, if that they may hym hente°!   *catch*
    Whan they han goon nat fully half a myle,
Right° as they wolde han treden° over a stile,   250   *Just have stepped*
An old man and a poure° with hem mette.   *poor*
This olde man ful mekely hem grette°   *greeted*
And seyde thus, "Now, lordes, God yow se.°"   *save*
    The proudeste of thise riotoures thre
Answerde agayn,° "What, carl°! With sory grace!°   *back churl Curse you!*
Why artow° al forwrapped° save thy face?   *are you wrapped up*
Why lyvestow° so longe in so greet age?"   *live you*
    This olde man gan looke° in his visage   *looked*
And seyde thus: "For° I ne kan nat fynde   *Because*
A man, thogh that I walked into Inde,°   260   *India*
Neither in citee ne in no village,
That wolde chaunge his youthe for myn age.
And, therfore, moot° I han myn age stille,   *must*
As longe tyme as it is Goddes wille.
    "Ne Deeth, allas, ne wol nat han° my lyf.   *have*
Thus walke I lyk a restelees caytyf,°   *wretch*
And on the ground, which is my modres° gate,   *mother's*
I knokke with my staf bothe erly and late,

And seye, 'Leeve° moder, leet me in.   Dear
Lo, how I vanysshe, flessh, and blood, and skyn. 270
Allas, whan shul my bones been at reste?
Moder, with yow wolde I chaunge my cheste,°   clothes-chest
That in my chambre longe tyme hath be,°   been
Ye,° for an heyre clowt° to wrappe me!'   Yes   hair rag
But yet to me she wol nat do that grace,
For which ful pale and welked° is my face.   withered
     "But, sires, to yow it is no curteisye
To speken to an old man vileynye
But° he trespase in word or elles° in dede.   Unless   else
In Holy Writ ye may yourself wel rede,   280
'Agayns° an old man, hoor° upon his heed,   Before hoary (*Lev.*, **xix**, 32)
Ye sholde arise.' Wherfore I yeve° yow reed°:   give   advice
Ne dooth° unto an old man noon harm now,   Don't do
Namoore than that ye wolde men dide to yow
In age, if that ye so longe abyde.
And God be with yow, wher° ye go° or ryde.   whether walk
I moot° go thider as° I have to go."   must where
     "Nay, olde cherl. By God, thow shalt nat so,"
Seyde this oother hasardour° anon.   gambler
"Thow partest° nat so lightly,° by seint John. 290   depart easily
Thow spak right now of thilke° traytour Deeth,   that same
That in this contree alle oure freendes sleeth.
Have here my trouthe,° as thow art his espye,°   oath spy
Telle wher he is, or thow shalt it abye,°   pay for
By God and by the holy sacrament!
For soothly thow art oon of his assent
To sleen° us yonge folk, thow false theef!"   slay
     "Now, sires," quod he, "if that yow be so leef°   eager
To fynde Deeth, turn up this croked wey.
For in that grove I lafte° hym, by my fey,°   300   left faith
Under a tree, and ther he wol abyde.
Nat for youre boost he wol hym° no thyng hyde.   himself
Se ye that ook°? Right ther ye shal hym fynde.   oak
God save yow, that boghte agayn° mankynde,   redeemed
And yow amende." Thus seyde this olde man.
And everich° of thise riotoures ran   each
Til they came to that tree, and ther they founde
Of floryns° fyne of gold y-coyned rounde   florins (coins)
Wel ny an eighte° busshels, as hem thoughte.°   Very nearly eight it seemed
                                                          to

No lenger thanne° after Deeth they soughte;   310   then
But ech of hem so glad was of the sighte,
For that the floryns been so faire and brighte,
That doun they sette hem° by this precious hoord.   themselves
The worste of hem he spak the firste word.
    "Bretheren," quod he, "taak kepe° what I seye.   heed to
My wit° is greet, thogh that I bourde° and pleye.   understanding   jest
This tresor hath fortune unto us yeven,°   given
In myrthe and jolitee oure lyf to lyven.
And lightly° as it cometh, so wol we spende.   easily
By Goddes precious dignytee, who wende°   320   would have believed
Today that we sholde han so fair a grace?
But, myghte this gold be caried fro this place
Hoom to myn hous, or ellis unto youres —
For wel ye woot° that al this gold is oures —   know
Thanne were we in heigh felicitee.
But, trewely, by daye it may nat be.
Men wolde seyn° that we were theves stronge°   say   violent
And for oure owene tresor doon us honge.°   have us hanged
This tresor moste y-caried be° by nyghte   must be carried
As wisly and as slyly as it myghte.   330
Wherfore I rede° that cut° among us alle   advise   cuts
Be drawe, and lat se° wher the cut wol falle.   let see
And he that hath the cut, with herte blithe
Shal renne° to the toune, and that ful swithe,°   run   quickly
And brynge us breed and wyn ful pryvely.°   secretly
And two of us shul kepen subtilly°   guard craftily
This tresor wel; and if he wol nat tarie,
Whan it is nyght, we wol this tresor carie
By oon assent wher-as us thynketh° best."   where it seems to us
    That oon° of hem the cut broghte in his fest,° 340   The one   fist
And bad hem drawe and looke wher it wol falle,
And it fil° on the yongeste of hem alle,   fell
And forth toward the toun he wente anon.°   at once
And also° soone as that he was agon,°   as   gone
That oon of hem spak thus unto that oother:
"Thow knowest wel, thow art my sworn brother.
Thy profit wol I telle thee anon.
Thow woost° wel that oure felawe is agon,   know
And heere is gold, and that ful greet plentee,
That shal departed° been among us thre.   350   divided

But, nathelees,° if I kan shape it so   nevertheless
That it departed were among us two,
Hadde I nat doon a freendes torn° to thee?"   turn
    That oother answerde, "I noot° how that may be.   don't know
He woot° that the gold is with us tweye.°   knows   two
What shal we doon? What shal we to hym seye?"
    "Shal it be conseil°?" seyde the firste shrewe.°   secret   wretch
"And I shal tellen in a wordes fewe
What we shul doon, and brynge it wel aboute."
    "I graunte," quod that oother, "out of doute, 360
That, by my trouthe, I wol thee nat biwreye.°"   betray
    "Now," quod the firste, "thow woost° wel we   know
      be tweye,
And two of us shul strenger be than oon.
Looke, whan that he is set, that right anoon°   at once
Arys ¹ as though thow woldest with hym pleye,
And I shal ryve° hym thurgh the sydes tweye,°   stab   two
Whil that thow strogelest with hym as in game.
And with thy daggere looke thow do the same,
And thanne shal al this gold departed be,
My deere freend, bitwixe me and thee.   370
Thanne may we bothe oure lustes al fulfille,
And pleye at dees° right at oure owene wille."   dice
And thus acorded been thise shrewes tweye
To sleen° the thridde, as ye han herd me seye.   slay
    This yongeste, which that wente to the toun,
Ful ofte in herte he rolleth up and doun
The beautee of thise floryns newe and brighte.
"O Lord," quod he, "if so were that I myghte
Have al this tresor to myself allone,
Ther is no man that lyveth under the trone   380
Of God that sholde lyve so myrie as I!"
And atte laste the feend, oure enemy,
Putte in his thoght that he sholde poyson beye,°   buy
With which he myghte sleen his felawes tweye,
For-why° the feend foond° hym in swich lyvynge   Because   found
That he hadde leve° hym to sorwe brynge.   permission (from God)
For this was outrely° his ful entente,   entirely
To sleen hem bothe and nevere to repente.

  ¹ Chaucer here seems to have mixed two constructions: (1) *Looke that thou arise,* "see to it that you arise"; and (2) *Whan that he is set, arys,* "when he is set, arise."

And forth he goth — no lenger wolde he tarie —
Into the toun unto a pothecarie,° 390 apothecary
And preyed hym that he hym wolde selle
Som poysoun that he myghte his rattes quelle,° kill
And eek ther was a polcat° in his hawe,° weasel hedge
That, as he seyde, his capouns° hadde y-slawe,° capons killed
And fayn° he wolde wreke hym,° if he myghte, gladly avenge himself
On vermyn that destroyed° hym by nyghte. annoyed
    The pothecarie answerde, "And thow shalt have
A thyng that, also° God my soule save, as
In al this world ther is no creature
That ete° or dronke hath of this confiture° 400 eaten preparation
Nat but the montaunce° of a corn° of whete, quantity grain
That he ne shal his lyf anoon forlete.° lose
Ye,° sterve° he shal, and that in lasse while Yes die
Than thow wolt goon a paas° nat but a myle, walk at footpace
The poysoun is so strong and violent."
    This cursed man hath in his hond y-hent° taken
This poysoun in a box, and sith° he ran then
Into the nexte strete unto a man
And borwed of hym large botels thre,
And in the two his poyson poured he. 410
The thridde he kepte clene for his drynke,
For al the nyght he shoop hym for to swynke° intended to work
In cariyng of the gold out of that place.
And whan this riotour — with sory grace!° — curse him!
Hadde filled with wyn hise grete botels thre,
To hise felawes agayn repaireth he.
    What nedeth it to sermone of it moore?
For right as they hadde cast° his deeth bifore, planned
Right so they han hym slayn, and that anon. 419
And whan that this was doon, thus spak that
    oon:
"Now lat us sitte, and drynke, and make us
    merye,
And afterward we wol his body berye."
And with that word it happed hym par cas° he happened by chance
To take the botel ther° the poysoun was, where
And drank, and yaf° his felawe drynke also, gave
For which anon they storven° bothe two. died
    But, certes,° I suppose that Avycen certainly

Wroot nevere in no canon ne in no fen [1]
Mo wonder signes° of empoysonyng   429   More wonderful symptoms
Than hadde thise wrecches two er hir° endyng.   before their
Thus ended been thise homicides two,
And eek the false empoysonere also.
    O cursed synne of alle cursednesse!
O traytours homicide! O wikkednesse!
O glotonye, luxurie, and hasardrye!
Thou blasphemour of Crist with vileynye
And othes grete of usage° and of pryde°!   habit   ostentation
Allas, mankynde, how may it bityde
That to thy Creatour, which that thee wroghte°   made
And with his precious herte-blood thee boghte, 440
Thow art so fals and so unkynde,° allas?   unnatural
    Now, goode men, God foryeve° yow youre tres-   forgive
        pas,
And ware yow fro° the synne of avarice.   beware of
Myn holy pardoun may yow alle warice,°   cure
So° that ye offre nobles° or sterlynges,°   Providing   nobles (6s.8d.)
                                                          silver pennies
Or elles silver broches, spones, rynges.
Boweth youre heed under this holy bulle!
Cometh up, ye wyves! Offreth of youre wolle°!   wool
Youre name I entre here in my rolle anon;
Into the blisse of hevene shul ye gon.   450
I yow assoille,° by myn heigh power,   absolve
Yow that wol offre, as clene and eek as cler
As ye were born. — And lo, sires, thus I preche.
And Jesu Crist, that is oure soules leche,°   leech (physician)
So graunte yow his pardoun to receyve,
For that is best. I wol yow nat deceyve.

Epilogue

    "But, sires, o° word forgat I in my tale.   one
I have relikes and pardon in my male°   wallet
As faire as any man in Engelond,
Whiche were me yeven by the Popes hond.   460
If any of yow wol, of° devocioun,   out of
Offren and han myn absolucioun,

---

[1] Avicenna, the eleventh-century Arabian philosopher, was the author of a widely studied work on medicine, divided into *fens* or sections, which contained the *canons* or rules of procedure appropriate to various illnesses, including poisoning.

Com forth anon, and kneleth here adoun,
And mekely receyveth my pardoun;
Or ellis taketh pardoun, as ye wende,°   travel
Al newe and fressh at every myles ende,
So° that ye offren, alwey newe and newe,°   Providing   again and again
Nobles or pens whiche that been goode and trewe.
It is an honour to everich° that is heer   each one
That ye mowe° have a suffisant° pardoner   470   can   adequate
T'assoille° yow, in contree as ye ryde,   To absolve
For aventures° whiche that may bityde.   incidents
Peraventure° ther may falle oon or two   Perhaps
Doun of° his hors, and breke his nekke atwo.   off
Looke which° a seuretee° is it to yow alle   what   security
That I am in youre felaweship y-falle,°   fallen
That may assoille yow, bothe moore° and lasse,°   high   low
Whan that the soule shal fro the body passe.
I rede° that oure Hoost shal bigynne,   advise
For he is moost envoluped° in synne.   480   enveloped
Com forth, sire Hoost, and offre first anon,°   at once
And thow shalt kisse the relikes everychon,°   each one
Ye,° for a grote.° Unbokele anon thy purs."   Yes   groat (4d.)
    "Nay, nay!" quod he. "Thanne have I Cristes curs!
Lat be!" quod he. "It shal nat be, so thee'ch.°   may I prosper (thee ich)
Thow woldest make me kisse thyn olde breech,
And swere it were a relyk of a seint,
Thogh it were with thy fundement depeynt.°   discolored
But, by the croys which that Seint Eleyne fond,[1]
I wolde I hadde thy coylons° in myn hond   490   testicles
In stede of relikes or of seintuarie.°   holy objects
Lat kutte hem of!° I wol thee helpe hem carie.   Have them cut off!
They shul be shryned — in an hogges toord°!"   turd
    This Pardoner answerde nat a word;
So wrooth° he was, no word ne wolde he seye.   wrathful
    "Now," quod oure Hoost, "I wol no lenger pleye
With thee, ne with noon° oother angry man."   nor with any

---

[1] "by the cross which St. Helena found." Helena, the mother of Constantine, the first Christian Emperor of Rome, was credited with having rediscovered the true Cross in Jerusalem in 326. She was especially revered in England since local legend claimed her to be of British origin.

But right anon the worthy Knyght bigan,
Whan that he saugh that al the peple lough,°   were laughing
"Namoore of this, for it is right ynough.   500
Sire Pardoner, be glad and murye° of cheere.   merry
And ye, sire Hoost, that been to me so deere,
I pray yow that ye kisse the Pardoner.
And, Pardoner, I pray thee, drawe thee neer.
And, as we diden, lat us laughe and pleye."
Anon they kiste, and ryden° forth hir weye.   rode

THE SECOND NUN'S TALE

[G 1–553. Here omitted.]

Like the Nun's Priest, the Second Nun is also overshadowed in the *General
Prologue* by the Prioress whom she serves, and she takes no part in the conversation of the pilgrims. Chaucer does, however, provide some suggestion of her character by the earnestness and piety of the preface to her tale, and by her choice, as
her subject, of a saint's legend celebrating chastity. But he adds nothing except
the rime-royal verse form to his source, which he faithfully translates; and he
does not connect the tale either by linkage or by subject matter with any preceding
group.

LINK

[G 554–719. Here translated.]

When the life of St. Cecilia was finished, before we had ridden fully
five miles, at Boughton under Blean [1] a man overtook us, who was dressed
in black, and underneath he was wearing a white surplice. His hackney,
which was dapple gray, was sweating so, it was a wonder to be seen. It
looked as if it had raced three miles. And the horse, too, that his yeoman
was riding on was sweating so much that it could hardly move. The foam
stood high around its collar, and it was flecked like a magpie with foam.
A double bag lay across the man's crupper. Evidently he carried very
little finery. This worthy was riding light for summer, and in my heart I
began to wonder what he was till I noticed that his cloak was sewed to
his hood. So, after I had pondered long, I judged him to be a canon of

---

[1] About five miles from Canterbury.

some sort.[1] His hat hung down behind his back on a cord, for he had been riding at more than a trot or a pace. He had kept racing as if he were mad. He had a burdock leaf under his hood to hold back the sweat and to save his head from the heat, but it was a joy to see him sweat. His forehead dripped like a still full of plantain and pellitory.[2] And when he had come, he began to shout. "God save this jolly company," said he. "I've ridden fast for your sake," said he, "because I wanted to overtake you, to ride in this merry company."

His yeoman was also full of courtesy and said, "Gentlemen, I saw you ride this morning out of your inn and warned my lord and master here, who is very eager to ride with you for his amusement. He loves conversation."

"Friend, for your warning may God prosper you," said our Host then, "for it certainly seems that your lord is wise, and indeed I would judge so. He's very jovial also, I dare say. Can he tell some merry tale or two, with which to gladden this company?"

"Who, sir? My lord! Yes, yes, in truth. He knows of mirth and jollity plenty and more. Believe me, sir, if you knew him as well as I do, you'd marvel how well and how cunningly he can work, and that in various ways. He has undertaken many a great enterprise which would be very difficult for any of you here to bring about unless you'd learned how from him. As homely as he rides among you now, it would be for your profit if you knew him. You wouldn't exchange his acquaintance for a great deal of wealth. I'd wager all I have in my possession on that. He's a man of high discretion. I warn you well, he's an ingenious man."

"Well," said our Host, "I beg you, tell me then. Is he a scholar or not? Tell us what he is."

"No. He is greater than a scholar, indeed," said the Yeoman. "And in a few words, Host, I'll reveal you something of his craft. My lord, I say, has such skill — but you can't learn all his craft from me, even if I do help somewhat in his work — he has such skill, I say, that all the ground on which we ride till we come to Canterbury he could turn completely upside-down and pave it all with silver and with gold."

And when the Yeoman had told this to our Host, he said, "Blessings! It's a wonderfully strange thing to me, since your lord has such high prudence, for which men should hold him in reverence, that he cares so

---

[1] Canons were, like monks, dedicated to a religious life but were much less restricted in matters of residence and discipline. For some families of canons the prescribed traveling attire consisted of cassock, linen surplice, and black cape.

[2] Plantain, a soothing herb, and wall pellitory, an irritant, were distilled to make medicinal extracts.

little for his presentability. His oversmock isn't worth a mite, in fact, for a man such as he. As I may thrive, it's all dirty, and torn to shreds, besides. Why is your lord so sluttish, I beg you, when he has the power to buy better cloth, if his actions are in keeping with your words? Tell me that, that's what I ask."

"Why?" said the Yeoman. "Why do you ask me? God help me, for he'll never prosper. But I won't admit what I say, so keep it secret, I beg you. Really, I believe, he is too wise. When something is overdone, it won't stand the test properly, as scholars say; it becomes a vice. And so, in this respect, I consider him foolish and ignorant, for when a man has too great a mind, it often happens that he misuses it. So does my lord, and it grieves me sorely. God amend it. I can't tell you any more."

"No matter, good Yeoman," said our Host. "Since you know about the cunning of your lord, tell how he works, I beg you heartily, since he's so clever and shrewd. Where do you live, if it can be told?"

"In the suburbs of a town," said he, "lurking in corners and dead-end lanes where by nature robbers and thieves make their secret, frightened residence. Like those that dare not show their presence, so we fare, if I'm to tell the truth."

"Now," said our Host, "let me talk to you still more. Why are you so discolored in the face?"

"By Peter," said he, "God grant it ill favor. I'm so accustomed to blow in the fire that it's changed my color, I suppose. I don't make a habit of peering in mirrors but labor hard and learn how to transmute metals into gold. We're always blundering and gazing in the fire, and, in spite of all that, we fail in what we desire, for we always fall short of our aim. To many people we perform an illusion and borrow gold, be it a pound or two, or ten or twelve, or many times more, and make them believe, at the very least, that from a pound we can make two, yet it's false. And we always have good hope of doing it, and we grope after it; but that knowledge lies so far beyond us that we can't overtake it, even though we had sworn we could, it slides away so fast. It'll turn us to beggars in the end."

While the Yeoman was talking thus, the Canon drew near him and heard everything the Yeoman said, for the Canon was always suspicious of men's talk. For Cato says that he who is guilty thinks that everything is certainly being said about him. That was the reason he drew so near to his Yeoman, to hear all his conversation. And he said to his Yeoman then as follows:

"Hold your peace, and speak no more, for if you do you'll pay for it dearly. You're slandering me here in this company and also revealing what you should hide."

"Yes," said our Host. "Tell on, whatever may happen. Don't bother a mite about all these threats."

"In faith," said he, "it's little I care."

And when the Canon saw there was no way out and that his Yeoman would tell his secrets, from very sorrow and shame he raced away.

"Ah," said the Yeoman, "now we'll have some fun. I'm now going to tell all that I can at once, since he has gone. May the foul fiend smite him, for never again am I going to meet with him for either penny or pound, I promise you. Before he die, may he that brought me first to that game have sorrow and shame, for, by my faith, the game to me is in earnest. That's how I feel, no matter what anyone says. And yet, for all my pain and all my grief, for all my sorrow, toil, and trouble, I could never at all give it up. Now would to God my brains could suffice to tell all that pertains to that craft, but nevertheless I'll tell you part. Since my lord has gone, I won't hold back. I'll reveal such things as I know."

THE CANON'S YEOMAN'S TALE

[G 720–1481. Translated on pp. 208–20.]

Chaucer introduces an unexpected variation in his narration by the sudden appearance of two new characters, and by the equally sudden disappearance of one of them, the fraudulent alchemist in threadbare canon's robes, whose deceptiveness is revealed to the suspicious Host by his companion. The leaden-faced Yeoman then ruefully describes his seven wasted years spent as the alchemist's assistant and narrates a most realistic tale, apparently original with Chaucer, about the tricks of alchemy.

As elsewhere, in his handling of scientific and pseudo-scientific matters, Chaucer shows that he is well acquainted with the scholarship, both ancient and recent, accepted as authoritative on the subject in his own day. Medieval thinkers assumed that all matter consisted of the four elements — fire, earth, air, and water — mixed in various proportions, gold being the noblest, silver the next, and so on. The aim of the alchemists was plausible enough, therefore, for they sought to isolate a fifth essence, the quintessence, by means of which they could transmute lesser metals into noble metals by altering the proportions of the elements they contained. But Chaucer also realized that alchemists, even if sincere, might be tempted to finance their costly experiments by exploiting the avarice of gullible acquaintances like the victim in the *Canon's Yeoman's Tale*.

LINK

[H 1–104. Here translated.]

You know, don't you, where there stands a little town called Bob-up-and-down under the Blean on the Canterbury road.[1] There our Host began to joke and play, and said, "Gentlemen, come, come. Dun is in the mire![2] Isn't there anyone here for request or for hire who'll awaken our companion away behind the rest? A thief could very easily rob and bind him. Look how he naps. Look, for Heaven's sake! He'll fall right off his horse. Is that a cook of London, curses on him! Have him come forward. He knows his penance, for he shall tell a tale, upon my faith, even if it isn't worth a bundle of hay. Wake up, you Cook," said he. "God give you sorrow! What ails you to be sleeping in the morning? Have you had fleas all night, or are you drunk, or have you labored with some wench all night, so that you can't hold up your head?"

The Cook, who was very pale, without a trace of red, said to our Host, "God bless my soul! Such a heaviness has fallen upon me, I don't know why, that I'd sooner sleep than have the best gallon of wine in Cheapside.[3]"

"Well," said the Manciple, "if it will help you, sir Cook, and not displease anyone that rides here in this company, and if our Host out of courtesy will agree, I'll excuse you of your tale just now. For, in faith, your face is very pale. Your eyes are dazed, too, it seems to me; and your breath, I know very well, smells very sour. That clearly shows you're indisposed. Certainly I'll not flatter you. See! Look how he yawns, this drunken fellow, just as if he wanted to swallow us right up. Keep your mouth shut, man, by your father's kin. May the Devil of Hell set his foot in it. Your cursed breath will infect us all. Fie, stinking swine! Fie! Shame upon you. Ah, gentlemen, take note of this fine man. Now, sweet sir, would you like to joust at the vane?[4] I should think you'd be in fine shape for it.

---

[1] Presumably a playful reference to Harbledown, near the Blean forest, less than two miles from Canterbury.

[2] The Host alludes to a game, the task in which is to move a heavy log by the help of as few contestants as possible. The game begins with the cry, "Dun is in the mire," that is, "our horse is stuck in the mud."

[3] London's shopping center.

[4] The contestant in the game of quintain, who was mounted on a horse, tried to hit the vane at one end of a pivoted bar with his spear without being hit afterwards by the weight hung at the other end of the bar.

I think you've drunk ape-wine, and that's the stage when men play with a straw.[1]"

And at this speech the Cook grew fierce and angry, and he began to nod hard at the Manciple for lack of words, and his horse threw him down, where he lay till some men picked him up. This was fine horsemanship for a cook! Alas that he hadn't held on to his ladle! And before he was back once more in his saddle, there was great shoving to and fro to lift him up, and much toil and care, so unwieldy was this pale, sorry ghost. And to the Manciple the Host then said, "By my salvation, since drink has power over this man, I think he'd tell his tale wretchedly. For, whether it was wine, or old ale, or new that he has drunk, he speaks in his nose and snorts hard, and he has a cold besides.

"Also, he has more than enough to do to keep himself and his nag out of the mire. And if he falls from his nag again soon, then we'll all have enough to do in lifting up his heavy, drunken body. Tell your tale. I'll not bother about him.

"But still, Manciple, you're certainly too rash, reproving him openly like that for his vice. Some other day he will perhaps call you in and bring you to lure.[2] I mean, he'll mention some little matter as if to find fault with your bookkeeping. That would be awkward, if it were put to the test!"

"Yes," said the Manciple. "That would be very serious. He could easily catch me in the snare that way. I'd sooner pay for the mare he rides on than have him fight with me. As I may thrive, I don't want to anger him. What I said, I spoke in jest. And do you know what? Here in a drinking horn I have a draught of wine from a ripe grape, indeed, and you're going to see a good joke right away. This Cook will drink it, if I can see to it. On peril of death, he won't say 'No' to me."

And in fact, to tell what happened, the Cook drank hard from the vessel. Alas, what need had he? He had drunk enough already. And when he had sounded this horn, he gave it back again. And the Cook was wonderfully pleased with the drink and thanked the Manciple as best as he could.

Then our Host began to laugh extremely loudly and said, "I clearly see that it's necessary to carry good drink with us wherever we go, for that

[1] Manciples, because of their professional interests as purchasing agents, were traditional enemies of cooks; and the present Manciple may have been intended to serve, moreover, as the butt of the Cook's unfinished tale. Here he takes advantage of his traditional rival and accuses him of suffering so early in the day from one of the last stages of drunkenness. Each temperament or "humor" had its own type of drunkenness, the sanguine man suffering from ape-wine. It was also said that the drinker passes successively through the stages of the lamb, the lion, the ape, and the sow.

[2] As a falconer attracts his hawk back to his wrist by showing a lure.

turns rancor and ill feeling into harmony and love, and appeases many a wrong. O Bacchus, blessed be your name, who can thus turn earnest into sport. Worship and thanks be to your deity. But you'll hear no more about this from me. Tell your tale, Manciple, I beg you."

"Well, sir," said he, "now listen to what I say."

THE MANCIPLE'S TALE

[H 105–362. Here omitted.]

The Manciple tells how the once white crow was turned to black because of its lack of discretion, and he then undertakes to interpret the story as an illustration of the lesson taught him by his mother. Oblivious of the quite uncalled-for abuse which he has just hurled at the defenceless Cook, he tells the pilgrims, in one of those moments of unconscious irony cherished by Chaucer, that his mother had always warned him, "Hold thy tongue, and think upon the crow."

As his source Chaucer uses a tale from Ovid's *Metamorphoses* which his friend John Gower also utilized in his *Lover's Confession*. Here, as with the *Wife of Bath's Tale*, a comparison of the methods followed by the two poets suggests that, while Gower knows how to adapt his borrowed material to his own expository theme, Chaucer knows how to adapt the story to the individuality of the narrator.

LINK

[I 1–74. Here translated.]

When the Manciple had finished his tale, the sun had descended so low from the line of the south that, to my eye, it was not so much as twenty-nine degrees in altitude. It was about four o'clock, I should think, for my shadow at that time and place was eleven feet long, or a little more or less, if one were to count as one foot the sixth part of my own height. And the moon's exaltation — Libra, I mean — was ascending as we were entering the end of a village.

Therefore our Host, since he was accustomed to direct our merry company in this matter, said as follows: "My lords each one, we now lack only one more tale. My judgment and my decree are fulfilled. I think we've heard from each rank. My ordinance is almost completely fulfilled. Pray God, may he truly prosper who has told this tale to us so pleasantly.

"Sir Priest," said he, "are you a vicar or are you a parson? On your faith, tell the truth. Whatever you may be, don't interrupt our sport, for everyone but you has told his tale. Unbuckle your wallet and show us what is in it, for certainly I should think by your appearance that you would knit up a great matter well. By God's bones, tell us a fable at once."

The Parson answered at once, "You'll get no fable told by me, for Paul in writing to Timothy reproves those that turn away from the truth and tell fables and such profanity. Why should I sow chaff from my fist when I can sow wheat if I care to? Therefore, I say, if you wish to listen to morality and virtuous matters and then will give me a hearing, I will very gladly out of reverence for Christ give you such permissible pleasure as I can. But, believe me, I am a Southerner. I can't compose rum-ram-ruff alliteratively [1]; and, God knows, I consider rime but little better. And therefore, if you wish, — I make no apology — I'll tell you a merry tale in prose to knit up all this feast and make an end. And may Jesus with his grace send me understanding to show you the way in this journey of that perfect, glorious pilgrimage which is called the heavenly Jerusalem. And, if you permit me, I'll begin at once on my tale. So, I pray you, give your opinion. I can say no more than that.

"But, nevertheless, I submit this meditation always to the correction of scholars, for I am not a learned reader. I remember only the general idea, believe me. I declare, therefore, that I am willing to stand corrected."

To this proposal we agreed at once, for it seemed to us the thing to do, to conclude on some virtuous note, and to give him opportunity and hearing. And we told our Host that he was to say to the Parson that we all wanted him to tell his tale. Our Host was spokesman for us all.

"Sir Priest," said he, "good fortune to you now. Say what you wish to, and we'll gladly listen." And then he said, "Tell us your meditation. But hurry," said he. "The sun will soon be down. Be fruitful, and that briefly. And may God send you his grace to do well."

THE PARSON'S TALE

[I 75–1080. Here omitted.]

The Parson's "merry tale in prose," as he jocularly calls it, recounts in systematic detail the sum and substance of two medieval treatises, one on Penitence and the other on the Seven Deadly Sins. Some modern critics, feeling that it provides an unsuitable means of "knitting up all this feast," have suggested that the tale was added at a later date to Chaucer's manuscripts by some pious scribe.

---

[1] Instead of rime the poetry composed in the Midlands of England during Chaucer's lifetime revived the Old English alliterative measure, as exemplified by the opening line of *Piers Plowman*: "In a summer season, when soft was the sun."

Yet, if we assume that it was recited just before the pilgrims reached Canterbury, it scarcely seems inappropriate to its fourteenth-century audience. The Host has promised that the pilgrims will celebrate their return from Canterbury to Southwark by joining in a supper party at his Inn, but he has not stipulated how they shall behave at Canterbury; and it is only reasonable to assume that even the roughest of the pilgrims would sense something of the solemnity of their approach to the revered shrine of St. Thomas Becket. The only really inappropriate circumstance is the time of day at which the Parson begins his tale — four o'clock in the afternoon, which is certainly a late hour to embark upon such an extensive address.

The sermon is appropriate, moreover, to what we have learned of the Parson both from the portrait in the *General Prologue* and from the two conversations contained in the links: the one after the *Man of Law's Tale* (p. 40), and the other preceding the *Parson's Tale*. By temperament he was not a popularizer. He repudiates fictitious compositions and poetic devices and may well feel that the *Pardoner's Tale* and the *Nun's Priest's Tale*, both of which might technically be called sermons, contain too much narrative and too little theology. But he also understands the minds of ordinary men and women. His sermon is couched in plain language and is full of everyday applications of the doctrine which it preaches. He complains, for instance, that the modern fashions in clothing encourage both shameful scantiness and wasteful superfluity, each in the wrong place. Those who wear overelaborate gowns, he says, allow the trailing ends to become "wasted, consumed, threadbare, and rotten" and in so doing waste a part which they might have saved for the poor. And he complains that the men who wear the tightly fitting hose fashionable in his day shamefully allow their buttocks to show "like the hinder part of a she-ape in the full of the moon." Such language does not belie Chaucer's characterization of the forthright Parson, who, we are told, was accustomed when necessary to rebuke any erring parishioner, whether he was of high or low degree.

Nor can we overlook the fact that at least several of the pilgrims may have been genuinely interested in theological exposition and would actually relish the *Parson's Tale* as a timely admonition. In the sermon, problems such as those raised by the Wife of Bath concerning marriage are solved in the perspective of that ideal order which may be said to epitomize the aspirations of medieval man, namely that order which would subordinate all human action to divine command.

CHAUCER'S PRAYER

[I 1081–1092. Here translated.]

Chaucer concludes the *Parson's Tale* by a brief prayer in prose, which here follows in translation. Modern editors have entitled this prayer *Chaucer's Retraction*, but there is no evidence that Chaucer himself gave it that title. Actually, it is something more than that. Having completed the Parson's "little treatise," to which he refers in his *Prayer*, Chaucer surveys his literary labors. He evidently feels that he has rounded out, at least in outline, his plan of the *Canterbury Tales;* and he has by now either abandoned or even forgotten his announced intention of preparing a set of tales for the pilgrims' homeward journey from Canterbury to London. But, in any case, what now concerns him is the spiritual merit and not the literary perfection of his work, and his piety forces him to renounce his secular compositions and to express satisfaction only with those of his writings which pertain to morality and devotion.

Some critics cannot believe that Chaucer would be willing to revoke his best compositions, and they therefore question the authenticity of the *Prayer*, but there is no real inconsistency in Chaucer's behavior, for he is simply acting, as any sincere Christian might, in accordance with the Parson's summons to repentance.

Now I beg all those who either hear or read this little treatise that, if there is anything in it that pleases them, they will thank our Lord Jesus Christ for it, from whom proceeds all knowledge and all good. And if there be anything that displeases them, I beg them also that they attribute it to my lack of skill and not to my good intentions, who would gladly have said better if I had had the skill. For our Book says, "All that is written is written for our doctrine." And that is my intention.

Therefore, I humbly beseech you, for the mercy of God, that you will pray for me that Christ have mercy on me and forgive me my trespasses, and especially that Christ from his great mercy forgive me the sin of translating and composing worldly vanities, which I revoke in my retractions, such as *Troilus and Criseyde*, the *House of Fame*, the *Legend of Good Women*, the *Book of the Duchess*, the *Parliament of Birds*, those of the *Canterbury Tales* that pertain to sin, the *Book of the Lion*,[1] and many another book, if I could remember them, and many a song, and many a lecherous lay.

But for the translation of Boethius's *Consolation* and for other books of saints' legends and homilies and morality and devotion I thank our Lord Jesus Christ and his Blessed Mother and all the saints of Heaven, beseeching them that, from henceforth unto my life's end, they send me grace to bewail my trespasses and to study for the salvation of my soul and that they grant me grace of true penitence, confession, and satisfaction so to do in this present life, through the benign grace of him who is King of Kings and Priest of all Priests and bought us with the precious blood of his heart, that I may be one of those at the Day of Judgment that shall be saved. *Qui cum Patre et Spiritu Sancto vivit et regnat in secula seculorum.*[2] Amen.

---

[1] This lost work was probably a translation of a poem by Guillaume de Machaut, from which Chaucer had borrowed elsewhere.

[2] "He who with the Father and Holy Spirit liveth and reigneth through all generations."

Three Canterbury Tales in Prose Translation

THE REEVE'S TALE

[B 3921–4324. Here translated. For commentary, see p. 35.]

At Trumpington, not far from Cambridge, there's a brook with a bridge over it, and on this brook there stands a mill. It's the real truth I'm telling you.

For many a day a miller lived there, who was as proud and gay as any peacock. He could pipe and fish and mend nets and turn cups on a lathe and shoot and wrestle well. He always carried a long cutlass on his belt, and the sword's blade was very sharp.[1] He carried a handsome dagger in his pouch. No one dared touch him for fear. He wore a Sheffield knife in his stocking. His face was round and his nose flat; his skull was as bald as an ape. He was an out-and-out wrangler at the market. No one dared to lay a hand on him, for he'd swear he'd pay for it at once. He was, for a fact, a thief of grain and meal, and a sly one at that, well accustomed to stealing. He was called proud Simkin.

He had a wife descended from nobility; her father was the parson of the town! And he gave many a pan of brass as dowry with her in order that Simkin would ally himself with the family.[2] She was reared in a convent, for Simkin didn't want any wife, as he said, who wasn't well nurtured and a maiden, in order to uphold his rank as yeoman. And she was as proud and pert as a magpie.

A pretty sight the two of them were. On holidays he would walk ahead of her with the tip of his hood wound around his head, and she walked behind in a red gown, and Simkin had a pair of hose of the same color.

No one dared call her anything but "dame." There was no passer-by so bold as to dare sport or toy with her unless he wanted to be stabbed by Simkin with cutlass, knife, or dagger, for jealous folk are always dangerous — or, at least, they'd like their wives to think so! And, besides, since she was somewhat besmirched, she was as dignified as ditch-water and full of pride and scorn. It seemed to her that a lady ought to respect her, what with her family connections and the education she'd acquired in the convent.

---

[1] According to the *General Prologue,* the Miller on the pilgrimage also could wrestle, wore a sword by his side, and played the bagpipes.

[2] The parson, who had broken his vows of celibacy, had to provide expensive kitchenware in order to marry off his illegitimate daughter.

Between them they had a daughter of twenty, and none other except for a half-year-old child. In the cradle it lay, and a fine lad it was. The wench was plump and well filled out, with a flat nose and eyes as blue as glass, broad buttocks and round, high breasts, and her hair was really lovely, I must say.

Because she was pretty, the parson of the town intended to make her the heir of his property and dwelling, and he was very particular about whom she should marry. His intention was to bestow her in high place with some family of distinguished ancestry, for Holy Church's goods must be spent upon Holy Church's blood, which is hereditary. Therefore he wanted to honor his holy blood even though he should devour Holy Church.

This miller had great milling rights, without question, including the right of grinding the wheat and malt of all the country around. In particular, there was a large college called Soler Hall in Cambridge,[1] and the college's wheat and malt too were ground at his mill. And once upon a time it happened that the business-agent of the college lay ill with a malady from which men seriously believed he would die. So the miller stole both meal and grain a hundred times more than before, for previously he stole only courteously, but now he was an outrageous thief. The college warden scolded and made a great to-do, but the miller didn't care a hang for that. He vaunted himself loudly and swore no such thing happened.

At that time there were two poor young scholars who lived in the hall which I mentioned. They were headstrong and eager for fun, and for sport and amusement they begged the warden persistently for permission to go to the mill for just a little while to see their grain being ground, and certainly they dared wager their necks that the miller wouldn't steal half a peck of grain from them by trickery or rob them by force. And at last the warden gave them permission. One was named John, and the other Alan. They were both born in the town of Strother,[2] far in the north, I can't just say where.

Alan made ready all his gear and at once threw the grain-sack on a horse. Then out set Alan the scholar and also John, with good swords and bucklers at their sides. John knew the way; he needed no guide. And at the mill he set the sack down. Alan spoke first. "Greetings, Simond, in good faith. How's your fair daughter and your wife?"

"Welcome, Alan, indeed," said Simkin, "and John also. How now? What are you doing here?"

---

[1] The name Soler ("Sunroom") Hall refers to King's Hall, Cambridge, which was founded shortly before Chaucer was born and was later merged with Trinity College.

[2] Strother was evidently located in Northumbria, although the place-name has now disappeared.

"Heavens, Simond," said John, "need has no equal. He must serve himself who has no servant, or he's a fool, as the scholars say. Our agent, I'm afraid, is going to die, the grinders are aching so hard in his head. And so I've come, and Alan too, to grind our grain and carry it home again. I beg you, speed us back again as fast as you can."

"In faith," said Simkin, "that shall be done. And what would you like to do while the job's under way?"

"By Heaven," said John, "I'll stand right at the hopper and see how the grain goes in. Indeed, I've never yet seen how the hopper wags back and forth."

Alan answered, "John, will you now? Well, indeed, then, I'll be beneath and see how the meal falls down into the trough. That'll be my amusement. For in faith, John, I must be of your kind. I'm as poor a miller as you!"

The miller smiled at their foolishness and thought to himself, "All this is just done for a trick. They think that no one can deceive them, but, by my thrift, I'll hoodwink them yet for all the cunning in their philosophy. The more quaint tricks they play, the more I'll steal while I'm at it. I'll still give them bran instead of flour. 'The greatest scholars are not the wisest men,' as the mare once said to the wolf.[1] I don't give a hoot for all their art."

Out of the door he went very secretly when he quietly noticed his time. He looked up and down till he found the scholars' horse standing tied under an arbor behind the mill, and right straight to the horse he went. He stripped off the bridle at once. And when the horse was loose, he set off for the marsh, where the mares run wild, and away with a "whee!" through thick and thin.

The miller went back. He said not a word but did his job and chatted with the scholars until their grain was well and properly ground. And when the meal was sacked and tied, John went out and found his horse gone. "Ho!" he shouted. "Help! Our horse is lost! Alan, for God's sake, step on your feet. Come on, man, right away. Our warden has lost his palfrey, alas."

Alan completely forgot both meal and grain; his economy had all gone out of his mind. "What!" he shouted. "What way's he gone?"

The wife came leaping in with a rush. "Oh, dear!" she said. "Your horse is off to the marsh with the wild mares as fast as he can go. Bad luck to the

---

[1] According to a well-known fable, the wolf asked the mare what was the price of her foal. "If you are a scholar and can read, come and see it on my hind hoof," she answered; and when he looked, she kicked him. Then she or, in other versions, her rueful victim, quoted the proverb mentioned here.

hand that tied him like that and to him that should have knotted the reins better!''

"Good grief," said John. "Alan, for Heaven's sake, put down your sword, and I will too. God knows, I'm as quick as a roe. By God, he'll not escape us both. Why didn't you put the nag in the barn? Curses! By God, Alan, you're a fool!''

The poor scholars ran as fast as they could toward the marsh, both Alan and John. And when the miller saw they were off, he took half a bushel of their flour and told his wife to go knead it into a cake. "I believe the scholars were afraid," he said. "A miller can still outwit a scholar for all his art. Yes, let them go their way. Look where he's going! Yes, let the children play. By George, they won't get him so easily.''

The poor scholars ran up and down with a "Hold, hold! Stop, stop! Here, here! Whoa there! You go whistle, and I'll watch for him here.''

But, in short, try as hard as they would, they couldn't catch their nag, he always ran so fast, till nighttime, when at last they caught him in a ditch.

Weary and wet as an animal out in the rain, poor John came back, and Alan with him. "Alas," said John, "the day I was born. Now we're driven to scorn and contempt. Our grain is stolen. They'll all call us fools, the warden and our fellows, and the miller in particular. Woe is me!''

Thus John complained as he went back to the mill with his steed in hand. The miller he found sitting by the fire, for it was nighttime; and they couldn't go farther but begged him, by the love of Heaven, for shelter and rest for their money.

The miller replied, "If there is any, such as it is, you shall have your share none the less. My house is cramped, but you've learned the art. By the arguments of logic *you* can make a place a mile broad out of twenty foot of space! Let's see now if this place'll suffice, or else make it roomier with talk, as your habit is.''

"Now, Simond," said John, "you're always joking, by St. Cuthbert,[1] and that's a good answer. I've heard tell that a man should take, of two things, either such as he finds or such as he brings. But I beg you especially, dear host, get us some food and drink, and entertain us, and truly we'll pay you in full. You can't lure hawks with an empty hand. Look, here's our silver ready to spend.''

The miller sent his daughter into town for ale and bread, and roasted a goose for them, and tied their horse so it wouldn't get loose again. And he

[1] Appropriately, John invokes the name of a fellow Northumbrian, St. Cuthbert, who was bishop of Lindisfarne in the seventh century and was widely commemorated in the north.

made up a bed, neatly spread with sheets and blankets, in his room, no more than ten or twelve feet from his own bed. His daughter had a bed all to herself nearby in the very same room. That's the best that could be done, and why? Because there wasn't any roomier accommodation in the place.

They supped, and they talked for amusement and kept drinking strong ale of the best. About midnight they went to bed.

The miller had oiled himself well. He'd lost his rosiness and turned all pale from drink. He hiccoughed, and he spoke through his nose as if he had asthma or a cold in the head. To bed he went, and with him went his wife. She was as light-headed and jovial as a jay, for she had wet her jolly whistle very well. The cradle was set at the foot of her bed so that she could rock it and give suck to the child. And when all that was in the crock was drunk, the daughter went right to bed. To bed went Alan and also John. There was no one else. No sleeping-draught they needed.

The miller had imbibed the ale so diligently that like a horse he snorted in his sleep, nor did he pay any attention to his tail behind. His wife played him an accompaniment full strong. You could hear their snoring a furlong off. The wench snored too for companionship.

Alan the scholar, who heard this melody, poked John and said, "Are you sleeping? Did you ever hear such a song before? Listen to that! Such a chorus among them all! May the wild fire [1] fall on their bodies! Who ever listened to such an uncanny thing? Indeed, they ought to get the richest of all bad fates. All this long night I'll get no rest. But never mind! All shall turn out well, for, John," said he, "as I may prosper, I'm going to lie with that wench, if I can. The law has provided us with some relief, for, John, there's a law says that if a man is harmed in one point, he shall be relieved in another. Our grain is stolen, that's a fact. There's no denying it. And we've had an ill turn today. And since I'm not to have any amends against my loss, I'm going to have relief. By God, there's no other way to it."

John answered, "Alan, have a care. The miller is a dangerous man, and if he woke out of his sleep, he could do us both some harm."

Alan answered, "I don't care a fly for him." And up he rose and crept in beside the wench. The wench was lying face-upwards and sleeping soundly until, before she knew it, he was so near that it would have been too late to cry out, and, to speak briefly, they were at one. Play now, Alan, for I'm going to speak of John.

John lay quiet for a moment or two and lamented and complained to himself. "Alas," said he, "this is a wretched joke. Now I can say that I'm just a fool, but my friend has something in return for his harm. He has the

[1] Epidemics of the highly contagious disease known as St. Anthony's fire, or erysipelas, were of common occurrence in the Middle Ages.

miller's daughter in his arms. He took a chance and succeeded, while I lie like a bag of straw in bed. And when this joke is told some other day, I'll be reckoned a simpleton and a fool. I'll get up, in faith, and take a chance. 'Nothing ventured, nothing gained,' they say." And up he rose, and quietly he went to the cradle and took it up in his hands and carried it quietly to the foot of his own bed.

Soon after, the wife stopped snoring and went out to make water and came back and couldn't find her cradle. She groped here and there but didn't come upon it. "Dear, dear," said she, "I almost went wrong. I almost went into the scholars' bed! Ah, bless me! then I'd have been in trouble!" And on she went till she found the cradle. She kept on groping with her hands and found the bed and thought nothing amiss, since the cradle was standing beside it and she didn't know where she was, for it was dark. But carefully she crept in beside the scholar and lay quietly and began to go to sleep. After a while John the scholar sprang up and set to it eagerly upon the good wife. She hadn't had so merry a turn for ages. He thrust as hard and deep as if he were mad.

This happy life the two scholars led until the third crowing of the cock. Alan grew weary in the dawn, for he had toiled all the long night, and said, "Farewell, Molly, dear creature. The day has come. I can't stay any longer. But, wherever I walk or ride, I am for evermore your very own scholar, as I may prosper."

"Go now, sweetheart dear," said she. "Farewell. But before you go, I'll tell you one thing. When you go home past the mill, right behind the entrance to the door you'll find a half-bushel cake that was made with your own flour, which I helped my sire to steal. And, sweetheart good, may God bless and keep you." And with these words she almost wept.

Alan arose and thought, "Before the dawn I'll go creep back beside my friend," and he found the cradle at once with his hand. "Heavens!" thought he, "I've gone all wrong. My head is so dizzy from my toil tonight that it makes me go astray. I know by the cradle I've gone amiss. Here lies the miller and his wife too." And on he went disastrously to the bed where the miller lay. He expected to creep in beside his friend John and at once crept in beside the miller. He caught him round the neck and softly spoke. "John, John," he said, "you swine's head, wake up and listen to a noble prank. For, by the lord we call St. James, three times in this short night I've served the miller's daughter as she lay stretched out, while you've been as timid as a coward."

"So!" said the miller. "False wretch! You have! O you false traitor, you false scholar," said he. "By God, you'll be killed. Who would be so bold as to dare shame my daughter who's descended from such ancestry!" And by the Adam's apple he seized Alan, who grappled with him fiercely in return and hit him on the nose with his fist. Down ran the bloody stream upon the miller's chest; and on the floor, with smashed nose and mouth, they wallowed like two pigs in a poke. And up they got and down again as fast until the miller tripped on a stone, and down he fell backwards on his wife. She knew nothing of this fine fight, for she had fallen asleep just a little while before with John the scholar, who had been awake all night. And, with the fall, she started from her sleep. "Help, holy cross of Bromholm,"[1] she said. "Into thy hands, O Lord! To thee I call. Wake up, Simond! The Fiend has fallen upon me! My heart is broken. Help! I'm all but dead. Someone's lying on my head and belly. Help, Simkin, for the false scholars are fighting."

John sprang up as fast as ever he could and groped back and forth along the wall to find a stick, and up she sprang too. She knew the quarters better than John did and found a stick at once by the wall and saw a little shimmering of light, for the moon was shining in brightly through a hole. By that light she saw the two of them, but certainly she didn't know who was who, except that her eye spotted a white thing. And when she spied this white thing, she thought the scholar was wearing a nightcap, and with the stick she drew nearer and nearer, and, expecting to hit Alan full-on, she struck the miller on his naked skull. Down he went and cried, "Help! I'm dead."

The scholars beat him well and left him lying there. They dressed and took their horse at once and their wheat-meal, too, and on their way they went. At the mill they took their cake, after all, well baked from half a bushel of flour.

Thus the proud miller was well beaten and lost the grinding of his wheat and paid thoroughly for the supper of Alan and John, who had beaten him well. His wife was served, and his daughter too. You see, thus it is for a miller to be false. And therefore this proverb is very truly spoken: "He must not expect good who does evil. A beguiler shall himself be beguiled." And may God, who sits on high in majesty, save all this company, high and low. And so I have paid back the Miller with my tale.

---

[1] A piece of wood reputed to be part of the true Cross was brought in the twelfth century to Bromholm in Norfolk, which consequently became a pilgrimage center.

THE CLERK'S TALE

[E 57–1162. Here translated. For commentary, see p. 123.]

I

On the west side of Italy, down at the base of Monte Viso the cold, there is a pleasant plain abounding in food where you may behold many a tower and town, founded in the time of the forefathers of old, and many another delightful sight; and this noble country is called Saluzzo.

A marquis was once lord of that land, as his worthy ancestors had been before him; and all his liegemen, both great and small, were obedient and always responsive to his control. Thus he lived happily and had long done so, through the favor of Fortune beloved and feared by his lords and commons. Moreover, to speak of lineage, he was the noblest born in Lombardy, handsome, strong, and young in years, and full of honor and courtesy, and sufficiently discreet to rule his country, except that in some respects he was at fault; and this young lord's name was Walter.

I blame him because he did not consider what might happen to him in the time to come but gave all his thought to present pleasures such as hawking and hunting everywhere. Almost all his other cares he let slide, and also — and this was worst of all — he would not take a wife, no matter what might occur. This one point the people so resented that they went to him one day as a body, and one of them who was the wisest in his learning — either the one whom the lord would most willingly allow to tell him what his people thought, or else the one who could explain such a matter well — said to the marquis as you shall hear:

"O noble marquis, your humanity assures us and emboldens us, as often as the occasion requires, to tell you of our grievance. Receive, lord, now, in your gentility, with pitiable heart, what we complain of to you, and let not your ears disdain my voice.

"Though I personally am not concerned in this matter any more than all the others in this place, yet in as much as you, my lord so dear, have always showed me grace and favor I dare the sooner ask you for an opportunity of audience, to show our request, and ask you, my lord, to do just as it may please you. For certainly, lord, so well are we satisfied with you and all your works, and always have been, that we could not of ourselves imagine how we could live in greater felicity, except for one thing, lord, if it be your will, namely, that you might be pleased to be a wedded man. Then would your people's hearts be supremely at ease.

"Bow your neck under that blissful yoke of sovereignty, not of service, which is called espousal or wedlock; and amid your wise thoughts, lord, consider that our days pass by in sundry ways, for though we sleep or wake or roam or ride, time always flees; it will await for no one. And though your green youth is still in flower, age, as still as stone, creeps on always, and death menaces every age and strikes in every estate, for no one escapes; and as certainly as we know each one that we shall die, so uncertain are we all of that day when death shall fall upon us.

"Accept, therefore, the true intentions of us who have never yet refused your command, and if you will assent, we will choose you a wife, lord, — in a short while at least, — born of the noblest and greatest in all this land, so that in our opinion it ought to seem an honor to God and to yourself.

"Free us from all this worrisome doubt, and take a wife, in the name of Heaven. For if it so happened — God forbid! — that through your death your line should expire, and a foreign successor should take your heritage, oh, woeful we should be! Therefore, we beg you, marry in haste."

Their meek prayers and their pitiful expressions made the marquis's heart feel pity.

"My own dear people," said he, "you will constrain me to do what I never thought of before. I rejoiced in my liberty, which is seldom found in marriage. Whereas I was free, I must now be in servitude. But, nevertheless, I see your true intention and trust your intelligence, and always have. And so I will assent of my own free will to marry as soon as I can. But though you have offered this day to choose me a wife, I release you from that choice and beg you to withdraw the offer. For, God knows, children often are unlike their worthy elders before them. Goodness comes entirely from God, not from the stock of which they were engendered and born. I trust in God's goodness, and therefore I commit my marriage and my estate and repose to him; he may do as he cares.

"Leave me alone in choosing my wife. I will endure that charge upon my own back. But I beg you and charge you upon your lives that, whatever wife I may take, you will promise me to respect her all her life in word and work, both here and everywhere, just as if she were an emperor's daughter. And, furthermore, this you shall swear, that you will neither grumble nor contend against my choice, for since I shall forego my liberty at your request, I will marry wherever my heart is set, as ever I may thrive. And, unless you will assent to this condition, I beg you, speak no more of the matter."

With good will they swore and assented to this entire stipulation, no one gainsaying; beseeching him that, before they went away, he would graciously grant them a certain day for his wedding as soon as ever he could, for the people still feared that the marquis would not take a wife. He granted them a day such as suited him, on which he would certainly be married, and said he did all this at their request. And they all thanked him humbly, obediently, kneeling on their knees most reverently. And thus they attained their purpose, and home again they went.

And hereupon he commanded his officers to prepare for the festivities and laid such charges upon his personal knights and squires as it pleased him to give; and they obeyed his commands, and each of them did his best to mark the festival with respect.

II

Not far from the honorable palace where the marquis prepared for his marriage, there stood a village on a delightful site where the poor of the village lived and kept their animals, and won their sustenance by their labors according as the earth yielded them abundance. Among these poor people there dwelt a man who was the poorest of them all; but the high God can sometimes send his grace into a little ox-crib. The people of the village called him Janicula. He had a daughter fair enough to look upon, and the young maiden's name was Griselda. But, to speak of the beauty of virtue, she was one of the fairest under the sun. Because she had been frugally reared, no lecherous passion ran through her heart. Much oftener she drank from the well than from the barrel, and because she wished to satisfy virtue, she was well acquainted with labor and not with idle ease.

But though this maid was of a tender age, yet in the breast of her virginity there was enclosed a mature and serious heart; and she had fostered her poor, aged father with great respect and kindness. While spinning, she tended a few sheep on pasture; she would not be idle until she went to sleep. And when she came homeward, she would often bring roots or other herbs, which she shredded and boiled for their sustenance, and she never made her hard bed soft, and she always sustained her father's life with all the obedience and diligence with which a child may pay respect to a father.

On Griselda, the poor creature, the marquis very frequently set his eye as perchance he rode hunting; and when it happened that he could see her, he did not cast his eyes upon her with the wanton looking of the foolish, but he would often consider her countenance seriously, commending in his heart her womanliness and also her virtue, in appearance and behavior surpassing anyone's of age so young. For though the people have no great insight into virtue, he considered her goodness very properly and decided that he would wed her only, if ever he were to wed.

The day of the wedding came, but no one could tell what woman it would be. Many a person marveled at this wonder and said, when in private, "Won't our lord abandon his folly yet? Won't he wed? Alas, alas, for this! Why will he beguile himself and us thus?"

But, nevertheless, the marquis had jeweled brooches and rings made, set in gold and azure, for the sake of Griselda; and by a maiden like her in stature he took the measure of her clothing and of all the other adornments that belong to such a wedding.

The time approached nine o'clock in the morning on the very day that the wedding was to take place, and all the palace was set in array, both hall and chambers, each in its rank. There you could see the storerooms of the household stuffed with abundance of the most dainty provisions to be found as far as Italy extends.

The royal marquis, richly arrayed, and the lords and ladies in his company who were invited to the feast, and the bachelor-band of his retinue, with many a sound of various melody, went in their splendor directly toward the village of which I have told you.

Griselda, completely unsuspecting, God knows, that all this array was destined for her, had gone to fetch water from a well and came home as soon as she could, for she had heard it said that on this very day the marquis was to marry, and she was very eager to see something of the sight, if she could. She thought, "I'll stand at our door with the other maidens that are my friends and see the marchioness, and so I'll try to finish the work I have to do at home as soon as I can; and then I can watch her at leisure if she passes this way to the castle."

And as she was about to pass in over the threshold, the marquis came and called her; and she at once set down her water-pitcher beside the threshold in an ox's crib and fell down on her knees and kneeled quietly with solemn countenance till she heard what her lord's will was. The thoughtful marquis spoke to the maid most soberly and said, "Where is your father, Griselda?"

And with reverence she humbly answered, "Lord, he is already here." And in she went without longer stay and brought her father to the marquis. He then took the old man by the hand and, after taking him aside, said, "Janicula, I neither can nor may hide the pleasure of my heart any longer. If you will permit it, then whatever may betide I will take your daughter, before I leave, as my wife unto my life's end.

"You love me, I know very well, and have conducted yourself as my faithful liegeman; and everything that pleases me, I dare say, pleases you. Therefore, answer me in particular the question I have just asked, if you will agree to take me as your son-in-law."

This sudden event so astonished Janicula that he turned all red; abashed and trembling he stood. He could hardly utter more than only, "Lord, my will is as your will, nor do I wish anything against your liking, you are my lord so dear. Direct this matter just as you please."

"I should still wish," said the marquis quietly, "that you and she and I might have a conference in your room, and do you know why? Because I wish to ask whether it is her will to be my wife and to agree with me. And all this shall be done in your presence. I do not wish to speak out of your hearing."

And while they were in the room discussing their agreement, about which you shall hear afterward, the people came to the house outside and marveled how honorably and attentively she had maintained her father dear. But well might Griselda marvel utterly, for never before had she seen such a sight. No wonder she was astonished to see so great a guest come to that place; she never was accustomed to such guests, and she watched with a pale face. But to pursue this matter briefly, these are the words that the marquis spoke to this benign, trustworthy, and faithful maid.

"Griselda," he said, "you must understand that it pleases your father and me that I should wed you; and it may also be, I suppose, that you are willing. But first I state these demands," said he, "that you will assent to, since it must be done hastily. Or do you wish to deliberate? This I ask, are you ready to accept with good heart whatever I wish, and to allow that I may freely make you laugh or grieve as seems best to me, and never to regret it night or day? And also when I say 'yes,' not to say 'no,' either by word or by frowning countenance? Swear this, and herewith I swear to our betrothal."

Marveling at this speech and quaking with fear, she said, "Lord, I am unworthy and unsuited for this honor which you offer me, but as you wish, so do I. And here I swear that I will never willingly disobey you in deed or thought, on pain of death, even though I were loath to die."

"That is enough, Griselda mine," said he. And forth he went with a most sober countenance out of the door, and she came out after; and to the people he said, "This is my wife who stands here. Honor her, and love her, I beg, whoever loves me. There is no more to say."

And in order that she should bring nothing of her old clothing into his house, he ordered that the women should undress her on the spot; nor were the ladies particularly glad to handle the clothes in which she was dressed. But nevertheless this maid so fair of hue they clothed all afresh from head to foot. Her hair they combed, which rudely lay untressed, and with their delicate fingers they arranged a coronet upon her head and decked her with jewelry great and small. Why should I linger over her array? The people hardly knew her for her beauty when she was transformed with such riches.

The marquis espoused her with a ring brought for the purpose and then set her on a horse, snow-white and well paced, and conducted her without longer stay to his palace with the joyful people who escorted and met her, and thus they spent the day in revel till the sun began to go down. And briefly to pursue the tale, to this new marchioness God in his grace sent such favor, I say, that it hardly seemed possible she was born and rudely nourished in a hut or ox's stall, as it were, rather than nurtured in an emperor's palace.

She became so dear to everyone and so worthy of respect that the people where she was born, who had known her from birth year by year, scarcely believed — and would indeed have sworn to the contrary — that she was the daughter of Janicula, whom I mentioned before; for, by conjecture, it seemed to them that she was another creature. For though she had always been virtuous, she increased in such excellence of fine morality, set in supreme goodness, and she became so discreet and fair of speech, so benign and so worthy of reverence and could so embrace the heart of the people, that everyone who looked upon her face loved her.

Not only in the town of Saluzzo was the goodness of her name made known, but also in many another region if one person spoke well of her another said the same. The fame of her supreme goodness spread so widely that men and women, both young and old, went to Saluzzo to look upon her.

Thus Walter, wedded humbly — nay, but royally — with fortunate distinction, lived at home in God's peace most comfortably, and he had outward grace in plenty. And because he had seen that virtue is often hidden under low degree, the people considered him a prudent man, and that very seldom happens.

Not only did Griselda through her intelligence know all the art of wifely humility, but also when the occasion required, she could redress the common interest. There was no discord, rancor, or oppression in all the land which she could not appease and wisely bring the people all to quiet and satisfaction. Even though her husband were absent at the time, if gentlemen or others in her country were angered, she would reconcile them. Such wise and mature words she had, and judgments of such equity, that it was believed she was sent from Heaven to save the people and amend every wrong.

Not long after Griselda was married, she gave birth to a daughter. Although she would sooner have borne a boy-child, the marquis and the people were glad of it, for though a girl-child came first, she could probably have a boy-child since she was not barren.

III

It happened, as it often does, when the child had suckled for a while, that the marquis so longed in his heart to test his wife in order to know her stability that he could not expel from his heart this remarkable desire to prove his wife. Needlessly, God knows, he decided to alarm her. He had tested her enough already and had always found her good. What need had he to try her more and more, even though some might praise it for a subtle thought? But, as for me, I say it is most unfitting to test a wife when there is no need and to put her in anguish and fear.

The marquis therefore did as follows. He came alone one night with a stern face and a troubled countenance to where she was lying and said, "Griselda, the day on which I removed you from your poor estate and raised you to the rank of high nobility — you haven't forgotten that, I suppose? This present dignity, I say, to which I've raised you, Griselda, doesn't make you forgetful, I assume, that I accepted you in the most humble poverty for whatever happiness you might know. Take heed of every word I say to you. There is no one who can hear except the two of us.

"You know yourself very well how you came here into this house, not so long ago. And though you are dear and beloved to me, to my nobles you are not so at all. They say that it is a great shame and grief to them to be subject and in servitude to you, who were born in a small village. And, without a doubt, they have spoken these words particularly since your daughter was born. But I desire, as I always have, to live my life with them in rest and peace. I cannot be indifferent in this matter; I must deal with your daughter as best may be — not as I would wish, but as my people would desire. God knows, I am loath to do so; but, nevertheless, without your knowledge I will not act. But I wish," said he, "that you would assent with me in this. Show your patience now in your behavior as you promised and swore to me in your village the day our marriage was arranged."

When she had heard all this, she responded in neither word, features, nor countenance, for apparently she was not distressed. She said, "Lord, all lies in your pleasure. My child and I are yours entirely, with hearty obedience, and you may save or destroy your own. Act according to your own will. Nothing can please you that can displease me, God save my soul, and I neither desire to have anything nor fear to lose anything except yourself alone. This intention is in my heart and always shall be. Neither length of time nor death can deface this or change my feelings in another direction."

Glad was the marquis of her answer, but he pretended not to be. His features and appearance were dreary as he left the room.

A little while after, he secretly told his entire plan to a man and sent him to Griselda. This private retainer was a sort of sergeant whom he had often found faithful in important matters, and such people can also execute bad matters well. The lord knew well that the man loved and feared him; and when the sergeant knew his lord's will, he stalked quietly into her room.

"Madam," he said, "you must forgive me though I do something I am compelled to do. You are so wise, you know very well that the commands of a lord cannot be feigned; they may very well be bewailed or lamented, but one must obey his pleasure, and so will I. There is no more to say. I am ordered to take this child."

And he said no more, but cruelly took up the child and acted as if he intended to slay it before he went.

Griselda had to suffer and consent to all, and she sat as meek and still as a lamb and let this cruel sergeant do his will. Suspect was the infamy of this man, suspect his face, and suspect also his word; suspect the time in which he began this. Alas, her daughter whom she loved so! She thought he intended to slay the child right then; but nevertheless she neither wept nor sighed, conforming to what the marquis wished. But at last she began to speak, and meekly she begged the sergeant, as he was a worthy, gentle man, that she might kiss her child before it died. And with a most sad face she laid the little child in her bosom and kissed it and lulled it and then made the sign of the cross over it. And thus she said in her benign voice:

"Farewell, my child! I shall never see you, but since I have marked you with the cross of the Father — blessed may he be, who died for us upon a cross of wood — I commit your soul to him, little child, for you are to die this night for my sake."

I am sure that for a nurse in this situation it would have been hard to witness this pitiful sight. Well might a mother then have cried "Alas!" But, nevertheless, so steadfast was she that she endured all adversity, and to the sergeant meekly she said, "Have here your little young maiden again. Go now," said she, "and carry out my lord's command. But one thing I will beg you, out of your compassion. Unless my lord forbade you, at least bury this little body in some place that beasts and birds will not destroy it."

But he would not say a word in that respect but took the child and went his way. The sergeant came back to the marquis and told him point for point, in short and plain, of Griselda's words and deportment and presented his lord with his dear daughter. The lord felt some compassion in his heart, but nevertheless he still held his purpose, as lords do when they wish to have their way; and he ordered the sergeant secretly to swathe and wrap the child quietly, and above all tenderly, and to carry her in a chest or wrapper. On pain of losing his head, he was not to let anyone know of his plan or whence he came or whither he was going, but he was to take her to Bologna to the marquis's dear sister, who was at that time countess of Panico, and explain the matter to her, beseeching her to exercise her diligence in fostering the child in all gentility. And whose child it was, he ordered her to conceal from everyone, no matter what might happen.

The sergeant went and fulfilled this order; but let us now return to the marquis. For now he went fully expecting to see by his wife's appearance or to detect by her words that she was changed; but he never could find her anything other than consistently steadfast and kind. And she was to him in every way as cheerful, as humble, as willing in service and in love, also, as ever she had been accustomed to be; nor did she speak a word of her daughter. No matter what the adversity, she showed no sign of any disturbance, nor did she ever name her daughter in jest or earnest.

IV

In this way there passed four years before she was with child, but, as it pleased God, she bore by Walter a boy-child, very gracious and fair to look on. And when the father was told, not only he but all his country too were delighted on account of the child, and God they thanked and praised.

When it was two years old and had been taken from its nurse's breast, one day the marquis became obsessed once more to test his wife yet again, if he could. Oh, needlessly was she put to the test! But married men know no moderation when they find a patient creature.

"Wife," said the marquis, "you have heard already, my people are dissatisfied with our marriage; and now, especially since my son is born, it is worse than ever before in our time. The rumor pierces my heart and spirit, for their voice comes so bitterly to my ears that it has very nearly destroyed my heart. Now they are saying, 'When Walter is gone, then the descendant of Janicula will succeed and be our lord, for we have no other.' Such words my people speak, in very truth. I certainly ought to pay heed to such a murmur, for I truly dread such an opinion, even though they do not speak openly in my hearing. I would like to live in peace, if I can. Therefore I have definitely decided; I intend to deal with the boy secretly just as I dealt with his sister at night. I warn you of this, so that you will not suddenly lose control of yourself because of your grief. Be patient, I beg you."

"I have said and always will," said she, "I do not want anything, nor ever shall, unless it pleases you. I am not grieved at all even though my daughter and my son be slain — at your command, that is. I have had no share of the two children except illness first and then pain and woe.

"You are our lord. Do with your own just as it pleases you. Do not ask advice from me. For, just as I left all my clothes at home when I first came to you, so I left my own will and all my freedom and took your clothing. Therefore I beg you, do your pleasure. I will obey your wish. And, certainly, if I had foreknowledge of your will before you were pleased to tell me, I would do it without fail; but now that I know all your pleasure and what you wish, I consider your desire established and fixed, for if I knew that my death would give you satisfaction, I would most gladly die to please you. Death can make no comparison with your love."

And when the marquis saw the constancy of his wife, he cast down his two eyes and marveled that she could suffer all this ordeal in patience; and forth he went with a dreary countenance, but it was a very great satisfaction to his heart.

In the same way that he had taken her daughter, or in a worse way, if it can be imagined, the ugly sergeant took her son, who was full of beauty. And she was always so consistently patient that she showed no trace of gloom but kissed her son and then made the sign of the cross over him. She did, however, beg the sergeant that, if he could, he would bury her little son in an earthen grave in order to protect his tender limbs, so delicate to look upon, from birds and beasts. But she could have no answer from him. He went his way as if he cared not at all; but he brought the child tenderly to Bologna.

The marquis marveled, ever the longer the more, at her patience; and, if he had not truly known before that she loved her children perfectly, he would have supposed that she suffered this with steadfast countenance through some trick or out of malice or cruel heart. But he knew well that, next to himself, certainly she loved her children best in every way.

But, now, I would like to ask of women whether these tests should not suffice. What more could a stern husband devise to test her wifeliness and her steadfastness, even if persisting in his sternness? But there are people who, when they have taken a certain purpose, cannot desist from their intention but, just as if they were bound to a stake, will not swerve from their original purpose. Just so, the marquis fully intended to test his wife as he had at first decided.

He watched to see whether by word or bearing she had changed in heart toward him, but he could never discover any variation. She was always the same in heart and in countenance; and ever, the more she advanced in age, the more faithful and the more devoted, if possible, she was to him in love. Hence it seemed that, between the two of them, there was only one will, for as Walter wished, the same desire was her pleasure too. And, God be thanked, all worked out for the best. She showed clearly that, no matter what her tribulation on earth, a wife should not in effect have any wishes of her own but should only wish what her husband wishes.

A repeated slander concerning Walter spread far and wide that he had murdered both his children secretly because he had married a poor woman. Such rumor was frequently heard among them, and no wonder, for there came no word to the people's ear but that they were murdered. So, whereas his people had previously loved him well, the slander of his infamy caused them to hate him because of it. To be a murderer is a hateful name, but nevertheless, he would not desist from his cruel purpose for earnest or jest. All his intent was set upon testing his wife.

When his daughter was twelve years old, he sent his messengers to the court of Rome, privily informed of his intention, commanding them to arrange for such papal bulls as would satisfy his cruel purpose, to the effect that the Pope ordered him to take another wife, if he were willing, for the satisfaction of his people. He ordered them, that is, to counterfeit papal bulls specifying that he had permission to leave his first wife by the dispensation of the Pope, in order to put a stop to the rancor and dissension between his people and himself. Thus said the edict, which they published in full.

The simple people, as well they might, fully believed that this was truly so; but when these tidings came to Griselda, I am sure her heart was woeful indeed. But she, ever consistently steadfast, was disposed, the humble creature, to endure all the adversity of Fortune, suffering always his desire and pleasure to whom she was devoted, heart and all, as her whole earthly sufficiency.

But — to tell the story briefly — the marquis wrote a special letter, in which he explained his intention, and sent it secretly to Bologna. He particularly requested the earl of Panico, who was at that time married to his sister, to bring home his two children openly in honorable estate. But one thing he requested him most emphatically, that he should not tell whose children they were, even though people asked, but that he should say that the maiden was to be married to the marquis of Saluzzo forthwith. And as the earl was requested, so he did, for at break of day he set out toward Saluzzo with many lords in rich array to escort the maiden and her young brother riding beside her. The fresh maid was arrayed for her marriage, covered with shining gems. Her brother, who was seven years old, was in his way also freshly arrayed. And so in great pomp and with glad countenances they rode on their way day by day, directing their journey toward Saluzzo.

V

Meanwhile, according to his grievous custom, to test his wife still more to the utmost extent of her spirit, in order to have complete assurance and knowledge that she was as steadfast as before, the marquis one day in open hearing said roughly to her as follows:

"Certainly, Griselda, I found pleasure enough in having you as my wife on account of your goodness, your faithfulness, and your obedience, and not for your extraction or your wealth. But now I know in very truth, when I consider carefully, that in various ways there is great servitude in great lordship. I cannot do as every plowman may. My people constrain me to take another wife and cry out day after day; and the Pope, also, consents — in order to assuage the rancor, I dare say. And this much I shall tell you, in truth: my new wife is on the way.

"Be strong of heart, and vacate her place at once, and take back the dowry which you brought me. Out of grace, I grant that. Return to your father's house," said he. "No one can have prosperity always. I advise you to endure with steady heart the stroke of Fortune or of chance."

And she answered patiently. "My lord," said she, "I know and always have known that no one either can or may make comparison between your magnificence and my poverty. There's no denial. I never considered myself worthy in any way to be your wife or even your chambermaid. And in this house, where you made me lady — I take the high God as my witness, and wisely may he comfort my soul — I never considered myself as lady or mistress but as a humble servant to your worthiness above every living person, and ever shall as long as my life endures.

"That out of your kindness you have upheld me so long in honor and nobility, where I was not worthy to be, I thank God — and you — whom I pray to repay you for it now. There is nothing more to say. I shall gladly return to my father and live with him to the end of my life. Where I was reared as a small child, till I die I shall lead my life, a widow pure in body, heart, and all. For since I gave you my maidenhood and am your faithful wife, without doubt, God forbid that the wife of such a lord should take another man as husband or mate!

"And may God in his grace grant you welfare and prosperity with your new wife. For I will gladly yield her my place, in which I used to be contented. For," said she, "since it pleases you, my lord, in whom all my heart's ease once rested, that I shall go, I will go when you wish.

"But, as you offer me such dowry as I brought at first, I well remember that it was my miserable and unattractive clothing, which would be hard for me to find now. Oh, dear God, how gentle and kind you seemed in speech and appearance the day we were married! But it is truly said — at least, I find it true, for it is proved in effect by my experience — that love when old is not as it was when it was new. But certainly, my lord, no matter what the adversity, including even death, it shall never be that I shall repent either in word or deed that I gave you my heart entirely.

"My lord, you know that in my father's home you had me stripped of my poor clothing and richly clad, out of your kindness. I brought you nothing more, in fact, than fidelity and nakedness and virginity; and here I return your clothes and your wedding ring for ever. The rest of your jewelry is ready in your room, I can truly say. Naked from my father's house I came, and naked I must return again. I will gladly follow your wishes entirely. But still I hope that it is not your intention that I should go from your palace without some smock. You could not do anything so dishonorable as to permit the womb in which your children were born to be seen bare before the people as I leave. I beg you, therefore, do not let me go on my way naked like a worm. Remember, my own lord so dear, I was your wife, even if I were unworthy. Therefore, in requital for my maidenhood which I brought and do not take away again, be pleased to give me as my reward only such smock as I used to wear so that I may cover the womb of her who was your wife. And here I take my leave of you, my own lord, lest I grieve you."

"Leave on the smock which you have on your back," said he, "and carry it away with you." But hardly had he said these words than he went away out of sorrow and pity.

Before the people she stripped herself, and in her smock, with bare head and feet, she set out for her father's house. The people followed her, weeping in her way, and ever they cursed Fortune as they went; but she kept her eyes dry from tears, nor did she at the time speak a word.

Her father, who soon heard the news, cursed the day and time that Nature had created him a living creature. For certainly the poor old man was always suspicious of her marriage, for he always thought from the beginning that when the lord had satisfied his desires, he would consider it a disparagement of his rank to descend so low and would expel her as soon as he could.

Quickly Janicula went to meet his daughter, for he knew of her coming by the noise of the people, and, sorrowfully weeping, he tried to cover her with her old coat as best could be, but he could not put it on her body, for the cloth was rough and she older by many days than at her marriage.

Thus this flower of wifely patience lived with her father for a certain time, so that neither by word nor appearance did she show, either before the people or in their absence, that offense had been done her. Nor, to judge by her countenance, did she have any remembrance of her high estate. Nor was it any wonder, for in her great estate her spirit was always filled with plain humility — no fastidious mouth, no delicate heart, no pomp, no appearance of regality, but patient kindness, discreet and prideless, ever honorable, and ever reliable and meek to her husband. Men speak of Job, and particularly for his humility — a subject on which clerks can well expound when they wish, especially concerning men. But in truth, though clerks praise women very little, no man can acquit himself in humility as a woman can, nor can be half so faithful as women are, unless it has just recently come to pass.

VI

From Bologna the earl of Panico came, and the news spread to high and low; and it reached the ears of the people one and all that he had brought with him a new marchioness in so much pomp and magnificence that such noble array was never seen by man's eye in all West Lombardy.

Before the earl arrived, the marquis, who had contrived and knew all this, sent his messengers for the poor, innocent Griselda; and with humble heart and cheerful countenance she came at his command, not with swollen thoughts in her mind, and set herself on her knees, and reverently and soberly greeted him.

"Griselda," said he, "it is my whole desire that this maiden that is to be wedded to me shall be received tomorrow as regally as is possible in my house, and also that everyone shall be honored according to his rank in seating and service and entertainment, as best I can devise.

"I have no women sufficient, certainly, to set the rooms in order according to my wishes, and so I should be glad that all this kind of arrangement should be in your hands. You know of old all my pleasure. Though your array be poor and ill becoming, at least do your duty."

"Not only am I glad, my lord," said she, "to do your pleasure, but I desire also to serve you and please you in my degree without fail, and forever shall. Nor shall the spirit within my heart, either for well or for woe, ever cease from loving you best with all my true intent."

And with these words, she began to prepare the house, to set the tables, and make the beds; and she took pains to do all that she could, begging the chambermaids to hasten, for the love of Heaven, and fast to sweep and shake. And she, the most serviceable of all, arranged his hall and every room.

At about nine o'clock in the morning the earl dismounted, bringing with him the two noble children, and the people ran to see the sight of their array, so richly equipped, and then for the first time they said among themselves Walter was no fool even if he did wish to change his wife, since that was for the best. For everyone agreed the new one was fairer than Griselda and more tender of age, and a fairer fruit would be produced from them, and a more pleasant, because of her high lineage. Her brother also was so fair of face that the people took delight in seeing him, commending now the marquis's planning.

"O stormy people! unstable and ever unfaithful, always indiscreet, and as changeable as a weather vane, delighting in every rumor that is new! For like the moon ever you wax and wane, ever filled with chatter, dearly bought at any price. Your judgment is false; your constancy badly fails the test. A great fool is he that believes in you." Thus sober persons in the city said, while the people gazed up and down, for they were glad, just for the novelty, to have a new lady for their town.

I shall make no more mention of this now but shall return to Griselda again and tell of her diligence and constancy.

Griselda was very busy in everything that pertained to the feast. She was in no way abashed by her clothing though it was rough and somewhat tattered, too, but went in good cheer to the gate with the other people to greet the marchioness and afterward carried on her work. She received her guests, each in his degree, with such good cheer and so adeptly that no one could discover any fault, but ever they wondered what she could be who was in such poor array and yet could show such honor and reverence, and with respect they praised her prudence.

Meanwhile she never ceased from commending the maiden and her brother, too, with all her heart in kindly intent, so that no one could improve upon her excellence. But at last, when the lords went to sit down to meat, the marquis called Griselda as she was busy in the hall.

"Griselda," said he, as if in jest, "how do you like my wife and her beauty?"

"Very well, my lord," said she, "for, in good faith, I never saw anyone more fair than she. I pray God give her prosperity, and I hope he will send you both pleasure in plenty to the end of your lives. One thing I beseech you, and warn you against also, that you will never goad this tender maid with torments as you have done others. For she has been reared more tenderly in her upbringing, and, I suspect, she could not endure adversity as could a poorly fostered creature."

And when Walter saw her patience, her good cheer, without trace of malice after he had so often done harm to her, though she had always remained as firm and constant as a wall, ever preserving her innocence in all things, then the stern marquis changed heart and took compassion upon her wifely steadfastness.

"This is enough, Griselda mine," said he. "No longer be afraid or grieved. I have tested your faithfulness and your kindness, both in high estate and poorly arrayed, as thoroughly as ever woman has been tested. Now I know, dear wife, your steadfastness." And he took her in his arms and kissed her, but in wonder she took no notice of it. She did not hear what he said to her. She acted as if she had just awakened from a sleep, till she was aroused from her confusion.

"Griselda," said he, "by God who died for us, you are my wife. I have no other, nor did I ever have before, God save my soul! This is your daughter, whom you supposed to be my wife. The other child, truly, shall be my heir, as I had always planned. In truth, you bore him in your body. At Bologna I kept them both secretly. Take them back, for now you can say that you have lost neither of your two children.

"And I warn those people who have said otherwise of me, I have done this deed out of no malice or cruelty but to test your womanhood, and not to slay my children — God forbid! — but to keep them quietly secreted until I knew your character and your determination."

When she heard this, she fell down swooning for pitiable joy, and after her swoon she called both her young children to her and, weeping pitifully, embraced them and, tenderly kissing them like a mother, she bathed their faces and their hair with her salt tears. Oh what a pitiable thing it was to see her swoon and to hear her humble voice!

"Much thanks, my lord," said she. "May God thank you for having saved my dear children for me. Now I do not even care if I die right here. Since I stand in your grace and love, I care not for death or when my spirit passes away.

"Oh, my tender, dear young children, your woeful mother firmly believed that cruel hounds or some foul creature had eaten you. But God, in his mercy, and your kind father have tenderly seen to your keeping." And with these words, she suddenly collapsed on the ground. And in her swooning, she held her two children so tightly when she embraced them that it was only with great difficulty and care that they were able to remove the children from her arms.

Oh, many a tear ran down on many a piteous face of those who stood beside her. They could hardly remain near her. Walter cheered her, and her sorrow ceased. Disconcerted, she rose up from her trance, and everyone encouraged and cheered her until she had recovered her countenance again. Walter was so diligently kind to her that it was a delight to see the happiness between the two, now that they were met together.

The ladies, when they saw their time, took her aside into a room and stripped her of her rude array; and in a cloth of gold that shone brightly, with a crown of many a rich stone upon her head, they brought her back into the hall, and there she was honored as she should be.

Thus this pitiful day had a blissful end, for every man and woman did his best to spend the day in mirth and revel till the starlight shone in the heavens. For, in everyone's sight, this feast was more magnificent and greater in expense than the revel for her marriage.

Full many a year in high prosperity the two lived, in concord and in peace, and the marquis married his daughter richly to one of the worthiest lords in all Italy. And in peace and quiet he kept his wife's father in his court till the soul stole away from Janicula's body.

Walter's son succeeded in his heritage in peace and quiet, after his father's day, and was also fortunate in marriage, even though he did not submit his wife to any severe test. There is no denying, this world is not so strong as it used to be in the old days of yore. And, therefore, listen to what the author of the tale says.

This story is told, not in order that wives should follow Griselda in humility, for that would be intolerable even if they were willing, but in order that everyone, whatever his rank, should be as constant in adversity as Griselda. That's why Petrarch wrote the story, which he narrates in elevated style. For, since a woman was so patient to a mortal man, we should so much the more receive submissively whatever God sends us. For there is good reason why he should test what he has made; but he never does tempt any man whom he has redeemed, as St. James says, if you read his *Epistle*.[1]

He tests people every day, no doubt, and allows us often to be beaten in various ways with sharp scourges of adversity in order to exercise us, not in order to discover our will, for certainly he knew all our frailty before we were born, and all his control is for our best. Let us then live in virtuous submission.

THE CANON'S YEOMAN'S TALE

[G 720–1481. Here translated. For commentary, see p. 175.]

PROLOGUE

I have lived with this Canon for seven years, and I'm none the better by his science. Through it I have lost all that I had, and, God knows, so have many more than I. While once I used to be fresh and gay in clothes and other good apparel, now I may well wear a stocking on my head; and while once my hue was both fresh and rosy, now it is wan and the color of

---

[1] "God cannot be tempted with evil, neither tempteth he any man: But every man is tempted, when he is drawn away of his own lust, and enticed." *James*, i, 13–14.

lead — whoever uses lead shall sorely rue it! — and my eyes are still bleary from my toil. You see what advantage there is in transmutation! That slippery science has made me so threadbare that I have no possessions wherever I go. And yet I'm so much in debt through it for the gold which I've borrowed that, truly, I shall never repay it while I live. Let everyone be warned by me for evermore! Whatever sort of person applies himself to it, if he persist, I maintain that he has put an end to thrift. For, so help me God, he'll not gain by it, but will empty his purse and thin his brains. And when, through his madness and folly, he has lost his own possessions by this gamble, then he will incite other people, too, to lose their possessions as he himself has done. For it is the joy and pleasure of a wretch to have his fellows in pain and misery. So I was instructed by a scholar. But no matter! I intend to speak about our work.

When we are gathered where we are to practice our magic craft, we seem wonderfully wise, so scholarly and learned are our terms. I blow the fire till my heart begins to fail. Why should I tell each proportion of the things we work on — such as ounces five or six of silver, let's say, or some other quantity — or why take the trouble to tell you the names of orpiment, burnt bones, and scales of rust that are ground into the finest powder; and how everything is put into an iron pot, and salt put in and pepper, too, before the powders that I've mentioned, and well covered with a sheet of glass; and of the many other things in it; and of the sealing of the pot and glass so that none of the air can escape; and of the slow fire and the quick one, too, which were made, and of the care and trouble we had in subliming our substances and in amalgamating and calcinating quicksilver, called crude mercury? Despite all our subtleties we cannot succeed. Our orpiment and our sublimated mercury, our litarge ground in porphyry — of each a certain number of ounces — they help us not at all; our labor is in vain. Nor can the ascension of our vapors, nor our matters that are consistently fixed, aid us at all in our undertaking, for all our labor and travail are lost. And — curses on it! — all the expense which we lay out on it is lost, too!

There are also many other things pertaining to our craft, though I can't rehearse them in order, because I'm an unlearned man. Yet I'll mention them as they come to mind even if I can't arrange them according to their properties, such as bole Armeniac, verdigris, borax, and various vessels made of earthenware and glass, our urinal-stills and our descensories, vials, crucibles, and sublimatories, distillation flasks and alembics too, and other such, dear at any price! There's no need to rehearse them all, — rubifying liquids, and ox-gall, arsenic, sal ammoniac, and brimstone; and many a herb too I could name, such as agrimony, valerian, and lunary, and other such, if I cared to linger; our lamps, burning both night and day to carry out our craft if we can; our furnace for calcinating, too, and albifying liquids; unslaked lime, chalk, and white of egg, various powders, ashes, dung, urine, and clay, waxed bags, saltpeter, vitriol, and various fires made of wood and coal; salt tartar, soda, and prepared salt, and combust and coagulated matters; clay made with human or horse's hair, and cream of tartar, rock alum, yeast, beer-wort, and crude tartar, realgar, and absorption of other matters; and precipitation of our matters, too, and citronising of our silver, our cementing and fermentation, our metal-molds, assaying vessels, and many more.

I will tell you, as was taught me also, the four spirits and the seven bodies in order, as I often heard my master name them.

The first spirit is called quicksilver, the second orpiment, the third sal ammoniac, indeed, and the fourth sulphur. The seven bodies, too, lo, hear them now: Sol is gold, Luna silver, and Mars iron, we assert; Mercury we call quicksilver, Saturn lead; and Jupiter is tin, and Venus copper, by my father's race!

Whosoever will practise this cursed craft shall attain no wealth that can suffice him, for all the wealth he spends upon it he shall lose. I have no doubt of that. Whoever cares to show his folly, let him come forth and learn transmutation; and everyone that has anything in his money-chest, let him appear and become a philosopher.[1] Maybe you think the craft is so easily learned? No, no! Whether he be monk or friar, priest or canon, or any other person, even though he sit at his book both day and night learning this strange, magical lore, God knows, all is in vain. And, what is more, by Heaven, to teach an unlearned man the mystery — ! Fie! Don't mention that, for it cannot be. And whether he has education or has not, in effect, he shall find it all the same. For both of them, upon my soul, succeed in transmutation equally well when they've done all they can. That is, both of them fail!

But still I forgot to rehearse the corrosive liquids, metal filings, mollification of bodies and their induration too, oils, ablutions, and fusible metal — to mention them all would exceed any Bible there is! And so, as is best, I shall take respite from all these names now, for I'm sure I've told you enough to summon up some devil as fierce as may be.

Oh, no, but wait! Every one of us seeks diligently for the philosopher's stone called elixir, for if we had it we'd be secure enough. But to God in Heaven I vow, despite all our craft and all our skill, when we've finished,

---

[1] The term *philosophy* in medieval usage could refer either to moral philosophy or natural philosophy. (See *General Prologue*, ll. 297–98, and n. 1, p. 17.) Throughout this tale, the term refers primarily to natural philosophy or science and, in particular, to the science of alchemy.

it won't come to us. It has made us spend much wealth, in regret for which we almost lose our minds, except that good hope creeps into our hearts, which always expect, no matter how sorely we suffer, to be relieved by the stone at length. Such expectation and hope are sharp and hard; I warn you well, they are never present but always to be sought. That future tense has caused those who trust in the stone to abandon all that ever they had. But still they can never become sated by the art, for to them it is a bitter-sweet, it seems, for if they had nothing but a sheet to wrap themselves in at night and a cloak to walk in by daylight, these they would sell and spend on the craft. They can't stop, until nothing is left. And from then on, wherever they go, they can be recognized by their brimstone smell. They smell, for all the world, like a goat; their savor is so rammish and so hot that, even though a man be a mile away from them, the savor will infect him, believe me. Thus, you see, by their smell and threadbare array those who care to may know these people. And if anyone will ask them confidentially why they are clothed so unprosperously, then right away they'll whisper in his ear and say that if they were noticed, men would kill them because of their science. Thus, you see, these people betray innocence!

Pass this by. I turn to my tale. Before the pot is put on the fire, my master tempers a certain quantity of metals, and no one else but he. (Now that he's gone, I can dare to speak boldly, for, as people say, he can work with real craft. At any rate, I know very well he has a reputation for it; but still he often gets into trouble.) And do you know how? As very often happens, the pot bursts, and farewell, all is gone! These metals are of such great violence, they penetrate so, our walls couldn't withstand them unless they were made of lime and stone. And through the wall they go! And some of them sink into the ground — at times we've lost pounds and pounds like that. And some are scattered all over the floor; some fly into the roof. Though the Fiend doesn't show himself in our sight, I think he's with us, that very scoundrel! The woe, rancor, and ire are no greater in Hell, where he is lord and master. When our pot is burst, as I've mentioned, everyone scolds and considers himself ill requited.

One says, "It was because of the fire-making." One says, "No. It was the way the fire was blown." And then I feel frightened because that is my job. "Bah!" says the third, "you're foolish and ignorant. It wasn't tempered as it should have been." "No," says the fourth. "Stop, and listen to me. As I prosper, this is the reason, and no other — because our fire wasn't made of beech!" *I* can't tell what the reason is; but I know there's certainly plenty of arguing among us.

"Well," says my master, "there's nothing more to be done. Hereafter I'll be on guard against these risks. I'm absolutely sure the pot was cracked.

But, be that as it may, don't be daunted. As usual, let's quickly sweep up the floor, pluck up our hearts, and be cheerful and happy."

The refuse is swept into a heap, a canvas thrown on the floor, and all this refuse tossed in a sieve and sifted and picked time and again.

"By Heaven," says one, "there's still some of our metal here, even though we don't have it all. And though this business has gone wrong this time, the next time it may be all right. We have to take risks with our resources. Heavens above! A merchant can't always stay prosperous, believe you me. Sometimes his goods are lost at sea, and sometimes they come safe to land."

"Peace!" says my master. "The next time I'll try to bring our craft to a different end; and if I don't, gentlemen, let me have the blame. There was a fault in something, I know very well."

Another says, "The fire was too hot." But, be it hot or cold, I dare say this, that we shall always have an unsuccessful conclusion. We fail in what we wish to have, and we continue to rave in our madness. And when we're all together, every one of us seems a Solomon. But not everything that shines like gold is gold, as I've heard tell, nor is every apple good that is fair to the eye, no matter what men may rant or rave. Exactly so, you see, it fares with us. He that seems the wisest is the greatest fool, by Heaven, when it comes to the proof, and he that seems the most trustworthy is a thief. That you shall know, before I leave you, by the time I have made an end of my tale.

THE TALE

There's a regular canon [1] among us who would infect a whole town though it were as large as Nineveh, Rome, Alexandria, Troy, and three more. His tricks and his infinite falsity no one, I suppose, could write down, though he lived for a thousand years. In all this world there is not his equal for falsehood, for in his terms he will so twist himself and will speak his words in so sly a manner when he converses with anyone that he will stupefy him at once, unless the person be a fiend, as he is himself. Many a man has he beguiled before this, and will beguile, if he may live a little longer; and yet men ride and walk many a mile to seek him out and to make his acquaintance, knowing nothing of his false behavior. And if you care to give me a hearing, I'll describe it here in your presence.

---

[1] In general, *regular* canons, that is, those living according to a *regula* or rule, were attached, somewhat like monks, to the residence belonging to their order. (*Secular* canons belonged to the secular clergy and might serve in a cathedral or large church.)

But, revered regular canons, don't think that I'm slandering your house, even though my tale is about a canon. There is some scoundrel of every order, Heaven knows, and God forbid that a whole company should regret one solitary man's folly. To slander you is in no way my intention, but to correct what is wrong I mean. This tale was not told for you alone but for others too. You know well that among Christ's twelve apostles there was no traitor but Judas alone. Then why should all the rest who were guiltless be blamed? I say the same in your case except for this, if you will listen: if any Judas be in your house, remove him at once, I advise you, if reputation or renown can awaken any concern. And don't be in any way displeased, I beg you, but hear what I have to say on this matter.

In London there was an annualer priest,[1] who had lived there for many a year, who was so pleasant and helpful to the wife where he boarded that she wouldn't allow him to pay anything for board or clothing, no matter how gaily he lived; and he had spending money in great plenty. But no matter! Now I want to proceed to tell my tale of the canon who brought this priest to confusion.

This false canon came one day to the room where the priest was staying, and begged him to lend him a sum of gold, which he would pay him back again. "Lend me a mark,[2]" he said, "for just three days, and I'll pay it back to you at the end of that time. And if you should find me false, have me hung by the neck the next day."

The priest gave him a mark at once, and the canon thanked him repeatedly and took his leave and went off on his way, and on the third day brought his money and gave the gold back to the priest, for which the priest was very well pleased and satisfied.

"Certainly," said he, "it doesn't bother me at all to lend a man two or three nobles, or whatever I happen to have in my possession, when he's so faithful in character that he won't break his agreement for any reason. Such a man I can never refuse."

"What!" said the canon. "Shall I be unfaithful! Nay, that would be something entirely new. I shall always keep faith till the day I creep to my grave. God forbid anything else! Believe this as surely as your creed. I thank God, and in due time let it be said, never yet was anyone dissatisfied because of gold or silver he lent to me, nor did I ever intend falsehood in

---

[1] Unlike the dutiful country Parson in the *General Prologue*, who did not seek his living in a "chantry for souls," the annualer priest was hired by private individuals to sing annual masses for the souls of the deceased on the anniversaries of their deaths.

[2] The pound (20*s.*) was divided for commercial purposes into thirds. The gold *noble* was equivalent to one-third (6*s.* 8*d.*); two *nobles* or two-thirds (13*s.* 4*d.*) were called a *mark*, but there was no *mark* coin.

my heart. And, now sir," said he, "confidentially, since you have been so kind to me and shown me such great consideration, I'll show you something to repay your kindness; and, if you care to learn it, I'll teach you openly my way of operation in philosophy. Pay careful attention. Before your very eyes you'll plainly see me perform a marvel before I go."

"Yes!" said the priest. "Really, sir? Will you? Heavens, I heartily pray you will."

"Faithfully, at your command, sir," said the canon, "and God forbid anything else."

Notice how the thief managed to offer his services. Most true it is that proffered service smells, as the sages of old showed; and I shall verify the fact immediately through the canon, this root of all treachery, who always takes delight and pleasure in how he may bring Christian people to harm, such fiendish thoughts well up in his heart. God guard us from his false deceptions!

The priest had no idea whom he was dealing with, nor did he suspect anything of the coming harm. O foolish priest! O foolish innocent! With covetousness you shall soon be blinded! O unfortunate, your senses are completely blind! You're completely unaware of the deception which this fox has prepared for you! His wily schemes you can't escape! To pass, therefore, to the outcome, which entails your discomfiture, unlucky man, I shall at once hasten to tell of your rashness and folly, and also of the other wretch's falsity, as far as my ability will serve.

You're thinking this canon was my master, sir Host? Truly, by the Queen of Heaven, it was another canon, and not he, who was a hundred times more subtle. Many a time has he deceived people; it wearies me to tell of his falsity. Whenever I speak of his deceptiveness, for shame of it my cheeks turn red — or, at least, they begin to glow, for I know very well there's no red left in my face. For various fumes of metals, as you've heard me explain, have consumed and wasted my redness. Now, notice the villainy of this canon!

"Sir," said he to the priest, "have your man go for quicksilver, so that we can have it right away, and have him bring two or three ounces. And as soon as he comes, you shall see a remarkable thing which you never saw before."

"Sir," said the priest, "certainly that shall be done." He ordered his servant to fetch him this, and the latter was ready at his bidding and set out, and soon came back with the quicksilver, to be brief, and gave the three ounces to the canon; and he set it carefully down and ordered the servant to bring coal so that he might set to work at once.

The coal was brought at once, and the canon took a crucible from his bosom and showed it to the priest. "This apparatus which you see," he said, "take in your hand, and put an ounce of this quicksilver in it yourself, and now, in the name of Christ, begin to become a philosopher. There are very few to whom I would offer to reveal so much of my science. For here, by experiment, you shall see me immediately mortify this quicksilver right before your very eyes, honestly, and make it into as good and pure silver as any in your purse or mine, or anywhere else, and make it malleable.[1] Otherwise, consider me false and unsuited to appear among people ever again. Here I have a powder, which cost me a lot, and it will do the job, for it's the basis of all the skill which I shall show you. Send away your man, and keep him outside, and shut the door while we're engaged in secrecy so that no one will spy on us as we work on this philosophy."

All was done just as he ordered. The servant went out directly, and his master at once shut the door, and quickly they turned to their labor.

At the bidding of this wretched canon, the priest set the thing on the fire, and blew the fire, and worked very busily. And the canon threw into the crucible a powder, made of I don't know what — either chalk, or glass, or something else not worth a fly — to confuse the priest; and directed him quickly to rake the coals up all around the crucible. "For, as a sign of my love for you," said the canon, "your own hands shall bring about all that shall be done here."

"Thank you very much," said the priest, and was very glad, and raked up the coals as the canon directed. And while he was busy, this fiendish wretch, this false canon — may the foul Fiend fetch him! — took from his bosom a coal of beech-wood, in which a hole had been very cunningly made, and in it there was an ounce of silver filings, and the hole was carefully stopped up with wax to keep the filings in. And, you understand, this false contrivance wasn't made there, but before; and I shall mention, afterwards, other things he had brought with him. Before he came, he planned to deceive the priest, and so he did, before they parted! Till he had skinned him, he just couldn't let up. It stupefies me when I speak of him. I'd love to avenge myself on his falsity, if I knew how, but he's here and there. He's so changeable, he doesn't stay anywhere.

But, gentlemen, attend now, for Heaven's sake! He took the coal which I mentioned, and he kept it secretly in his hand. And while the priest was busily bedding the coals, as I told you already, the canon said, "My friend, you're doing that wrong. That isn't bedded as it ought to be, but I'll soon fix it," he said. "Now, let me rake there just a moment, for I'm sorry for you, by St. Giles. You're certainly hot; I can see how you're sweating.

[1] Alchemists hoped to discover how to mortify (kill) the quick (living) nature of quicksilver and thus convert it into solid, malleable silver.

Have a cloth here, and wipe away the wet." And while the priest wiped his face, the canon took his coal — curses on him! — and laid it directly above the center of the crucible, and then blew hard till the coals began to burn fast.

"Now give us a drink," said the canon then. "Soon all shall be well, I guarantee. Let's sit down and enjoy ourselves." And when the canon's beech-wood coal was burnt, all the filings fell out of the hole down into the crucible; and so they had to, of course, since the coal was bedded directly above it. But the priest knew nothing of this, alas! He thought all of the coals were equally sound, for he understood nothing of that trick. And when the alchemist saw his time, "Rise up," said he, "sir Priest, and stand beside me. And, since I know very well you haven't a metal-mold, set out. Go and bring us a chalk stone, for I'm going to make it into the same shape as a mold, if I can manage. And also bring with you a bowl or pan full of water, and then you shall see very well how our work is to turn out and prosper. But yet, so that you won't feel any distrust or wrongful suspicion of me while you're away, I won't leave your presence but go with you and come back with you." To be brief — they opened the door of the room, and shut it and went their way, and they carried the key away with them, and came back directly. Why should I linger all the day long? He took the chalk and shaped it like a mold, as I shall explain.

He took a plate of silver, just one ounce in weight, let me tell you, out of his own sleeve — may evil fall upon him! And notice now his cursed trick.

He shaped his mold the length and breadth of this plate so slyly, you may be sure, that the priest didn't notice. Then he hid the plate again in his sleeve and removed his material from the fire and, with cheerful face, poured it into the mold. This he then threw into the water-vessel at his convenience, and at once told the priest, "See what's there. Put in your hand and feel. You'll find silver, I expect. What the devil else should it be? The shaving of silver is silver, Lord knows!"

The priest put in his hand and took out a plate of fine silver, and when he saw that it was so, he was happy through and through. "The blessings of God and of the Holy Mother and All Saints, too, be upon you, Sir Canon," said the priest, "and their curse upon me if I don't serve you in all that I can, if you will vouchsafe to teach me this noble craft and this mystery."

"I'm still going to make a test the second time," said the canon, "so that you can observe and become expert at this and, if necessary, put this discipline and this crafty science to the test yourself in my absence some day. Let's take another ounce of quicksilver," he then said, "without further words, and do with it as you have done previously with the first lot that is now silver."

The priest busied himself as best he could to do what the canon, cursed man, ordered, and hard he blew the fire to gain the result he wished. And in the meanwhile the canon was quite ready to beguile the priest all over again, and for his imposture he held in his hand a hollow stick — notice and beware! — in the end of which were put one ounce and no more of silver filings, just as had been before in his coal, well stoppered with wax to keep in every bit of his filings. And while the priest was busy, the canon moved over toward him with his stick, and cast in his powder as he had done before — I pray to God, the Devil will flay his skin for his deceit, for he was always false in thought and deed — and with this stick, equipped with this false contrivance, he stirred the coals above the crucible till the wax began to melt from the heat, as everyone but a fool knows it must, and everything in the stick ran out and fell swiftly into the crucible.

Now, good sirs, what better could you want? When the priest was thus beguiled again, supposing nothing but the truth, indeed, he was so glad that I'm quite unable to express his joy and gladness; and to the canon once again he promised his body and substance. "Yes," said the canon at once, "poor though I be, you'll find me crafty. I warn you, there's still more to come. Is there any copper here?" said he.

"Yes, sir," said the priest. "I'm quite sure there is."

"Otherwise, go and buy us some, right away. Now, good sir, set out and hurry."

He went his way and came back with the copper, and the canon took it in his hands and weighed out just one ounce of the copper.

My tongue is much too simple a minister to my wit to pronounce the duplicity of the canon, the root of all cursedness! To those that did not know him, he seemed friendly, but he was malevolent both in thought and action. It wearies me to tell of his falsity, and yet, none the less, I will describe it with the intention that men may thus be warned, and certainly for no other reason.

He put this ounce of copper in the crucible and set it at once on the fire and threw in powder and made the priest blow the coals and had him stoop down low at his work, as he did before — and yet it was all just a sham. He made a fool of the priest just as he wished! And afterwards he poured the metal into the mold and finally put it in the pan of water and then put in his own hand. And he had up his sleeve (as you've heard me mention before) a silver plate. He slyly took it out, this cursed trickster, without the priest's knowing anything of this craftiness, and he left it in the bottom of the pan and groped to and fro in the water; with remarkable secrecy he also picked up the copper plate, without the knowledge of the priest, and hid it, and seized him by the chest and spoke to him thus in his game: "Bend down, for goodness' sake. You're remiss. Help me now as I helped you before. Put your hand in, and see what's there."

The priest at once picked up the silver plate, and then the canon said, "Let's go to some goldsmith with the three plates we've made and find out if they're anything special. For, by my hood, I wouldn't want them to be anything but silver good and true, in faith, and that shall be discovered immediately."

To the goldsmith they went with the three plates and submitted them to the test by fire and hammer. No one could deny but that they were as they ought to be.

Who was gladder than the deluded priest? No bird was ever gladder of the day, nor was any nightingale ever more willing to sing in the Maytime, nor lady more eager to carol or speak of love and womanliness, nor knight-at-arms to do a hardy deed in hope of his dear lady's grace, than was the priest eager to learn this sorry craft. And to the canon thus he said: "For the love of God who died for us all, and as I may deserve it of you, what will this recipe cost? Tell me now."

"By our Lady," said the canon, "it's expensive, I warn you. For apart from myself and one friar, no one in England knows how to make it."

"No matter," said he. "Now, sir, for God's sake, what shall I pay? Tell me, I beg you!"

"Indeed," said he, "it's very expensive, as I said. Sir, in a word, if you want to have it, you must pay forty pounds, so help me God! And if it weren't for the kindness you showed me earlier, you'd certainly have to pay more."

The priest at once brought the sum of forty pounds in nobles and gave them all to the canon for this recipe. All his doings were nothing but fraud and imposture.

"Sir Priest," said he, "I don't care to have any notoriety because of my craft, for I'd like it kept hushed. And, as you love me, keep it secret. For, if men knew all my subtlety, they'd feel so envious of me, by Heaven, on account of my philosophy, that I'd be dead! There are no two ways about it!"

"God forbid!" said the priest. "What are you saying? I'd sooner spend all the wealth that I have, or else I'm losing my mind, than that you should fall into such disaster."

"For your good wishes, sir, may you have the best of results," said the canon. "Farewell, and many thanks." He went his way, and the priest never saw him again after that. And when the priest decided to try out this recipe at his convenience, farewell! It would not work! Thus it is the canon introduces himself, to bring people to destruction.

EPILOGUE

Observe, sirs, that in every rank of society there is such strife between men and gold that there's hardly any gold. This transmutation deceives so many that, in good faith, I believe it's the greatest cause of such scarcity. Philosophers speak so mistily in this craft that men can't come near it, with such wits as men have now-a-days. They may very well chatter like jays and turn their interest and concern toward technical terms, but they'll never attain their goal. A man can easily learn, if he has anything, how to transmute — and reduce all his goods to nothing!

Lo, such is the gain in this gay sport: it will turn a man's mirth to gloom, and empty great and heavy purses, too, and cause men to earn the curse of those who have lent them their goods on account of it! Oh, fie, for shame! Those that have been burnt, alas, can't they flee from the heat of the fire? You that follow it, I advise you, abandon it lest you lose all, for it's better late than never. Never to prosper would be too long a time to wait. Though you search continually, you never shall find it. You're as bold as Bayard [1] the blind, who blunders on and senses no danger. He's just as bold at running against a stone as passing around it on the road. Those of you who transmute are just the same, I'd say. If your eyes can't see properly, make sure that your mind doesn't lack its sight. For no matter how far and wide you look and stare, you'll never gain anything at that business, but waste everything that you can snatch and grab. Draw back from the fire lest it burn too hard. Meddle no longer with that art, I mean, for if you do, your thrift will be gone completely. And with haste I'll tell you now just what philosophers say on the matter.

Lo, thus says Arnold of the New Town, according to his *Rosary* [2]; he says this very thing, for a fact: "No man can mortify mercury unless it be with the knowledge of mercury's brother." He tells that he who first said this was the father of philosophers, Hermes [3]; and that Hermes had said that the dragon, certainly, does not die unless he is slain along with his brother; and, that is to say, by the dragon he meant mercury, and by the dragon's

---

[1] *Bayard* was a proverbial name for a horse.

[2] Arnold of Villanova, a French writer on medicine and allied subjects who died in 1314, was the author of various works on alchemy including the *Philosophers' Rosary* and the *Philosophers' Stone.* It is from the latter treatise that the Yeoman's quotations are drawn.

[3] Hermes Trismegistus, or "thrice-great Hermes," as Milton calls him, was the reputed author of the so-called *Hermetical Books* (compiled in the third century A.D.), which dealt with mystical lore of various kinds, including alchemy.

brother, sulphur, which were drawn out of Sol and Luna.[1] "And therefore," he said, — notice this saying! — "let no one strive to seek this art unless he can understand the meaning and language of philosophers. Otherwise he is a foolish man, for this science and knowledge," said he, "is indeed of the secret of secrets."

Moreover, there was a disciple of Plato who once questioned his master, as the book entitled *Senior*[2] will bear witness, and, truly, this was his request: "Tell me the name of the secret stone."

And Plato at once answered him, "Take the stone called Titan."

"What is that?" said he.

"The same as Magnesia," said Plato.

"Indeed, sir, is that so? This is *ignotum per ignotius*.[3] What is Magnesia, good sir, I pray you?"

"It's water made of the four elements,[4] I tell you," said Plato.

"Tell me the basis of that water, good sir, if you will," he then said.

"No, no," said Plato. "I certainly won't. The philosophers have sworn one and all never to reveal it to anyone or to write it down in books in any way. For it is so dear and precious to Christ that he doesn't want it to be revealed except when it pleases his deity to inspire men, and also to prohibit whomever he wishes to. Lo, this is the end."

Therefore I conclude thus: since God in Heaven does not wish the philosophers to specify how a man shall attain this stone, let it go. This is the best I can advise, for whoever makes God his adversary by doing anything contrary to his will shall certainly never thrive, even though he transmute for the rest of his life. And here let us stop, for my tale is finished. God send every honest man relief from his misfortune!

---

[1] This typically mystical statement concerning the alchemists' hope of mortifying quicksilver (see p. 215, n. 1) implies that quicksilver, one of the four spirits, can never be mortified unless its brother-spirit sulphur is also involved in the transmutation, and that both must in some unexplained way be affected by the two noblest of the seven bodies, Sol or gold, and Luna or silver, which were known as the father and mother of the philosopher's stone. Wisely, the Yeoman does not pretend to understand its ambiguous meaning.

[2] By *Senior* Chaucer refers to a tenth-century Arabic alchemical treatise written by Muhammad ibn Umail the Physician, called by his Latin translator ibn Umail Senior.

[3] "The unknown through the more unknown." An explanation of the unfamiliar by reference to something still less familiar.

[4] That is, a special kind of water miraculously made of the four basic elements, fire, earth, air, and water, of which all matter was believed to consist.

APPENDIX

The Pronunciation of Chaucer's Language

[See Introduction, pp. xxv–xxvii.]

For those readers who wish really to master the details of Chaucer's language, there is no short cut. They must become familiar with Chaucer's entire set of distinctive sounds and the various methods of representing those sounds in spelling. This information is tabulated below. But the beginner will find his task lighter if he works gradually, studying first the long vowels and diphthongs, then practicing reading aloud, and then studying the short vowels. The consonants present fewer real difficulties and should be studied last, a few at a time.

In the first column of the following tables each separate sound or sound-group is provided with a reference number, and the normal varieties of spelling for each separate sound are listed. Some sounds are consistently represented by one spelling only (No. 20, for instance); other sounds, by as many as four different spellings (No. 5). Moreover, one and the same spelling symbol may be used for several different sounds. Chaucer's *e*, for example, represents four different sounds (Nos. 3, 4, 15, and 16), not counting its presence in three arbitrary combinations of letters (Nos. 5, 6, and 13) used to represent diphthongs. Letters or combinations of letters thus used for more than one sound are distinguished by means of small subscript numerals.

The second column provides, whenever possible, a modern counterpart to the sounds listed, the relevant sound within the modern word being indicated by means of italics. The pronunciation intended is that shown as standard in modern dictionaries. Where counterparts are lacking in our standard dialect of modern English, descriptions or foreign examples are supplied. Information is also given enabling modern readers to determine, when the spelling is ambiguous, which sound Chaucer was using. Sometimes the modern survival of the sound in the word containing the spelling ambiguity will suffice to decide. Sometimes modern usage in spelling is the only ready guide.

The third column provides at least one example of each sound as it occurs in a common Chaucerian word; and the modern English survival of each example, even though changed in pronunciation, is added in parenthesis. Sometimes the survival of a Chaucerian sound, as in "nam*e*" (No. 16) or "*k*now" (No. 21), is merely orthographic, representing a vanished sound. Sometimes it differs entirely in sound from its Chaucerian counterpart, as in modern "n*a*me" (No. 1); sometimes it is identical, as in modern "fr*e*sh" (No. 15).

Some words in Chaucer's time, particularly those borrowed from French, were accented on a syllable other than that now accented, as, for instance, *coráge* (now *courage*), and the accentuation of examples is therefore indicated throughout the third column. But accentuation presents no problem to the modern reader, for the metrical pattern of Chaucer's verse usually indicates it clearly enough.

LONG VOWELS AND DIPHTHONGS

Chaucer's spelling	Modern approximation	Chaucerian example (and survival)
1. a_1, aa	f*a*ther (with vowel more prolonged than No. 14)	námè (name)
2. au, aw	h*ou*se	cáusè (cause)
3. e_1, ee_1	*a*ble	félè (feel)
4. e_2, ee_2	*e*bb (with vowel more prolonged than No. 15). (Distinction in pronunciation between Nos. 3 and 4 has not survived, but survivals of No. 4 can often be recognized by the spelling *ea*.)	heeth (heath)
5. ei, ey, ai, ay	a glide from "*e*bb" (No. 15) to "*i*t" (No. 17)	fáillè (fail)
6. eu_1, ew_1	a glide from "*e*bb" (No. 15) to "p*u*ll" (No. 19) (Cf. No. 13.)	kn*ew* (kn*ew*)
7. i_1, y_1	mach*i*ne	rídè, rýdè (ride)
8. o_1, oo_1	n*o*te	fódè (food)
9. o_2, oo_2	n*au*ght (Nos. 8 and 9 can be identified by their survivals, which still have distinct sounds.)	boot (boat)
10. oi, oy	b*oy*	b*oy* (b*oy*)
11. ou_1, ow_1	a glide from "*o*ft" (No. 18) to "p*u*ll" (No. 19)	sówlè (soul)

Chaucer's spelling	Modern approximation	Chaucerian example (and survival)
12. ou_2, ow_2	rule (Nos. 11 and 12 can be identified by their survivals, which still have distinct sounds.)	hous (house)
13. u_1, eu_2, ew_2	yule (French borrowings, distinguishable from No. 6 because survivals are spelt u, not ew.)	cúrė (cure) réulė (rule)

SHORT VOWELS

14. a_2	A short variety of No. 1, as in Irish dialect pronunciation of "man," or in German "Mann"	man (man)
15. e_3	ebb (with vowel less prolonged than No. 4). (In stressed syllables.)	fressch (fresh)
16. e_4	Stella (with final vowel unemphasized), raven (In unstressed syllables.)	námė, námės (name, names)
17. i_2, y_2	it	lítėl (little)
18. o_3	oft	oft (oft)
19. u_2, o_4	pull	púllė (pull) sónė (son)

All the long vowels and diphthongs except for No. 10 require the modern reader's particular attention since they have changed in modern English and since three of them (Nos. 5, 6, and 11) do not approximate any diphthong now in use.

Chaucer's short vowels, which have changed not nearly so significantly, are indistinguishable from his long vowels in spelling except when the letters a, e, or o are written double. But it will be noticed that their modern survivals differ in pronunciation from survivals of the long vowels. Thus, if in doubt, we can tell that the o in Chaucer's word softè represents the short vowel No. 18 and not the long vowels Nos. 8 or 9 because modern English has soft, not sooft or soaft.

PRONUNCIATION

CONSONANTS

Chaucer's spelling	Modern approximation	Chaucerian example (and survival)
20. b	*b*oy	*b*oy (*b*oy)
21. c_1, k	*c*alm, *k*eep (c_1 and *k* survive unchanged in pronunciation except that *k* has disappeared before *n*. Cf. No. 38.)	cálmĕ (*c*alm) képĕ (*k*eep) knówĕ (*k*now)
22. ch, cch	*ch*ild	*ch*ild (*ch*ild) fé*cch*ĕ (fet*ch*)
23. d	*d*eem	dé mĕ (*d*eem)
24. f	*f*eel	fé lĕ (*f*eel) o*f* (o*f*, o*ff*)
25. g_1, gg_1	*g*ame (g_2, gg_1 survive unchanged in pronunciation except that g_1 initially in native English words has disappeared before *n*. Cf. No. 32.)	gámĕ (*g*ame) dó*gg*ĕ (do*g*) *g*náwĕ (*g*naw)
26. g_2, gg_2, j	*g*entle, *j*udge (g_2, gg_2, *j* survive unchanged in pronunciation.)	*g*éntil (*g*entle) *j*ú*gg*ĕ (*j*u*dg*e)
27. gh	More strongly breathed than *h* in "how," as in Scottish dialect pronunciation of "lo*ch*" (not "lo*ck*"), or in German "Ba*ch*" (not "ba*ck*").	ni*gh*t (ni*gh*t)
28. h_1	*h*ome	*h*oom (*h*ome)
29. h_2	silent as in "*h*onest" (h_2, which occurs in words borrowed from French, has usually remained silent.)	*h*ónĕst (*h*ónest)
30. l	*l*arge (*l* was pronounced even before *f*, *k*, and *m*.)	lárgĕ (*l*arge) ha*l*f (ha*l*f)
31. m	*m*ore	mórĕ (*m*ore)
32. n_1, gn	*n*ame, si*gn* (*gn* pronounced as *n* occurs in words borrowed from French. Cf. *gn*–, No. 25.)	námĕ (*n*ame) sí*gn*ĕ (si*gn*)
33. n_2g	fi*ng*er (not "si*ng*er," "thi*ng*")	thi*ng* (thi*ng*)
34. n_2k	thi*nk*, u*nc*le (not "u*nc*outh")	thí*nk*ĕ (thi*nk*)
35. p	*p*age	*p*ágĕ (*p*age)

Chaucer's spelling	Modern approximation	Chaucerian example (and survival)
36. qu	queen	quéné (queen)
37. r	rage	rágè (rage)
38. s_1, ss, c_2	service (s_1 occurred only at the beginning or end of a word or before a consonant. c_2 survives unchanged in pronunciation. Cf. No. 21.)	sèrvýcè (service) cértein (certain) kíssè (kiss) was (was)
39. s_2, z	cause, gauze (s_2 occurred only between vowels.)	cáusè (cause) zódiak (zodiac)
40. sh, sch	ship	ship (ship)
41. t	teach	téchè (teach)
42. th_1	thin (not then) (th_1 occurred only at the beginning or end of a word or before a consonant.)	thínkèth (thinketh) then (then) thrówè (throw)
43. th_2	then (not thin) (th_2 occurred only between vowels.)	óther (other)
44. v	vice	výcè (vice)
45. w	was (w was pronounced even before l or r.)	was (was) wrécchè (wretch)
46. wh	whale (not "wail")	what (what) who (who)
47. x	six	six (six)
48. y_3	your	your (your)

There are few real problems in the rendering of Chaucer's consonants, although some trifling ambiguities are worthy of mention. The pronunciation of initial g (Nos. 25 and 26) can only be determined by its modern survival; but *Dorigen*, the name of the heroine in the *Franklin's Tale*, has not survived, and we shall therefore never know whether Chaucer pronounced the name with a g_1 or a g_2.

In Chaucer's time the final s (No. 38) in unstressed words of high relative frequency such as *was, is,* and *as* was already changing to z (No. 39) in sound, though not in spelling; and the initial sound *th* (No. 42) of unstressed words of high relative frequency such as *then, they, this, though* was already changing to the *th* (No. 43) of the modern survivals in these words. The older pronunciation recommended in the tables for *was* and *then* is arbitrarily chosen for the sake of consistency.